SEXUAL ETHICS

SEXUAL ETHICS

A Theological Introduction

TODD A. SALZMAN
AND
MICHAEL G. LAWLER

Georgetown University Press
Washington, DC

6/11/13
Lan
$ 24.95

Library of Congress Cataloging-in-Publication Data

Salzman, Todd A.
   Sexual ethics : a theological introduction / Todd A. Salzman and Michael G. Lawler
       p.   cm.
   Includes bibliographical references and index.
   ISBN 978-1-58901-913-3 (pbk. : alk. paper)
   1. Sex—Religious aspects—Catholic Church.   2. Catholic Church—Doctrines.   3. Sexual ethics.   I. Lawler, Michael G.   II. Title.
   BX1795.S48S249   2012
241'.66088282—dc23

                                        2011037930

15 14 13 12   9 8 7 6 5 4 3 2 First printing

This book is dedicated to our students,
past and present, from whom
we have learned so much.

Contents

Abbreviations for Sources

AAS	*Acta Apostolicae Sedis: Commentarium Officiale (Roma: Typis Polyglottis Vaticanis)*
Can	Code of Canon Law
CCC	*Catechism of the Catholic Church*
CCE	Congregation for Catholic Education
CDF	Congregation for the Doctrine of the Faith
CRP	CDF, *Considerations regarding Proposals to Give Legal Recognition to Unions between Homosexual Persons*, *AAS* (2003), 41–57
DS	*Enchiridion Symbolorum Definitionum et Declarationum de Rebus Fidei et Morum*, ed. H. Denziger and A. Schoenmetzer (Fribourg: Herder, 1965)
DV	*Dei verbum*, Vatican Council II, *Dogmatic Constitution on Divine Revelation*
EGHL	*Educational Guidance in Human Love: Outlines for Sex Education*, CCE (Roma: Typis Polyglottis Vaticanis, 1983)
EV	*Evangelium vitae*, John Paul II, *The Gospel of Life*, *AAS* 87 (1995), 401–522
FC	*Familiaris consortio*, John Paul II, *Exhortation on the Role of the Christian Family*, *AAS* 74 (1982), 81–191
GS	*Gaudium et spes*, Vatican Council II, *Pastoral Constitution on the Church in the Modern World*

HV	*Humanae vitae*, Paul VI, *On Human Life*, AAS 60 (1968), 481–503
LG	*Lumen gentium*, Vatican Council II, *Dogmatic Constitution on the Church*
MD	*Mulieris dignitatem*, John Paul II, *On the Dignity of Woman*, AAS 80 (1988), 1653–1729
OT	*Optatum totius*, Vatican Council II, *Decree on Priestly Formation*
PG	*Patrologiae Cursus Completus: Series Graeca*, ed. J. P. Migne
PH	*Persona humana*, CDF, *Declaration on Certain Questions concerning Sexual Ethics*, AAS 68 (1976), 77–96
PL	*Patrologiae Cursus Completus: Series Latina*, ed. J. P. Migne
SRS	*Sollicitudo rei socialis*, John Paul II, *The Social Concern of the Church*, AAS 80 (1987), 513–86
ST	*Summa Theologiae Sancti Thomae de Aquino*
TS	*Theological Studies* (Marquette University)
USCCB	United States Conference of Catholic Bishops
VS	*Veritatis splendor*, John Paul II, *The Splendor of Truth*, AAS 85 (1993), 1133–1228

All translations from languages other than English are the authors'.

Prologue

Our earlier book, *The Sexual Person: Toward a Renewed Catholic Anthropology*, was highly acclaimed by its academic critics and was selected by the Catholic Press Association as the best theological book of 2009. That book, however, was written primarily for our fellow theologians, and that, countless readers told us, made it a difficult read for those who were not theologically trained. That complaint, allied to a fairly common request for a Catholic book on sexual morality that "people in the pews" and "my students" can understand, is the origin of this book. It is offered to the general educated Catholic population in the hope that it will be more readable and therefore more enlightening on common questions about sexual morality as they arise for Catholics in the contemporary world. Twenty-first-century sexual science, perhaps especially the critiques offered by feminist scholars, have made clear to us that ancient assumptions about sexuality and sexual intercourse are not entirely accurate. The advice of Pythagoras, to "keep to the winter for sexual pleasures, in summer abstain; sexual pleasures are less harmful in autumn and spring, but they are always harmful and not conducive to health," will surely make twenty-first-century adults smile, but the pain and disaster daily experienced in the sexual area, especially by the young, indicates that we have more to do than smile.[1] We must understand more about our sexuality and the principles that direct it morally and make it truly human than did Holden Caulfield, J. D. Salinger's tortured protagonist in *The Catcher in the Rye*. It is to facilitate that dual understanding that this book is offered.

Two magisterial principles capture the essence of the Catholic moral, sexual tradition. The first principle received its modern articulation in

Pope Paul VI's encyclical *Humanae vitae* (*HV*): "Each and every marriage act must remain open to the transmission of life."[2] The second was enunciated by the Congregation for the Doctrine of the Faith (CDF): "Any human genital act whatsoever may be placed only within the framework of marriage."[3] In the Catholic tradition, moral sexual activity is institutionalized within the confines of marriage and procreation, and sexual morality is marital morality.

These two principles do not have the same theoretical underpinning. The first is founded in what is called "*nature*" or *natural order*: the structure of sexual acts reveals to the attentive and rational person the form that each and every sexual act must take to be in accord with "nature" and the will of nature's Creator. The second is founded in human *reason*: attention to and understanding, evaluation, and rational judgment of the various aspects of an issue reveal to attentive, rational, and responsible human beings what right sexual conduct ought to be. These two different ways of arriving at moral principles have a long history in the Catholic moral tradition. Thomas Aquinas argued, for example, that there are two ways in which a sexual act is rendered unbecoming. "First, through being contrary to right *reason*. . . . Secondly, because, in addition, it is contrary to the *natural order* of the sexual act as becoming to the human race."[4]

In his influential 1951 speech to Italian midwives, Pope Pius XII argued from the same two sources. On the one hand, he did not condemn the prevention of procreation in a *marriage*; on the other hand, he condemned artificial prevention of procreation in *marital intercourse*.[5] In the first case, *right reason* dictates how a married life should be lived; in the second, the "*nature*" of the sexual act dictates how it should be performed within marriage. These two ways of arriving at moral principle and judgment on sexual ethical questions are evident throughout Catholic tradition and will recur regularly throughout this book. They reflect a tension within that tradition between methodological developments in approaches to ethics and anthropological developments in understanding the sexual person, and the norms that are formulated and justified in light of those developments. This tension and its implications for a living and evolving Catholic tradition, and theologians within that tradition, are well illustrated in Bernard Lonergan's concept of conversion.

Lonergan introduced the important notion of conversion in his groundbreaking *Insight*, and further developed it in his important *Method in Theology*.[6] Conversion is a process that involves "a radical about-face in which one repudiates characteristic features of one's previous horizon or perspective"; it may be threefold.[7] *Intellectual conversion* abandons "the myth that fully human knowing is to be conceived on an analogy with seeing" (that is, that knowing is simply looking) and replaces it with the affirmation that one knows only when one comes to understand correctly.[8] *Moral conversion* is "a shift in the criterion of one's decisions and choices from satisfaction to values."[9] *Religious conversion* is simply "falling in love with God."[10] Lonergan's initial analysis of conversion occurred within the analysis of the development of the human knower in general, and reoccurred within the analysis of the theologian-knower in particular. Conversion, it is important to note, is not a development in what the theologian *says* but "a fundamental and momentous change in the human reality that a theologian *is*."[11] Conversion changes what the theologian *is*; it is a radical development of personal foundations and perspectives.[12] From different foundations and perspectives, unconverted and converted theologians will interpret the Catholic tradition, and the methodological and anthropological developments of that tradition, in different ways and will draw radically different conclusions from it. Dialogue between theologians will recur throughout this book, with no implied judgment as to which theologian is converted and which is not.

The conversion that we explore in this book is primarily intellectual conversion that stimulates and leads to moral and religious conversion. In examining the tradition of Catholic sexual teaching, we note a conversion in that tradition that is reflected in a disconnect. The disconnect is between many of the Magisterium's absolute proscriptive sexual norms and the methodological and anthropological developments explicitly recognized and endorsed in Catholic tradition, especially since the Second Vatican Council. The conversion is marked by these methodological and anthropological developments, which invite a reconsideration of norms and their justification. Methodological developments include a fundamental shift from a primarily classicist worldview to a primarily historically conscious worldview. A classicist worldview asserts that reality is static, necessary, fixed, and universal. The method utilized, anthropology formulated, and norms taught in this worldview are timeless, universal, and immutable, and the acts condemned by those norms are always so condemned. A historically conscious worldview fundamentally challenges this view of reality. In a historically conscious worldview, reality is dynamic, evolving, changing, and particular. The method utilized, anthropology formulated, and norms taught in this worldview are contingent, particular, and changeable, and the acts condemned by those norms are morally evaluated in light of evolving human knowledge and understanding.

The shift from a classicist to a historically conscious worldview is reflected, for example, in the Magisterium's endorsement of the historical-critical method for interpreting scripture articulated in *Divino afflante spiritu* and *Dei verbum*, which requires that scriptural texts be read in the "literary forms" of the writer's "time and culture."[13] While this method is clearly established and marks an explicit shift in the Catholic tradition in how scripture is to be read, interpreted, and applied to ethical issues, magisterial teaching continues to proof-text scripture to justify absolute norms condemning certain sexual acts. Proof-texting happens when a biblical text is cited to justify a doctrinal or ethical conclusion that is already held and reached on the basis of some reason other than the accurate interpretation of the biblical text.

The *Catechism of the Catholic Church*, for example, cites Genesis 19:1–29, the story of Sodom and Gomorrah, as a scriptural foundation for the absolute prohibition of homosexual acts.[14] Most biblical scholars, however, relying upon the Vatican II–approved historical-critical method, as we shall see in chapter 5, assert that the central meaning of this passage is about hospitality or homosexual rape and has little relevance to the discussion of the sexual activity of gays and lesbians of a homosexual orientation in stable, monogamous, committed, just, and loving relationships. While the Magisterium espouses the historical-critical method for interpreting scripture and advocates utilizing other methodological resources such as the sciences to formulate its teaching, it fails to fully consider and integrate the normative implications of those methodological developments into that teaching, especially with regard to many of its absolute sexual norms.[15] It continues to cite certain scriptural passages to condemn sexual acts, while its own method indicates these passages are peripheral, if not irrelevant, to the acts it is condemning. The historical-critical method does not support this classicist approach to justifying norms.

A similar disconnect exists between sexual anthropological developments in the Catholic tradition and the formulation and justification of absolute sexual norms. *Gaudium et spes* (GS) marks a radical evolution in Catholic sexual teaching and, by implication, the sexual anthropology reflected in that teaching, by eliminating the language of the hierarchy of the ends of marriage. Prior to the Second Vatican Council, procreation was advanced as the primary end of marriage, and union between spouses was advanced as its secondary end. In *Gaudium et spes*, hierarchical language for the two ends of marriage is rejected, and "the nature of the human person and his acts" is posited as the foundational principle for harmonizing the ends of marriage.[16] This marked a fundamental shift and development in Catholic sexual teaching and anthropology, but there is little evidence that the Magisterium has fully incorporated this shift into its sexual anthropology or into its formulation and justification of sexual norms. As we will demonstrate throughout this book, the emphasis in that teaching continues to be on the "nature" of the act rather than on the meaning of the act for the human person.

This book has two objectives, one explicit and one implicit. The explicit objective is to explore the normative implications for sexual ethics of the methodological and anthropological developments in Catholic tradition. Given the importance of history in the process of conversion, we begin by providing a historical overview (chapter 1) of the Christian understanding of human sexuality, which spans from Genesis to Vatican II. This historical overview provides a context and foundation for our own anthropology, which draws insights from tradition and utilizes methodological resources in that tradition to formulate a foundational sexual ethical principle (chapter 2). The following chapters apply that principle to marriage and contraception (chapter 3), premarital sex (chapter 4), homosexuality (chapter 5), and reproductive technologies (chapter 6).

The implicit objective of this book is to stimulate dialogue about sexual morality between Catholic laity, theologians, and hierarchy. John Paul II teaches that dialogue is rooted in the nature and dignity of the human person. It "is an indispensable step along the path towards *human self-realization*, the self-realization of *each individual* and of *every human community*."[17] We agree that every dialogue involves the subjectivity of each person in the dialogue. Each must, therefore, attend carefully to the data emerging in the dialogue, must marshal the data as fully as possible, come to understand it, formulate that understanding in mutually understandable concepts, and eventually pass judgment on the truth or falsity of his or her understanding. It is only after this rational judgment is passed that any true knowledge is achieved in the dialogue. After the passing of judgment, there is the final step of considering possible courses of action, evaluating them, making a decision about which course of action to follow, and then translating that decision into action. In all of this, the participants in the dialogue must be equal partners, with none being privileged over any others, for it is only on the basis of this equality that any individual in the dialogue may reach intellectual and, perhaps, also moral conversion.

We are wide open to dialogue in this book. We have to be, given the theological positions we embrace in it and in our theological lives. We are like two men at a third-story window getting only a restricted third-story perspective on the landscape outside the window, and we have to be open to the complementation of perspectives provided by women and men at sixth-, ninth-, and twenty-first-story windows. In theological parlance, therefore, we situate this book in the category of *quaestio disputata*, the disputed question, so beloved of the medieval Scholastics. The Scholastic master had three tasks: *lectio*, or commentary on the Bible; *disputatio*, or teaching by objection and response to a

theme; and *praedicatio*, or proclamation of the theological word.[18] Peter
Cantor speaks for all of them when he argues that "it is after the *lectio* of
scripture and after the examination of the doubtful points thanks to the
disputatio, and not before, that we must preach."[19] It is important for the
reader to be aware that this book seeks to be *lectio*, accurate interpretation of biblical and doctrinal texts, and *disputatio*, elucidation of themes
by objection and response, before it is *praedicatio*, pastoral proclamation
of the theological word.

We freely confess that it is not for theologians alone to formulate
the theological or moral doctrine and practice of their church. That
task is for the whole communion-church. The task of the theologian
in the church is a different and critical one. In the words of the CDF's
International Theological Commission, it is the task of "interpreting
the documents of the past and present Magisterium, of putting them
in the context of the whole of revealed truth, and of finding a better
understanding of them by the use of hermeneutics," that is, interpretive
tools that rely on scripture, tradition, reason and the sciences, and human
experience.[20] The theologian "is charged with developing the tradition
beyond its current state so that it can meet new questions, needs, and
circumstances."[21] It is that difficult and frequently dangerous theologian's
task of "maintaining the balance between 'immobilism' and 'eccentricity'"
we seek to fulfill, positively and not destructively, in this book.[22] Since
we believe that genuine and respectful dialogue about sexual morality,
and indeed about all that is involved in the life of Christian discipleship,
is sorely needed to clarify Christian truth today, we intend this book to
be part of a genuine dialogue.

There is a broad division of moral theologians in the contemporary
Catholic tradition. "Traditionalist" is the general label given to moral
theologians who support and defend absolute magisterial norms prohibiting certain types of sexual acts such as premarital sex, artificial birth
control, artificial reproductive technologies, masturbation, and homosexual acts. The traditionalist school is contrasted with the revisionist
school. "Revisionist" is the general label given to moral theologians who
question many of these absolute norms and propose alternative norms.

These two groups disagree on many specific sexual norms because they disagree, more fundamentally, on the methodology and sexual anthropology that either supports these norms or questions their legitimacy and credibility. Our dialogue partners in the book, as you will discover as you proceed, are theologians who argue from different starting points and reach different conclusions about sexual morality than we do. Our intent is neither to prove ourselves right nor to prove them wrong. Convinced of the central role that love, desire, and fertility play in a human life, and therefore also in a life of Christian discipleship, we seek only to suggest a sexual anthropology that might lead to the enhancement and flourishing of human sexual relationships.[23] What we suggest is to be read as submitted to the experience, attention, intelligence, reasonableness, and response of our fellow believers in the communion-church. Since we do not dare suggest, in a pilgrim Church, that the Spirit of God has breathed the final word about either the communion-church or the sexuality of its members, we invite our dialogue partners to be as critical in their reading as we are in our writing.[24] Both our critiques and theirs, however, should be such that they are not destructive of the communion instituted by Christ and constituted by the Spirit of Christ, who, as the Spirit of God, is also the Spirit of "righteousness and peace and joy" (Rom. 14:17).

"NATURE" DEFINED

Since there will be much talk of "nature" in this and following chapters, we must first confront a difficulty with any argument from "nature." We cannot draw conclusions from what just *is* to what morally *ought to be*, from the biological structure of sexual intercourse, for example, to moral obligation, for even after determining what just *is*, we still have to determine whether it is right or wrong. To draw an immediate conclusion from what is to what morally ought to be is a logical fallacy; a "naturalistic fallacy" Moore calls it; a "theological fallacy" Frankena calls it.[25] All we can understand from "nature" is the naked fact of a reality—sexuality and sexual intercourse, for instance—nothing else. "Nature" reveals to our attention, understanding, judgment, and decision only its naked fact, not our moral obligation. Everything beyond "nature's" fact is the result of interpretation by attentive, rational, and responsible human beings.[26]

In reality, we have no access to the pure, unembellished experience of "nature;" we experience "nature" only as interpreted by rational, social beings.[27] When we derive moral obligations from "nature," we are actually deriving them from our interpretation and evaluation of "nature." It is, of course, inevitable that different groups of equally rational human beings may derive different interpretations of "nature" and moral obligation deriving from "nature," and that any given interpretation may be wrong. That is a fact that has been demonstrated time and again in history, including Catholic history.[28] It is also something taken for granted in the social scientific enterprise known as the sociology of knowledge. One of the founders of this discipline, Alfred Schutz, presents its widely taken-for-granted principle: "It is the *meaning* of our experiences and not the *ontological structure* of the objects that constitutes reality."[29] "The potter, and not the pot," Alfred North Whitehead adds metaphorically, "is responsible for the shape of the pot."[30] The uninterpreted experience of "nature," as of every other factual reality, is restricted to its mere fact and is void of meaning, a quality that does not inhere in "nature" but is assigned to it by rational beings in interpretive acts. The decisive criterion for the meaning of any human action, including any moral action, for instance, sexual intercourse, is the project of the actor.[31] Meaning is what is or was meant by the *actor*, who is always to be understood not as an Enlightenment radical *individual* but as an Aristotelian-Thomistic radically *social being*. Since "nature" is not pure, uninterpreted nature, since it is, as philosophers and sociologists say, socially constructed, throughout this book we speak of it always within quotation marks, that is, as "nature."

PERSPECTIVISM VERSUS RELATIVISM

To many people, such an approach to reality and truth raises the specter of relativism. With Lonergan, however, we prefer to speak of *perspectivism* rather than relativism. "Where relativism has lost hope about the attainment of truth, perspectivism stresses the complexity of what the historian is writing about and, as well, the specific difference of historical from mathematical, scientific and philosophic knowledge."[32] While relativism concludes to the falsity of a judgment, perspectivism concludes to its *partial* truth. According to Lonergan, perspectivism in human knowledge arises from three factors. First, human knowers are finite, the information available to them is incomplete, and they do not attend to or master all the data available to them. Second, the knowers are selective, given their past socialization, personal experience, and range of data offered to them. Third, knowers are individually different, and we can expect them to make different selections of data. The theologian-knower trained in the philosophy of Plato, for instance, Augustine, will attend to different data, achieve different understanding, make different judgments, and act on different decisions than the theologian-knower trained in the philosophy of Aristotle, for instance, Aquinas. They produce different theologies, both of which will be necessarily partial and incomplete explanations of a very complex reality. They are like two viewers at first-story and fifteenth-story windows of a skyscraper; each gets a different, but no less partial, view of the total panorama that unfolds outside the building.

Every judgment of truth, including, perhaps especially, every judgment of theological truth, is a limited judgment and commitment based on limited data and understanding.[33] "So far from resting on knowledge of the universe, [a judgment] is to the effect that, no matter what the rest of the universe may prove to be, at least *this* is so."[34] It is precisely the necessarily limited nature of human, sociohistorical sensations, understandings, judgments, and knowledge that leads to perspectivism, which is not, to repeat, as a source of falsity but as a source of partial truth. Though he said it on the basis of God's incomprehensibility, Augustine's restating of earlier Greek theologians is apropos and accurate here: "*Si comprehendis non est Deus*"—if you have understood, what you have understood is not God.[35] Aquinas agrees: "Now we cannot know what God is, but only what God is not; we must, therefore, consider the ways in which God does not exist rather than the ways in which God does."[36]

"NATURE," KNOWLEDGE, AND NORMS

This epistemological overview of object and objective knowledge has profound implications for how we understand "nature" and the norms and principles we derive from that understanding. First, depending on the meaning derived from the dialectic of interdependence among object, individual, and society, "nature" includes a variety of meanings and partial truths. These meanings must be judged morally, as *Gaudium et spes* correctly notes, in light of the objective criterion of the human person who is a relational, incarnated, enculturated, historical subject.[37] These epistemological considerations caution against positing a one-size-fits-all morality deduced directly from "nature," and they have implications for the norms we formulate to guide sexual persons.

Second, Fuchs allies our foregoing discussion of "nature" to moral norms in the following manner. He asks what is meant by the objectivity of moral norms and gives two answers. First, a negative answer: "Objectivity does not derive from formal revelation, tradition, or the authentic documents of the magisterium." Second, a positive answer: "If the norms of moral rightness derive from a process of knowledge, evaluation and judgment [and with Lonergan he assumes they do], then it must be admitted that they are determined not only by the elements of the world-object but also by elements of the judging subject that necessarily enter into this process."[38] The human subject cannot make a genuinely moral judgment without careful hermeneutics, that is, without attention to, and understanding, judgment, and affirmation of, both the world and himself or herself in the world. "It is only in this way that a norm is truly objective—whether it is discerned by society or by a single person."[39] This concept of objectivity is different from the one that calls a norm "objective" if it is generally accepted in a society, for example, the church, or is proposed by a social authority, for example, the Magisterium. It is, however, the only concept of objectivity that takes account of the true "nature" of not only physical acts but also the rational subject who performs the acts.

We agree with the majority of Catholic moral theologians that an absolute ethical principle exists and that such an absolute principle dispels all possible confusion. We agree also, however, with the Catholic moral theologian Dietmar Mieth that the only absolute principle is that "good is to be done and evil left undone," and that every other ethical judgment requires concrete, empirical judgment.[40] Fuchs also agrees: "There is no discrepancy of theories and opinions within Catholic moral theology about the one ethical *absolutum*; the translation of the ethical *absolutum* into the [concrete] *material plurality* of human reality is, however, a different matter."[41] The hermeneutic for that translation is controlled, as it is always in the Catholic moral tradition, by human reason seeking to be attentive, intelligent, rational, and responsible in the actual sociohistorical situation.[42] It cannot be otherwise for free persons who live in a world that is both physical and human and that is subject to historicity.

With regard to these matters, the Second Vatican Council taught that lay persons are not to imagine that their pastors "are always such experts that to every problem which arises, however complicated, they can readily give a concrete solution, or even that such is their mission." The clear acknowledgment is that they are not. The Council goes on to advise laypersons, "enlightened by Christian wisdom and giving close attention to the teaching authority of the Church," to take on their own distinctive role.[43] That distinctive role, it teaches with regard to the moral norms of married life, is to reach "objective" judgments based on the "nature" not only of the acts but also of the human person, "*ex personae eiusdem actuum natura.*"[44] Acknowledging the evident plurality of objective moral judgments in the modern world, the Council enjoins "the entire People of God, especially pastors and theologians, to hear, distinguish, and *interpret* the many voices of our age, and to judge them in the light of the divine word. In this way, revealed truth can always be more deeply penetrated, better understood, and set forth to greater advantage."[45] These magisterial teachings suggest to us that the concept of objectivity we have proposed lies well within the Catholic tradition. That it does is already underscored by our prior consideration of historicity.

CONSCIENCE

Earlier we spoke of the need for human moral agents to rationally reflect on what they believe they ought to do, to marshal as fully as possible the evidence for or against their belief, to pass judgment on its truth or falsity, and finally to translate that judgment into a decision for action. That final, practical judgment that this is what I ought to do in this situation is what the Catholic tradition universally calls *conscience*, the "most secret core and sanctuary of a man," where "he is alone with God."[46] Conscience is, as the *Catechism of the Catholic Church* teaches, "a judgment of reason by which the human person recognizes the moral quality of a concrete act," that is, recognizes what he or she ought to do here and now in this situation.[47] Conscience, Richard Gula writes, is "me coming to a decision."[48] Timothy O'Connell's division of conscience into conscience/1, conscience/2, and conscience/3 has become classic.[49] These three "consciences" are not three different realities but three tasks that articulate fully the one reality of conscience.

Conscience/1 is the human's intrinsic capacity to know what is good and to do it; without this intrinsic capacity judgments and decisions of conscience would not be possible. Conscience/2 is accurate marshaling and understanding of the evidence or data and right moral reasoning with respect to it. Conscience/3, conscience in the proper sense, is the practical judgment and decision that this is what I ought to do in this particular situation. In and through that decision, I am and become the person I freely choose to be and become. Once a decision is made to act in this way rather than that way, what we call evaluative conscience takes over, evaluates the decision and its impact on human flourishing, and completes the process of conscience/2 formation by integrating into it the knowledge and understanding gained from the decision. Once conscience/3 has made its judgment of truth and decision to act, the Catholic tradition universally teaches, it is always to be obeyed. Other teachers and authorities, the Church's Magisterium, for instance, may assist conscience/2 in marshaling and understanding the evidence, but once conscience/3 has made its judgment and decision, the individual person stands "alone with God" in carrying it out.

Nobody, the *Catechism of the Catholic Church* teaches, is to "be forced to act contrary to his conscience," and nobody is to "be prevented from acting according to his conscience, *especially in religious matters.*"[50] Pope Benedict XVI, when he was theologian Joseph Ratzinger, articulated in the strongest terms what was and continues to be the universal and consistent Catholic teaching about conscience. "Over the Pope as the expression of the binding claim of ecclesiastical authority there still stands one's own conscience, which must be obeyed before all else, if necessary even against the requirement of ecclesiastical authority."[51]

Even if the practical judgment of conscience/3 is erroneous, because conscience/2 has either not marshaled the data fully or not understood it correctly or not drawn logical conclusions from it, the judgment and decision of conscience/3 is still morally binding. Every prudent effort should be made to marshal and consider the evidence fully, to draw logical conclusions from it, and to make an honest, faithful judgment and decision with respect to what is moral for me to do in this particular situation. It is always possible, however, for the judgment of conscience to be in error, but even if it is in error, the Catholic tradition universally teaches, it is to be followed, and to act against it is immoral. It is precisely to help Catholics marshal all the evidence about human sexuality and make honest, faithful, and true judgments of conscience about moral sexual behavior that the analyses in this book are offered.

QUESTIONS FOR REFLECTION

1. What is the difference between a classicist worldview and a historically conscious worldview? What difference, do you think, do the two worldviews make to the articulation and understanding of Catholic sexuality?

2. Why is honest and open dialogue so critical for the attainment of the truth about Catholic sexuality? Who should be involved in such dialogue in the Church, and how should it be conducted?

3. What do you understand by *nature* and our presentation of it as *"nature"*? What is the role of human reason in reading the meanings of nature?

4. How do you understand *perspectivism*? How is it different from *relativism*? What correction does perspectivism offer to your understanding of magisterial teaching?

5. What do you understand by *conscience*? What is the obligation to reach, and how should one reach, a well-formed conscience?

6. What other questions arise for you from reading this prologue?

NOTES

1. Diogenes Laertius, *Lives of Eminent Philosophers*, VIII, 1, 9.
2. HV, 11.
3. PH, 7.
4. *ST*, II–IIae, 154, 11 corp.
5. *AAS* 43 (1951), 835–54.
6. Bernard J. F. Lonergan, *Insight: A Study of Human Understanding* (London: Longman's, 1957), especially 431–87, *Method in Theology* (New York: Herder and Herder, 1972), 237–44, 270–71.
7. Robert M. Doran, *Theology and the Dialectics of History* (Toronto: University of Toronto Press, 1990), 35.
8. Ibid., 36.
9. Ibid.
10. Ibid.
11. Lonergan, *Method in Theology*, 270; emphasis added.
12. See Michael G. Lawler, *What Is and What Ought to Be: The Dialectic of Experience, Theology, and Church* (New York: Continuum, 2005), 18–20.
13. DV, 12; and Pius XII, *Divino afflante spiritu*, AAS 35 (1943), 297–325.
14. CCC, 2357, n. 140.
15. GS, 62.
16. Ibid., 51.
17. John Paul II, *Ut unum sint*, 28; emphasis added.
18. See Jean-Pierre Torell, *St. Thomas Aquinas*, vol. 1 (Washington, DC: Catholic University of America Press, 1996), 54–74.
19. Peter Cantor, *Verbum abrreviatum*, 1, PL 205, 25; emphasis added.

20. International Theological Commission, *Theses on the Relationship between the Ecclesiastical Magisterium and Theology* (Washington, DC: USCC, 1977), 6.

21. Johann Sebastian Drey, *Brief Introduction to the Study of Theology with Reference to the Scientific Standpoint of the Catholic System*, trans. Michael J. Himes (Notre Dame: University of Notre Dame Press, 1994), xxv.

22. Ibid., xxvi.

23. For a recent exemplar of this approach, see Julie Hanlon Rubio, "Beyond the Liberal/Conservative Divide on Contraception," *Horizons* 32 (2005), 270–94.

24. See *LG*, 48.

25. G. E. Moore, *Principia Ethica* (Cambridge: Cambridge University Press, 1903), 64; W. K. Frankena, *Ethics* (Englewood Cliffs, NJ: Prentice Hall, 1963), 101.

26. See Jean Porter, *Nature as Reason: A Thomistic Theory of Natural Law* (Grand Rapids, MI: Eerdmans, 2005), 123–25.

27. Ibid., 117.

28. See John T. Noonan Jr., *A Church That Can and Cannot Change: The Development of Catholic Moral Teaching* (Notre Dame, IN: University of Notre Dame Press, 2005); Michael G. Lawler, *What Is and What Ought to Be* (New York: Continuum, 2005), 127–29.

29. Alfred Schutz, *Collected Papers* (The Hague: Martinus Nijhoff, 1964–67), 1:230; emphasis added.

30. Alfred North Whitehead, *Symbolism: Its Meaning and Effect* (New York: Putnam's, 1959), 8.

31. See, for example, Thomas Luckmann, *The Invisible Religion: The Transformation of Symbols in Industrial Society* (New York: Macmillan, 1967); Peter L. Berger and Thomas Luckmann, *The Social Construction of Reality: A Treatise in the Sociology of Knowledge* (New York: Doubleday, 1966).

32. Lonergan, *Method in Theology*, 217.

33. On limit language, see David Tracy, *Blessed Rage for Order: The New Pluralism in Theology* (New York: Seabury, 1975); *The Analogical Imagination: The Culture of Pluralism* (New York: Crossroad, 1987); *Plurality and Ambiguity: Hermeneutics, Religion, and Hope* (San Francisco: Jossey-Bass, 1987).

34. Lonergan, *Insight*, 344; emphasis added. See also *Method in Theology*, 217–19.

35. *Sermo* 52, 16, *PL* 38, 360. For a detailed analysis, see Victor White, *God the Unknown* (New York: Harper, 1956); and William Hill, *Knowing the Unknown God* (New York: Philosophical Library, 1971).

36. *ST*, I, 3, preface.

37. *GS*, 51.

38. Joseph Fuchs, *Moral Demands and Personal Obligations* (Washington, DC: Georgetown University Press, 1993), 103.

39. Ibid., 104.

40. Dietmar Mieth, *Moral und Erfahrung. Beitrage zur theologisch-ethischen Hermeneutik* (Freiburg: 1977), 34.

41. Fuchs, *Moral Demands*, 27. Emphasis in original.

42. Lonergan, *Method in Theology*, 20.
43. GS, 43.
44. Ibid., 51.
45. Ibid., 44; emphasis added.
46. GS, 16.
47. CCC, 1778 and 1796.
48. Richard M. Gula, *Reason Informed by Faith: Foundations of Catholic Morality* (New York: Paulist, 1989), 131. For an extended discussion of conscience, see 123–62.
49. Timothy O'Connell, *Principles for a Catholic Morality* (New York: Seabury, 1978), 88–93.
50. CCC, 1782 and 1800; emphasis added.
51. Joseph Ratzinger, "The Dignity of the Human Person," in *Commentary on the Documents of Vatican II*, ed. H. Vorgrimler (New York: Herder, 1969), 134. For a discussion of two models on the relationship between the formation of conscience and magisterial teaching, see Todd A. Salzman, "Signs of the Times: Ethical Method, Noninfallible Magisterial Teaching, and the Formation of Conscience: Two Divergent Models," *New Theology Review* 17, no. 4 (November 2004): 76–77.

CHAPTER I

❧

Sexual Morality in the Catholic Tradition
A Brief History

Human sexual activity and the sexual ethics that seeks to order it are both sociohistorical realities and are, therefore, subject to historicity. Before we embark on a presentation of contemporary Catholic sexual anthropology and ethics, therefore, it behooves us to look at their past history. We will do that in two stages. First, and briefly, we will consider the pre-Christian history that helped to shape Western understanding of human sexuality, sexual activity, and sexual ethics. Second, and more extensively, we will consider their understanding in specifically Catholic history. Before embarking on the history, however, we must first say a word about historicity.

HISTORICITY

Bernard Lonergan lays out "the theoretical premises from which there follows the historicity of human thought and action." They are as follows: "(1) that human concepts, theories, affirmations, courses of action are expressions of human understanding. . . . (2) That human understanding develops over time and, as it develops, human concepts, theories, affirmations, courses of action change. . . . (3) That such change is cumulative, and (4) that the cumulative changes in one place or time are not to be expected to coincide with those in another."[1] From these premises flows the conclusion that the articulations of the moral values, norms, and actions of one sociohistorical era are not necessarily those of another era or, indeed, of different groups in the same era. The world—both world free of every human intervention and the human world fashioned by socially constructed meanings and values—is in a permanent state of change and evolution. It is essentially for this reason that Joseph Fuchs argues, correctly in our judgment, that anyone who wishes to make a moral judgment about any human action in the present on the basis of its givenness in the past has at least two facts to keep in mind.

First, the past simply did not know the entire reality of the human person from its emergence to its full development in the future or its individual elements from the mysterious powers of the physical universe to the possibilities of human sexuality considered physiologically, psychologically, and sociohistorically. "If one wishes to make an objective moral judgment today," Fuchs points out, "then one cannot take what Augustine or the philosophers of the Middle Ages knew about sexuality as the exclusive basis of a moral reflection."[2] Second, "we never simply 'have' nature or that which is given in nature." We know "nature," rather, "always as something that has already been interpreted in some way."[3] The understanding, interpretation, and judgment of rational persons about "nature" and what it demands, never simply the pure givenness of "nature" alone, is what constitutes *natural law*. In the Catholic moral tradition, argument is never from "nature" alone or reason alone, but always from "nature" *interpreted by* reason. For the human person subject to historicity, moral decision making and action is always the outcome of a process of interpretation controlled by reason. It is never the outcome of the mere fact of "nature."

Lonergan was convinced that something new was happening in history in the twentieth century and that, since a living theology ought to be part of what is taking place in history, Christians were living in a new theological age that required a new theological approach. That new approach, he prophesied correctly, would be necessarily historical and empirical. Lonergan's distinction between a classicist and an empirical notion of culture has itself become classical. "The classicist notion of culture was normative ... there was but one culture that was both universal and permanent"; the empirical notion of culture is "the set of meanings and values that informs a way of life."[4] Classicist culture is static; empirical culture is dynamic. Theology, which is necessarily part of culture, mirrors this distinction.

In its classicist mode, moral theology is a static, permanent achievement that anyone can learn; in its empirical mode, it is a dynamic, ongoing process requiring a free person who is committed and trained. The classicist understanding, Fuchs writes, conceives of the human person as "a series of created, static, and thus definitively ordered temporal facts"; the empirical understanding conceives of the person as a subject in process of "self-realization in accordance with a project that develops in God-given autonomy, that is, along a path of human reason and insight."[5] Classicist theology sees moral norms coming from the Magisterium as once and for all definitive; sexual norms enunciated in the fifth or sixteenth centuries continue to apply absolutely in the twenty-first century. Empirical theology sees the moral norms of the past not as facts for uncritical acceptance but as partial insights providing bases for critical understanding, evaluation, and decision in the present sociohistorical situation. What Augustine and his medieval successors knew about sexuality cannot be the exclusive basis for a moral judgment about sexuality today.

The Catholic Magisterium has two approaches to making moral judgments. In sexual ethics it follows the classicist approach enshrined, for instance, in the writings of Pope John Paul II; in social ethics it follows the historical approach validated by the Second Vatican Council. The *Catechism of the Catholic Church* teaches that "the Church's social teaching proposes *principles for reflection*; it provides *criteria for judgment*; it gives *guidelines* for action."[6] This trinity of principles for reflection, criteria for judgment, and guidelines for action came into Catholic social teaching via Paul VI's *Octogesima adveniens* in 1971.[7] It was repeated in the Congregation for the Doctrine of the Faith's (CDF) important *Instruction on Christian Freedom and Liberation* in 1986,[8] and underscored again a year later in John Paul II's *Sollicitudo rei socialis*. This sociomoral teaching introduces a model of personal responsibility that increasingly emphasizes the responsibility of each person. John Paul accentuates this point of view by teaching that, in its social doctrine, the Church seeks "to *guide* people to *respond*, with the support of rational reflection and of the human sciences, to their vocation as *responsible* builders of earthly society."[9] The relationship of Magisterium and individual believer advanced in this teaching merits close attention. The Church guides.[10] Responsible persons, drawing on this guidance, their own intellectual abilities, and the findings of the human sciences, respond responsibly.

The notion of responsibility introduces an important personal and important dimension of human freedom and autonomy to the unnuanced notion of response.[11] In social reality, the Magisterium does not pretend to pronounce on every last detail or to impose final decisions; it understands itself as informing and guiding believers, and leaving the final judgment and application to their faithful and responsible conscience.[12] Sociomoral principles are guidelines for reflection, judgment, and action, not unchanging moral imperatives demanding uncritical obedience to God, "nature," or Church. John Paul adds what the Catholic moral tradition has always taken for granted. On the one hand, the Church's social teaching is "constant." On the other hand, "it is ever new, because it is subject to the necessary and opportune adaptations suggested by the changes in historical conditions and by the unceasing flow of the events which are the setting of the life of people and society."[13] Principles remain constant. Criteria for judgments and guidelines for actions might well change after reflection on changed sociohistorical conditions and the data of the social sciences.

In *social morality*, then, the Catholic Church offers principles for reflection, criteria for judgment, and guidelines for action. In *sexual morality*, however, it offers propositions from past tradition, not as principles and guidelines for reflection, judgment, and action but as laws and absolute norms to be universally and uncritically obeyed. How this can be is, at least, debatable. Since social and sexual morality pertain to the same person, this double and conflicting approach seems illogical.

In fact, because the whole personality is more intimately involved in the sexual domain, should it not "be *more than any other* the place where all is referred to the informed conscience."[14] The choice between the two moral approaches is neither self-evident nor free from risk, but it is a choice that must be made to find the best theological and pastoral approach to the experience of contemporary women and men.

SEXUALITY AND SEXUAL ETHICS IN ANCIENT GREECE AND ROME

Though generalizations about ancient Greece and Rome are fraught with difficulties, both because their histories were in general written by elite males to the detriment of women's sexual histories and because we know today more about Athens and Rome than about any other Greek or Roman city, we can safely say that in both societies sexuality was generally accepted as a natural part of life and that attitudes toward sex were permissive, especially for men.[15] In both societies, marriage was monogamous and regarded as the foundation of social life, but sexual activity was not restricted to marriage. Judith Hallett demonstrates that, at least among elite men and women, erotic intercourse could be sought with partners other than spouses.[16] And concubinage, male and female prostitution, and male intercourse with slaves were also permitted and common. The ancient aphorism attributed to Demosthenes is famous: "Mistresses we keep for the sake of pleasure, concubines for the daily care of our persons, but wives to bear us legitimate children and to be faithful guardians of our households."[17] Divorce was readily available in Greece and the later Roman Empire, with both societies legislating for the economic situation of divorced women. Abortion and infanticide were commonly accepted forms of birth control. Marriage was not about love, which is not to say that marital love was never present between spouses. Men were expected to marry to produce an heir, but for them the greatest love was to be had in relationship, sexual or otherwise, with other men, for between men there was an equality that a man could never attain with a woman.

Both Greece and Rome were male-dominated societies in which women were regarded as inferior to men, indeed as belonging to men, first to their fathers and then to their husbands. Male homosexual activity was accepted in both as a function of a patriarchal ethos, and female homosexual activity was regarded as adultery, because wives were the property of their husbands.[18] The approved male homosexual activity was not because some men had an intrinsic homosexual orientation, which was unknown at the time, but because men were considered more beautiful than women, and a man might reasonably be attracted to the more beautiful. It is misleading, however, to speak of sexual relations between men; relations were most often between adult men and boys. Those relations were to cease when the boy reached a certain age, not because homosexual relations per se were problematic, but because adult *male passivity* was problematic.[19] We will encounter this same problematic later when we consider the biblical texts proscribing male homosexuality.

Greek and Roman attitudes toward sexuality were fashioned in large part by their great philosophers. The Greek dualism between body and soul, with the body being the inferior component, led to a distrust of physical sex and the categorization of sexual pleasure. Both Plato and Aristotle judged sexual pleasure to be a lower pleasure shared with other animals.[20] Plato urged its transcendence for the sake of higher pleasures of good, beauty, and truth; Aristotle urged its moderation. It was not, however, Plato or Aristotle who had the greatest influence on the Christian approach to sexuality. It was the Stoics. We deal with these in some detail in the next section; here we make only two summary statements. The Stoic Musonius Rufus, in his *Reliquiae*, and Seneca, in his *Fragments*, considered sexual desire and activity to be irrational and liable to excess. They sought, therefore, to rationally order it by situating it in a larger context of human meaning, and they did this by asking about its *telos*, its purpose or end. That end, they judged, was the procreation of children, and therefore sexual activity was moral *only* when it was engaged in for the sake of procreation. The later Stoics went further. Not only was sexual activity for procreation, but also it was to be limited to marriage; there could be no moral sex outside of marriage. Stoic philosophers both "conjugalized" and "procreationalized" sexual relations.

SEXUALITY AND SEXUAL ETHICS IN THE CATHOLIC TRADITION

In 1968, in *Humanae vitae*, Pope Paul VI asserted that in marriage "each and every marriage act must remain open to the transmission of life."[21] In 1976 the Congregation for the Doctrine of the Faith asserted that, to be moral, "any human genital act whatsoever may be placed only within the framework of marriage."[22] In traditional Catholic sexual morality, therefore, every sexually moral act takes place only within the institution of marriage, and within marriage each and every such act must be open to procreation. Traditional Catholic sexual morality is essentially *marital* morality; sexuality is carefully confined in marriage, and every intentional genital act outside of marriage is seriously sinful.[23]

The consonance of that teaching with Stoic philosophy is clear. It would be wholly inaccurate, however, to assume that Greek philosophy is the only root of Catholic sexual morality. Catholicism's first instinct is to consult not ancient Greek philosophers but its ancient sacred text, the Bible, believed to be the word of God. As Catholic theologians, it is also our first instinct, and so we begin our analysis of the development of traditional Catholic sexual morality with an exploration of first the Old and then the New Testament. Following the lead of the Second Vatican Council, we then follow the biblical tradition through its subsequent history, in which, under the grace of the Spirit of God, "there is a growth in insight into the realities and words that are being passed on."[24]

READING SACRED SCRIPTURE

The Pontifical Biblical Commission's 1994 document *The Interpretation of the Bible in the Church* insists, "Holy scripture, inasmuch as it is 'the Word of God in human language,' has been composed by human authors in all its various parts and in all the sources that lie behind them. Because of this, its proper understanding not only admits the use of [the historical-critical] method but actually requires it."[25] It acknowledges the historicity of the biblical texts, insisting that "religious texts are bound in reciprocal relationship to the societies in which they originate. . . . Consequently, the scientific study of the Bible requires as exact a knowledge as possible of the social conditions distinctive of the various milieus in which the traditions recorded in the Bible took shape."[26] The very nature of the biblical texts requires the use of a historical methodology for their correct interpretation.

Of particular relevance to this book is the Commission's applications of its principles for biblical exegesis to moral theology. Though the Bible is God's word to the church, "this does not mean that God has given the historical conditioning of the message a value which is absolute. It is open both to interpretation and being brought up to date"; it follows, therefore, that it is not sufficient for moral judgment that the scripture "should indicate a certain moral position [e.g., the practice of polygamy, slavery, or divorce, or the "prohibition" of homosexual acts] for this position to continue to have validity. One has to undertake a process of discernment. This will review the issue in the light of the progress in moral understanding and sensitivity that has occurred over the years."[27] And so Fuchs writes that what Augustine, Jerome, Aquinas, and Trent said about sexuality cannot exclusively control what moral theologians say today.

Scriptural and traditional doctrinal formulations are the result of reflexive, critical, human construal and have to be, therefore, as historically conditioned as its construers themselves.[28] It cannot be otherwise. If God is to be really revealed to historical women and men, there is no alternative but for the revelation to be mediated in their sociohistorical symbols. If the foundational revelation is to be expressed in human language, oral or written, as it is in scriptural, doctrinal, and theological formulations, there is no alternative but for the expression to be in a language that is historically mediated. There is no transhistorical, transcultural language valid for all times and for all peoples. Since the scriptural rule of faith and the theological writings derived from it are historically and culturally conditioned, they will require translation, interpretation, and enculturation to truly disclose God in every different historical and cultural situation. Since the translators, interpreters, and enculturators may stand in different sociohistorical contexts, their interpretations of the classic tradition will almost certainly be pluriform, which will lead to debate. That debate will be resolved only by theologians in respectful dialogue.

Discovering what scripture says about sexual morality, therefore, is never as straightforward as simply reading the text. The reader must get behind the text to understand how the Church and its theologians construe scripture and what authority they assign to it. We begin our analysis with the Catholic teaching of how the four Gospels came to be and how they are to be interpreted. They came to be in a four-stage process: a first generation of followers construed their experience of the life, death, and resurrection of Jesus of Nazareth as religious and revelatory of God; further construals grew up around that experience; those traditions were preserved in written form in the third generation.[29] And certain of those writings were ultimately canonized as authoritative Church scripture.[30] How theologians understand this four-stage process determines how they construe scripture and its authority in theology.

The Second Vatican Council embraced this four-stage scheme with respect to the writing of the four Gospels and issued instruction on how the scriptures of both testaments are to be read. "Those who search out the intentions of the sacred writers," it teaches, "must, among other things have regard for 'literary forms.' For truth is proposed and expressed in a variety of ways, depending on whether a text is history of one kind or another, or whether its form is that of prophecy, poetry, or some other type of speech. The interpreter must investigate what meaning the sacred writer *intended to express and actually expressed* in particular circumstances as he used contemporary literary forms in accordance with the situation of his own time and culture."[31] It is never enough simply to read the text to find out what it says about sexual morality. Its original sociohistorical context must first be clarified, and then the text can be translated, interpreted, and enculturated in a contemporary context. An example of how sexual morality and sociohistorical context are connected appears from an analysis of patriarchy.

The dominant characteristic of patriarchy is that it describes women in relation to men, and in ways that serve and further men's interests. Patriarchy is the "social order in which women are declared to be the possessions of, first, fathers and, later, husbands."[32] It is "the systematic social closure of women from the public sphere by legal, political, and economic arrangements which operate in favor of men."[33] Patriarchal assumptions abound in both testaments, and the New Testament uses them to enforce women's subordination to men (1 Cor. 11:7–12; Col. 3:18), to silence them in church, and to suggest the way for women to atone for their collective guilt in causing men to sin is to bear men children (1 Tim. 2:12–15). Genesis 2–3 is the mythical justification for all patriarchy in the Bible. In this account, the earlier creation account, woman is created as an afterthought *from* man and *for* man. She is to be "a helper fit for him" (Gen. 2:20). A quite different perspective is given in the later account in Genesis 1, where both male and female are created together "in [God's] own image" and together are declared to be *'adam*, humankind (Gen. 1:27). This presumed equality between male and female as human vanishes in Genesis 3, where the woman is blamed for the man's sin (Gen. 3:12) and condemned to be under the man's rule (Gen. 3:16).

If we accept the Bible as a source for moral judgments about sexual morality, the Catholic tradition requires that we first examine the cultural assumptions that underpin what is said about sexual morality. If what is said is inseparably linked to the underpinning judgment that the proper relationship between a man and a woman is a patriarchal relationship with the man as superior, then a careful process of separating what is true but culturally limited and what is transculturally true must be undertaken. For Christians, the criterion for such a refining process is provided by the New Testament and Jesus's behavior toward women, the woman with the issue of blood (Mark 5:25–34), the sinful woman in the house of the Pharisee (Luke 7:36–50), and the Samaritan woman at Jacob's well (John 4:8–30). Jesus deals with and speaks to none of these women in a demeaning or patriarchal way. It was but a small further step to Paul's egalitarian judgment that for Christians in the fictive family of Jesus ("whoever does the will of God is my brother, my sister, my mother" (Mark 3:35), "there is neither male nor female, for you are all one person in Christ" (Gal. 3:28).

OLD TESTAMENT TEACHING

Old Testament teaching on sexuality and marriage must be situated in the context of the ancient Near Eastern cultures with which the biblical peoples had such intimate links. Underlying the themes of sexuality and marriage in the cultures surrounding Israel are the archetypal figures of the god-father and the goddess-mother, the sources of universal life in the divine, the human, and the natural realms. Myths celebrated the marriage, the sexual intercourse, and the fertility of this divine pair, simultaneously divinizing sexuality and legitimating the marriage, the intercourse, and the fertility of every earthly pair. Rituals acted out the myths, establishing a concrete link between the divine and the earthly worlds, enabling men and women to share in both the divine action and the efficacy of that action. This is especially true of sexual rituals, which bless sexual intercourse and ensure that the unfailing divine fertility is shared by a man's plants and animals and wives, all important elements in his struggle for survival in those primitive cultures.

The Hebrew view of sexuality and marriage makes a radical break with this polytheistic perspective.[34] Sexuality is not divinized. There is no god–goddess couple, only Yahweh who is unique (Deut. 6:4). In the later Priestly account, God creates merely by uttering a creative word (Gen. 1) and, in the earlier Yahwist account, by shaping creation as a potter (Gen. 2–3). At the apex of Yahweh's creation stands 'adam, man and woman together: "male and female he created them and he blessed them and named them 'adam" (Gen. 5:2). The fact that Yahweh names male and female together 'adam, that is, earthlings or humankind, founds the equality of man and woman as human beings. They are "bone of my bones and flesh of my flesh" (Gen. 2:23), and because they are equal they can marry and become "one body" (Gen. 2:24). In marriage, equal man and woman take on the unequal gendered roles of husband and wife, which gives a foundation for biblical patriarchy.[35]

Equal man and woman, and their separate sexualities, do not derive from a divine pair whom they are to imitate. They are called into being by the creative action of the sovereign God. "It was not the sacred rites that surrounded marriage that made it a holy thing. The great rite which sanctified marriage was God's act of creation itself."[36] It was God alone, unaided by any partner, who not only created 'adam with sexuality and for marriage but also blessed him and her, making them fundamentally good. That a man and a woman become one body in marriage has often been restricted in the Western tradition to only one facet of marriage, namely, the act of uniting bodies in sexual intercourse. That facet is undoubtedly included in becoming one body but it is far from all there is, for body in Hebrew implies the entire person. "One personality would translate it better, for 'flesh' in the Jewish idiom means 'real human life.'"[37] In the debate on sexuality and marriage at the Second Vatican Council, biblical scholar Cardinal Alfrink pointed out that "the Hebrew verb dabaq, in Greek kollao, does suggest physical, bodily, sexual union, but it suggests above all spiritual union which exists in conjugal love."[38] In marriage a man and a woman unite in an interpersonal union, not just a sexual or genital one. In such a union they become one coupled social person and one life, so complementing one another that they become again, as in the beginning, 'adam, one social person.

The older Yahwist creation account in Genesis 2–3 situates sexuality in a relational context. "It is not good that the male should be alone," God judges, "I will make a helper fit for him" (2:18). The importance of the helper to the one helped may be gleaned from the fact that twice in the Psalms (30:10 and 54:4) God is presented as such a helper of humans. The equality of the partners in this helping relationship is underscored. Male and female are "bone of my bones and flesh of my flesh" (2:23), they have the same strengths and the same weaknesses, and the myth asserts that it is precisely because of their equality and, therefore, potential intimacy that male and female may marry. Significantly, they are presented as being totally comfortable with each other's sexuality, for they "were both naked and not ashamed" (1:25), a comfort that is celebrated frankly in that great Jewish love song, the Song of Songs.

About four hundred years later, the Priestly tradition has God bless *'adam*, male and female, and enjoin them to "be fruitful and multiply, and fill the earth and subdue it" (1:28). Male and female, their sexuality, and their fertility are blessed by God; ever afterward there can be no doubt that sexuality is good. The Priestly myth situates sexuality in a procreative context, that is, a context of cooperation with the Creator in both the creation of children and caring providence for them. Raymond Collins notes that "procreation was valued in Israel insofar as large Israelite families were considered to be the fulfillment of the promise made to Abraham."[39] From the beginning of the biblical tradition, therefore, sexuality as created by God is linked to two perspectives, to the relationship of mutual help between male and female and to their procreative activity together. These two perspectives are the ones we found also in the Greco-Roman, Stoic tradition. They will have convoluted histories in the postbiblical, Catholic tradition.

Central to the Hebrews' notion of their special relationship with God was the idea of the covenant. Yahweh is the God of Israel; Israel is the people of Yahweh. Together Yahweh and Israel form a union of salvation, a union of grace, a union, one could say, of one body. It was probably only a matter of time until the people began to image this covenant relationship in terms drawn from marriage, and the first to speak of marriage as image of the covenant was the prophet Hosea. He preached about the covenant relationship of Yahweh and Israel within the biographical context of his own marriage to his wife, Gomer. Hosea found in marriage, either in his own marriage or in marriage in general, an image in which to represent the steadfastness of Yahweh's covenantal love for the people of Israel. On a superficial level, the marriage of Hosea and Gomer is like any other marriage. But on a deeper level, it serves as prophetic symbol, revealing and celebrating in representation the covenant relationship between Yahweh and Israel. Yahweh's covenant fidelity becomes a characteristic to be imitated, a challenge to be accepted, first, in every Jewish marriage and, later, in every Christian one.

Another Old Testament book, the Song of Songs, is intimately related to any biblical analysis of sexuality. The Song has always been an embarrassment for interpreters, posing the difficulty of deciding whether it is a celebration of divine or human love. For centuries, under the shadow of the negative presuppositions about sexuality that developed in the postbiblical Church, Christian commentators opted for a spiritualized meaning. The Song, they prudishly explained, was about the love of Yahweh for Israel, even the love of God for the individual soul. This argument ignores the historical fact that the Song was included in the Hebrew canon before there was any suggestion of an allegorical interpretation, which in itself provides "a powerful argument for believing that Israel's faith did not see its profane nature as an impediment to its acceptance as 'biblical literature.'"[40] Embodied men and women need no elaborate literary or philosophical argument; they need only listen to the extraordinarily explicit words and imagery of sexual love to know what the poetry means.

"I am sick with love," the woman exclaims (2:5; 5:8). "Come to me," she cries out in desire for her lover, "like a gazelle, like a young stag upon the mountains where spices grow" (2:17; 8:14). When he comes and gazes upon her nakedness, he is moved to poetry. "Your rounded thighs are like jewels . . . your vulva is a rounded bowl that never lacks wine.[41] Your belly is a heap of wheat encircled with lilies. Your two breasts are like fawns, twins of a gazelle. . . . You are stately as a palm tree and your breasts are like its clusters. I say I will climb the palm tree and lay hold of its branches" (7:1–8). Her response is direct and far from coy. "I am my beloved's and his desire is for me. Come, my beloved, let us go forth into the fields. . . . There I will give you my love" (7:10–13). No woman or man who has ever been sick with love and desire can doubt the origin of the language or its intent. Karl Barth, who argued that the Song was a "second Magna Carta" that develops the relationship view hinted at in Genesis 2, notes the equality between the man and the woman in the Song.[42] "It is to be noted that in this second text we hear a voice which is lacking in the first. This is the voice of the woman, to whom the man looks and moves with no less pain and joy than she to him, and who finds him with no less freedom . . . than she is found. Implicitly, of course, this voice is heard in Genesis as well. But now it finds expression in words. And what words!"[43]

Such explicitly erotic language has always raised doubt about the claim that the Song is about divine love, and today a consensus has emerged among scholars that its clear and literal meaning is the one enshrined in any human love song.[44] The Song may be an allegory about divine love, but only secondarily; it may be about spiritual love, but only derivatively. It is primarily about human, erotic love, love that makes every lover "sick with love" (2:5). This love is celebrated as image of the love of the creator God who loves women and men as the two lovers love each other. It is celebrated as good, to honor both the Giver and the gift, and also the lovers who use the gift to make both human and, in representation, divine love. Sexuality is no more divinized in the Song than anywhere else in the Old Testament; it may provide the basis for spiritual analogy, but the basis remains a secular, profane, and good reality. Barth notes an item of importance, namely, the woman speaks as openly as the man, and just as often. "There is no male dominance, no female subordination, and no stereotyping of either sex."[45] Nor is there any mention of marriage or procreation to justify sexuality. The Song is a far cry from Plato's and Aristotle's downgrading of sexual desire and pleasure; it is a celebration of human love and of the sexual desire of the lovers. Christian history will seriously patriarchalize the equal sexual relationship between male and female, will institutionalize it within the confines of marriage and procreation, and will follow Plato and Aristotle in their suspicion of sexual pleasure.

NEW TESTAMENT TEACHING

Sexuality, as we have seen, plays a relatively small role in the Old Testament. Lisa Cahill judges it "striking" that it also "plays a relatively small role in the New Testament at all. Only twice does Jesus direct his concern toward it [John 8:1–11 and Matt. 5:31–32], and in both cases he protects women from the customs of his day and culture."[46] The New Testament provides no more of a systematic code of sexual ethics or even an approach to a sexual ethics than does the Old Testament. The most extensive New Testament teaching about sexuality is in Paul's first letter to the Corinthians, apparently in response to a question the Corinthians had asked: "Is it better for a man not to touch a woman?" (7:1). Paul's answer, under the mistaken apprehension that the last days have arrived (7:31), is a mixed message. He prefers celibacy over marriage in the situation of the last days, but "because of the temptation to sexual immorality, each man should have his own wife and each woman her own husband" (7:2). It is "better to marry than to be aflame with passion" (7:9). Marriage is good, even for Christians, he seems to say, against the ascetical Encratites and Gnostics, who urged celibacy on all Christians, even if only as a safeguard against sexual sins (7:5–9).

Much more telling, however, than his grudging affirmation of marriage and sex in the circumstances of his time is Paul's counter-cultural assertion of equality between husband and wife in marriage. "The husband should give to the wife her conjugal rights, and likewise the wife to her husband. For the wife does not rule over her own body, but the husband does; likewise, the husband does not rule over his own body, but the wife does" (7:3–4). Theodore Mackin accurately comments.

> A modern Christian may wince at finding the apostle writing of sexual intercourse as an obligation, or even a debt, owed by spouses to one another, and writing of husbands' and wives' marital relationship as containing authority over one another's bodies. But Paul's contemporaries—at least those bred in the tradition of Torah and of its rabbinic interpreters—would have winced for another reason. This was Paul's assertion of equality between husbands and wives, and equality exactly on the juridical ground of authority and obligations owed.[47]

When a Christian man and a Christian woman marry, first-century Paul suggests, the covenant they make with each other is a covenant of equal and intimate partnership, and it embraces their human sexual activity within it. It is a suggestion that the Second Vatican Council will pursue twenty centuries later.[48]

Hosea's conception of marriage as a prophetic symbol of the mutually faithful covenant relationship is continued in the New Testament, with a change of characters, from Yahweh–Israel to Christ–church. Rather than presenting marriage in the then-classical Jewish way as a symbol of the covenant union between Yahweh and Israel, the writer of the letter to the Ephesians presents it as an image of the relationship between the Christ and the new Israel, his church.[49] This presentation is of central importance to the development of a Christian view of marriage and sexuality and, unfortunately, has been used to sustain such a diminished Christian view that we have to consider it here in some detail.

The passage in which the writer offers his view of marriage (5:21–33) is situated within a larger context (5:21–6:9), which sets forth a list of household duties that exist within a family in his historical time and place. This list is addressed to wives (5:22), husbands (5:25), children (6:1), fathers (6:4), slaves (6:5), and masters (6:9). All that concerns us here is what is said to wives and husbands. There are two similar lists in the New Testament, one in the letter to the Colossians (3:18–4:1), the other in the first letter of Peter (2:13–3:7), but the Ephesians' list opens with a singular injunction. "Because you fear [or stand in awe of] Christ give way to one another" or, in the weaker translation of the Revised Standard Version, "be subject to one another out of reverence for Christ" (5:21). This injunction, commentators agree, is an essential element of what follows. Mutual giving way is required of all Christians, even of husbands and wives as they seek holiness together in marriage, and even in spite of traditional patriarchal relationships that permitted husbands to lord it over their wives.

As Christians have all been admonished to give way to one another, there is no surprise in the instruction that a Christian wife is to give way to her husband, "as to the Lord" (5:22). There is a surprise, however, at least for the ingrained male attitude that sees the husband as lord and master of his wife and appeals to Ephesians 5:22–23 to ground and sustain that un-Christian attitude, that a husband is to give way to his wife. That follows from the general instruction that Christians are to give way to one another. It follows also from the specific instruction given to husbands. That instruction is not that "the husband is the head of the wife," the way the text is frequently cited, but rather that "*in the same way* that the Messiah is the head of the church the husband is the head of the wife." A Christian husband's headship over his wife is to be modeled upon and model of Christ's headship over the Church, and the way Christ exercises authority is never in doubt: "The Son of Man came not to be served but to serve, and to give his life as a ransom [redemption] for many" (Mark 10:45).

Diakonia, service, is the Christ way of exercising authority; it was as a servant that "Christ loved the church and gave himself up for her" (5:25). A Christian husband, therefore, is instructed to be head over his wife by serving, giving way to, and giving himself up for her. Marital authority modeled on that of Christ does not mean control, giving orders, making unreasonable demands, reducing another person to the status of servant or, worse, of slave to one's every whim. It means loving service. The Christian husband-head, as Markus Barth puts it so beautifully, becomes "the first servant of his wife."[50] It is such a husband, and only such a one, that a wife is to hold in awe (v. 33b) as all Christians fear or hold in awe Christ (v. 21b). There is no reversal of Paul's judgment of equality between spouses in marriage, but rather a confirmation of it from another perspective, that of mutual and equal service, in every part of their life, including the sexual. A husband is further instructed to love his wife, for "he who loves his wife loves himself" (v. 28b; cp. v. 33a). This love is essential to marriage, and the marriage it founds reveals a profound mystery about Christ and Church. The mystery, most scholars agree, is embedded in the text of Genesis 2:24 cited in 5:31. As the Anchor Bible translation seeks to show, "this [passage] has an eminent secret meaning," which is that it refers to Christ and Christ's Church.

THE FATHERS OF THE CHURCH

The doctrine about sexuality and marriage in both Old and New Testaments was a Jewish doctrine, developed in the originating Jewish culture of the Christian movement. The developing Christian Church soon moved out of that Jewish culture into a Greco-Roman one in which Greek and Latin Fathers of the Church shaped the biblical doctrine about marriage and sexuality within their own cultural contexts and established the Catholic approach to sexuality we noted at the outset, namely, sexual morality as marital morality. To understand fully the Christian tradition about sexuality and marriage that came down to our day, we must seek to understand not only their teaching but also the historical situation in which it developed. As we have already discovered for the Bible, there was no systematic and full treatment of either sexuality or marriage as a social and Christian institution. The Fathers' teaching was almost exclusively a defense of marriage and marital sexuality against certain errors that threatened both its Christian value and its future. The majority of these errors had Gnostic sources, and it will be to our benefit to consider, however briefly, the Gnosticism from which they came.

Gnosticism, a Hellenistic religious philosophy characterized by the doctrine that salvation is achieved through a special knowledge (*gnosis*), antedated Christianity and exercised a great influence on many Christian communities in the Mediterranean Basin. Christian Gnostics looked upon themselves as the only faithful interpreters of the Jesus movement. They preached a dualistic and pessimistic view of the world, a view in which good and evil are equally real. Both of these views affected their attitude toward sexuality and marriage and therefore the Fathers' expositions on them in response. Because matter, and therefore sexuality and marriage with their very material bodily intercourse and bodily outcome, was essentially evil, Gnostics believed, it could not have been created by a good God. That meant they had to revise the classic Jewish approach to creation, a task that was accomplished by Marcion, who taught there had to be two gods, one who created evil, the other who created good. The god who created evil is Yahweh, the god of the Old

SEXUAL MORALITY IN THE CATHOLIC TRADITION

Testament; the god who created good is the Father of Jesus, who alone reveals him. The Old Testament, therefore, should be rejected, along with all its doctrines and its laws. Among these doctrines is the one that men, women, sexuality, and marriage were created good by God; among such laws are those that legislate the relationships of men and women and their mutual sexual activity. Such attitudes generated, on the one hand, a negative, ascetic approach to sexuality and marriage and, on the other hand, a licentious, permissive approach, known as antinomianism. The second- and third-century Fathers had to defend marriage against attacks on both these fronts.

By the middle of the second century of the Christian era, Alexandria had become established as the intellectual capital of the Hellenistic world. We would expect to find powerful Gnostics there, and our expectation is verified via the writings of Clement, the bishop of Alexandria. He tells us of the two kinds of Gnostics we have noted, namely, the ascetics who abstained from marriage and sexual intercourse because they believed them to be evil, and the antinomians who believed they are saved by their special *gnosis*, no matter what, and are therefore above any law regarding sexuality and marriage.[51] Clement declares the opinions of the Gnostics "impious" and responds with a simple argument.

There is only one God, and that God is good; sexuality and marriage were created by the one God and, therefore, are good from their origin. Irenaeus of Lyons employs this same argument in his extensive refutation of the Gnostics. He accuses Gnostics of frustrating the ancient plan of God and of finding fault with him "who made both male and female for the begetting of men."[52] Marriage is primarily for procreation, and also for a wife to bring help to her husband in the funding of his household, particularly in his sickness and old age.[53] The early Greek Christian understanding of the nature of sexuality resembles that of the Stoic philosophers, represented in a statement from the Christian African, Lactantius: "Just as God gave us eyes, not that we might look upon and desire pleasure, but that we might see those actions that pertain to the necessity of life, so also we have received the genital part of the body for no other purpose than the begetting of offspring."[54] By its very nature, therefore, sexual intercourse is for the procreation of children, and any intercourse for purposes other than procreation is a violation of nature and therefore immoral. From this established position Christian Fathers would argue that Gnostics, or anyone else, engaging in sexual intercourse for any purpose other that procreation, love-making, for instance, or pleasure, were in violation of nature. It is an argument Latin Church Fathers continue to make into the twenty-first century.

The Latin Father Tertullian argued that abstinence from sexual activity is the surest way to the grace of God. Commenting on Paul's "It is better to marry than to burn with passion" (1 Cor. 7:9), Tertullian adds that "it is better neither to marry nor to burn with passion."[55] Virgins, he goes on, have "full holiness," because "continence is more glorious" than marriage.[56] Tertullian seems to have been the first to make this evaluation of virginity as holier than marriage, but in the fourth century that theological judgment was concretized in a new ascetic practice, the rejection of marriage and the embracing of virginity as a way to live a Christlike, holy life. It was not that the Fathers of the time were opposed to marriage; they were not. It was rather that they expressed their preference for virginity. John Chrysostom can say, "I believe that virginity is a long way better than marriage, not because marriage is evil, for to those who would use it correctly [for procreation] it is the doorway to continence."[57] Basil also affirms the goodness of sexual intercourse in marriage that is "entered into according to the sacred scriptures and legitimately," that is, for procreation, but he also excoriates marital intercourse sought for pleasure.[58]

Marriage is good, especially when sought for procreation; it has to be good, since God created it. But virginity is better. This ambiguity about the goodness of sexuality and marriage, introduced early into the Catholic tradition, perdures to the present time. Writing an Apostolic Exhortation *On the Family*, John Paul II, citing Chrysostom as above, removes any ambiguity about the Church's position. "[T]he Church throughout her history has always defended the superiority of this charism [virginity] to that of marriage, by reason of the wholly singular link which it has with the Kingdom of God."[59] When it comes to a comparison of sexual intercourse and marriage with virginity, one could say that John Paul has removed the Greek ambiguity.

AUGUSTINE

When we reach Augustine, the fifth-century bishop of Hippo, we reach the systematic insight into sexual morality and marriage that was to mold and control the doctrine of the Catholic Church down to our own day. His influence is always present in Catholic talk about marriage. Since Augustine's influence on the doctrine of marriage is beyond doubt, we must look closely at it. His teaching too must be viewed in its historical context, a context that is again largely a defense against attack. As the Alexandrians defended sexuality and marriage against the attacks of the Gnostics, so did Augustine defend them against the attacks of the Manichees, who at root were Gnostics, and Pelagians. We need to say a word, therefore, about these two.

The Manichees took their name from Mani, born in Babylonia about the year 216 CE. Manichaeism is a dualistic system, the dual opposites being, as always, good and evil, light and darkness, spirit and matter. Sexuality is listed among the evil, dark, and material realities. Sexuality and marriage, as material, are evil in themselves and therefore to be avoided. Against this approach Augustine repeated the argument of Clement and Irenaeus: sexuality and marriage, created by God, must be essentially good. Pelagianism derived its name from a Briton, Pelagius, who lived in Rome around the year 380. The Pelagian debate centered around the extent of 'adam's original fall from grace. Augustine taught that the original sin seriously impaired human nature, so that after the Fall men and women could not do without grace what they had been able to do without it before the Fall. Pelagius, on the contrary, taught that the Fall left human nature unimpaired, so that men and women could do after the Fall what they had been capable of doing prior to the Fall without any help from grace. Against the Pelagians Augustine taught that the results of the Fall make it very difficult to avoid sin in sexual intercourse, even in marriage.

Augustine's basic statement about sexuality and marriage is ubiquitous, firm, and clear. Contrary to those Manichee heretics who hold that sexuality is evil and who condemn and prohibit marriage and sexual intercourse, he states that sexuality and marriage were created good by a good God and cannot lose that intrinsic goodness.[60] He specifies the good of marriage as threefold and insists that even after the Fall the marriages of Christians still contain this threefold good: fidelity, offspring, sacrament.[61] In this triple good Augustine intends the mutual fidelity of the spouses, the procreation of children, and indissolubility. Procreation has priority because "from this derives the propagation of the human race in which a living community is a great good."[62] Alongside the tradition of the threefold good of marriage, Augustine advances another good, that of friendship between the sexes. In *The Good of Marriage*, after asserting that marriage is good, he gives an interesting explication of why it is good. "It does not seem to me to be good only because of the procreation of children, but also because of the natural companionship between the sexes. Otherwise, we could not speak of marriage in the case of old people, especially if they had either lost their children or had begotten none at all."[63] In this opinion, Augustine has falsified in advance the claim of those modern commentators who say that only in modern times have sexual intercourse and marriage been seen in the context of the relationship of spouses. But the source of what appears problematic in Augustine's teaching about marriage seems always to derive from what he says against the Pelagians. To this, therefore, we now turn.

The basic position can be stated unequivocally, and there can be no doubt about it: sexual intercourse between a husband and a wife is created good by God. It can, as can any good, be used sinfully, but when it is used sinfully, it is not the good itself that is sinful but its disordered use. Augustine explains carefully: "Evil does not follow because marriages are good, but because in the good things of marriage there is also a use that is evil."[64] Sexual intercourse is good in itself, but there are uses that can render it evil. The condition under which it is good is the classic Stoic condition we have already seen in the Alexandrians, namely, when it is for the begetting of a child. Any other use, even between the spouses in marriage, is at least venially sinful. "Conjugal sexual intercourse for the sake of offspring is not sinful. But sexual intercourse, even with one's spouse, to satisfy concupiscence [disordered desire] is a venial sin."[65] It is not the sexual appetite that is sinful; it is good. It is disordered and unreasonable sexual desire that is sinful, not sexual intercourse per se. "Whatever, therefore, spouses do together that is immodest, shameful, filthy, is the vice of men, not the fault of marriage."[66] And what is "immodest, shameful, and filthy" is the disordered desire for sexual pleasure.

Pope Gregory the Great shared Augustine's judgment that, because of the presence of concupiscence, even genital pleasure between spouses in the act of procreation is sinful. He went further and banned from the church those who had just had pleasurable intercourse. "The custom of the Romans from antiquity," he explained, "has always been, after sexual intercourse with one's spouse, both to cleanse oneself by washing and to abstain reverently from entering the church for a time. In saying this we do not intend to say that sexual intercourse is sinful. But because every lawful sexual intercourse between spouses cannot take place without bodily pleasure, they are to refrain from entering the holy place. For such pleasure cannot be without sin."[67] Again, it is clear that it is sexual pleasure that is sinful, and it is not difficult to see how such a doctrine could produce a strong ambivalence toward sexuality and marriage. That ambivalence weighed heavily in subsequent history on the theory and practice of Christian marriage.

In summary, though the relational and procreational meanings of sexual activity we found in Genesis remain, they have been seriously prioritized. Though the judgment remains that sexuality and sexual activity are good because they were created good by the good God, their goodness is threatened by the pleasure associated with sexual intercourse and by the concupiscence engendered by sin. This might be the place, however, to introduce a linguistic caveat. Medieval Latin had no words for the modern concepts of "sex" and "sexuality." Pierre Payer, therefore, correctly states, "In the strictest sense there are no discussions of sex in the Middle Ages." He goes on to point out that Michel Foucault's claim that "the relatively late date for the invention of sex and sexuality is . . . of paramount significance. The concept of sex and sexuality as an integral dimension of human persons, as an object of concern, discourse, truth, and knowledge, did not emerge until well after the Middle Ages."[68] This caveat has significance for all that has gone before and all that comes after in this book.

THE PENITENTIALS

Many of the attitudes and teachings of the Fathers with respect to sexuality and marriage can be found in the manuals known as Penitentials, which flourished in ecclesiastical use from about the sixth to the twelfth century CE. The Penitentials were designed to help confessors in their pastoral dealings with penitents in confession, providing lists of sins and corresponding penances. They were, however, more than just lists of sins and penances. They were also manuals of moral education for the confessor; and what the confessor learned, of course, his penitents also learned. Penitentials took the abstract moral principles of the Church and particularized them at the level of practice, in this case the practice of the new confession introduced by the Celtic monks in the sixth century. They are sure guides for us as we explore the moral teaching of the Church at the time of their publication with respect to sexuality and marriage.

The general rule for sexual behavior in the Penitentials is the ancient Stoic one and the one we have found in the Christian tradition from Clement onward: sexual intercourse is permitted only between a man and a woman who are married and, even then, only for procreation. Every other sexual act is proscribed, and, therefore, nonprocreative intercourse is prohibited. Both oral and anal sex are also prohibited, most frequently between male homosexuals but also between heterosexuals. The Anglo-Saxon canons of Theodore (ca. 690) prescribe, "Whoever emits semen into the mouth shall do penance for seven years; this is the worst of evils."[69] And, "If a man should practice anal intercourse he must do penance as one who offends with animals," that is, for ten years.[70]

Masturbation falls into the category of nonprocreative sexual behavior and is therefore prohibited. The Celtic Penitential of Columban (ca. 600) prescribes, "If anyone practices masturbation or sins with a beast, he shall do penance for two years if he is not in [clerical] orders; but if he is in orders or has a monastic vow, he shall do penance for three years unless his [tender] age protects him."[71]

Theodore also proscribes male homosexuality with severe penances: "A male who commits fornication with a male shall do penance for ten years." The "man who commits this sexual offense once shall do penance for four years; if he has been in the habit of it, as Basil says, fifteen years."[72] There is some mitigation, however, for what may be seen as experimentation: if a boy engages in homosexual intercourse, the penance is two years for the first offense and four years if he repeats it. Adultery is prohibited but the penances, except for higher ecclesiastics, are relatively short. Finnian decrees, "If any layman defile his neighbor's wife or virgin daughter, he shall do penance for an entire year on an allowance of bread and water and he shall not have intercourse with his own wife."[73] Sexual intercourse between a husband and a wife is not always a good thing. Cummean prescribes that "he who is in a state of matrimony ought to be continent during the three forty-day periods [prior to Christmas, prior to Easter, and after Pentecost] and on Saturday and Sunday, night and day, and in the two appointed week days [Wednesday and Friday], and after conception, and during the entire menstrual period."[74] A quick calculation reveals that few days remain available for intercourse.[75]

An obvious summary and conclusion emerges from this medieval analysis: a strong Catholic negativity toward sexuality, even between a husband and a wife in marriage. Richard Gula's judgment is accurate. The Penitentials helped shape "a moral perspective which focused on individual acts, on regarding the moral life as a matter of avoiding sin, and on turning moral reflection into an analysis of sin in its many forms."[76] The act-centered morality of the Penitentials, and their ambivalence toward sexuality and marriage, was perpetuated in the manuals of moral theology published in the wake of the reforms of clerical education mandated by the Council of Trent.[77]

SCHOLASTIC DOCTRINE

Augustine's teaching controlled the approach to sexuality and marriage in the Catholic Church until the thirteenth century, when the Scholastic theologians made some significant alterations to it. The Scholastic sexual ethic remained an ethic for marriage, and Aquinas took over Augustine's three goods of marriage and transformed them into three ends of marriage. "Marriage," Aquinas argues, "has as its principal end the procreation and education of offspring . . . and so offspring are said to be a good of marriage." It has also "a secondary end in man alone, the sharing of tasks which are necessary in life, and from this point of view husband and wife owe each other faithfulness, which is one of the goods of marriage." There is another end in believers, "the meaning of Christ and Church, and so a good of marriage is called sacrament. The first end is found in marriage insofar as man is animal, the second insofar as he is man, the third insofar as he is believer."[78] The terminology, *primary end–secondary end*, came to dominate discussion of the ends of marriage in Roman Catholic manuals for the next seven hundred years, but we should note that it is a curious argument, for it makes the claim that the primary end of specifically *human* marriage is dictated not by man's specifically *human* nature but by his generically *animal* nature. It was precisely this curious argument that would be challenged in the twentieth century, leading to a more personal approach to the morality of both sexual activity and marriage.

Some ambivalence toward sexual desire, activity, and pleasure remains. As in Plato and Aristotle, they are "occupations with lower affairs which distract the soul and make it unworthy of being joined actually to God,"[79] but they are not sinful at all times and in all circumstances. Indeed, within the ends of marriage they are meritorious, and Aquinas asserts explicitly that to forgo the pleasure and thwart the end would be sinful.[80] That is a far cry from Augustine and Gregory. It is also a move toward both the liberation of marriage, legitimate sexual intercourse, and sexual pleasure from any taint of sin and their recognition as a sign and a cause of grace, that is, as a sacrament.

The early Scholastics did not doubt that marriage was a *sign* of grace but, because of their negative evaluation of sexual activity, they seriously doubted that it could ever be a *cause* of grace. They hesitated, therefore, to include it among the sacraments of the Church, which were defined as both sign and cause of grace. The Dominicans Albert the Great and Thomas Aquinas had no such hesitations, and they firmly established marriage among the sacraments of the church. In his commentary on Lombard, Albert characterizes as "very probable" the opinion that holds that marriage "confers grace for doing good, not just any good but that good specifically that a married person should do."[81] In his commentary on Lombard, Aquinas goes further, characterizing as "most probable" the opinion that "marriage, insofar as it is contracted in faith in Christ, confers grace to do those things which are required in marriage."[82] In his *Contra gentiles*, he is even more positive, stating bluntly that "it is to be believed that through this sacrament [marriage] grace is given to the married."[83] By the time he achieves his mature thought in the *Summa Theologiae*, he lists marriage among the seven sacraments with no demur whatsoever about its grace-conferring qualities, and by the Reformation his opinion was held universally by theologians. A further scholastic teaching about marriage that was to become central to marriage discussions in the twentieth century should be noted here, namely, the personal relationship and equality between husband and wife. Aquinas understood, at least inchoately, that the relationship between men and women should be one of friendship and that sexual intercourse enhances that friendship as well as being a means to procreation;[84] Bonaventure calls the friendship between spouses the sacrament of the relationship between God and the soul.[85]

THE MODERN PERIOD

When Cardinal Gasparri first codified Catholic law in the 1917 Code of Canon Law, the section on marriage developed three prominent notions: marriage is a contract; the object of the contract is the permanent and exclusive right of each spouse to the body of the other for sexual intercourse leading to procreation; and the primacy of procreation over every other end of marriage. None of these notions was traditional in magisterial teachings; they were all novel opinions in Gasparri's work and therefore in the Code that he dominated. With respect to the notion of marriage as contract, even Gasparri himself acknowledged that marriage was never considered a contract in either Roman or European law.[86] With respect to the right to the use of the other's body for procreative intercourse, David Fellhauer demonstrates that there is no magisterial source "which presents the juridical essence of marriage as the *ius in corpus* (right to the body) for procreation or which identifies the object of consent in similar terms."[87] With respect to the ends of marriage, Urban Navarette points out that, in the documents of the Magisterium and in the corpus of canon law itself, "we find hardly anything about the ends of marriage precisely as goals until the formulation of Canon 1013, 1."[88] He further notes that a preliminary version of Canon 1013 indicated no hierarchy of ends and concludes that the 1917 Code of Canon Law is the first official document of the Catholic Church to embrace the terminology *primary end–secondary end*.

In December 1930, in response to the Anglican Lambeth Conference's approval of artificial contraception as a moral action in certain situations, Pope Pius XI published an important encyclical on marriage, *Casti connubii*. In it, predictably, he insisted on everything in Gasparri's *Code*, but, unpredictably, he did more. He retrieved and gave a prominent place to a long-ignored item from the *Catechism of the Council of Trent*, marriage as a union of conjugal love and intimacy. By emphasizing the essential place of mutual love in a marriage, Pius placed the Catholic view of marriage on the track to a more personal definition. Marital love, Pius teaches, does not consist "in pleasing words only, but in the deep attachment of the heart [will] which is expressed in action, since love is proved by deeds."[89] So important is the mutual love and interior formation of the spouses, he continues, that "it can, in a very real sense, as the Roman Catechism teaches, be said to be the *chief reason and purpose of marriage*, if marriage be looked at not in the restricted sense as instituted for the proper conception and education of the child, but more widely as the blending of life as a whole and the mutual interchange and sharing thereof."[90] In these wise words, Pius directs us to see that there is more to marriage than can be contained in the cold, legal categories of the Code of Canon Law. European thinkers were poised to point in the same direction, most influentially two Germans, Dietrich von Hildebrand and Heribert Doms.

VON HILDEBRAND AND DOMS

In the opening paragraph of his work *Marriage*, written in 1939, Dietrich von Hildebrand states the problem precisely. The modern age, he suggests, is guilty of a terrible antipersonalism, "a progressive blindness toward the nature and dignity of the spiritual person." This antipersonalism expresses itself in all kinds of materialism, the most dangerous of which is biological materialism, which considers man as a more highly developed animal. "Human life is considered exclusively from a biological point of view and biological principles are the measure by which all human activities are judged."[91] The Catholic legal approach to marriage, with its insistence on rights over bodies and their physiological functions, is wide open to the charge of biological materialism. So too is the centuries-old Stoic-cum-Christian doctrine that argues from physiological structure to human "nature" and to "natural" ends. So too is Aquinas's position that founds the primary end of *human* marriage in the *biological* structure of men and women. In contrast to this biological approach, von Hildebrand introduced a radical innovation in thinking about marriage, claiming Pius XI and *Casti connubii* in support of his central thesis that marriage is for the building up of loving communion between the spouses. Conjugal love, he claims, is the primary meaning and ultimate end of marriage.[92]

In marriage, von Hildebrand argued, the spouses enter an interpersonal relationship, in which they confront one another as I and Thou, as Ego and Other, and "give birth to a mysterious fusion of their souls."[93] This fusion of their innermost personal beings, not merely the fusion of their physical bodies, is what the oft-quoted "one body" of Genesis intends. It is this interpersonal fusion that is the primary meaning of the spouses' mutual love and of their sexual intercourse, which is the symbol of that love, and intercourse achieves its end when it expresses and leads to interpersonal union. "Every marriage in which conjugal love is thus realized bears spiritual fruit, becomes *fruitful*—even though there are no children."[94] Heribert Doms agreed with von Hildebrand in that what is natural or unnatural for human animals is not to be decided on the basis of what is natural or unnatural for nonhuman animals. Human sexuality is essentially the capacity and the desire to fuse, not merely one's body but one's very self, with an other person. Sexuality drives a human to make a gift of herself or himself (not just of her or his body) to an other, in order to create a communion of persons and of lives that fulfills them both.

The primary end of sexual intercourse in this perspective is the loving communion between the spouses, a communion that is both signified and enhanced, or "made," in the intercourse. Popular language is correct: in their sexual intercourse spouses "make love." This primary end is achieved in every act of intercourse in which the spouses actually enter into intimate communion. Even in childless marriages, marriage and intercourse achieve their primary end in the marital communion of the spouses, their *two-in-oneness* as Doms would have it. He summarizes his case in a clear statement. "The immediate purpose of marriage is the realization of its meaning, the conjugal two-in-oneness. . . . This two-in-oneness of husband and wife is a living reality, and the immediate object of the marriage ceremony and their legal union." The union of the spouses tends naturally to the birth and nurture of new persons, their children, who focus the fulfillment of their parents, both as individuals and as a two-in-oneness. "Society is more interested in the child than in the natural fulfillment of the parents, and it is this which gives the child primacy among the natural results of marriage."[95] Since Doms wrote, social scientific data demonstrate that the well-being of the child is a function of the well-being of its parents, suggesting that the relationship between the spouses is the primary natural result of marriage, since all other relationships in the family depend on it.[96]

The Catholic Church's immediate reaction to these new ideas, as has been so often the case in theological history, was a blanket condemnation, which made no effort to sift truth from error. In 1944, the Holy Office condemned "the opinion of some more recent authors, who either deny that the primary end of marriage is the generation and nurture of children, or teach that the secondary ends are not essentially subordinate to the primary end, but are equally primary and independent."[97] In 1951, as the opinions of von Hildebrand and Doms persisted and attracted more adherents, Pope Pius XII felt obliged to intervene again. The truth is, he taught, that "marriage, as a natural institution in virtue of the will of the Creator, does not have as a primary and intimate end the personal perfection of the spouses, but the procreation and nurture of new life. The other ends, inasmuch as they are intended by nature, are not on the same level as the primary end, and still less are they superior to it, but they are essentially subordinate to it."[98] This approach was seriously altered by the Second Vatican Council's document *Gaudium et spes*.

SECOND VATICAN COUNCIL

The direction of the debate on marriage at the Second Vatican Council may be summed up in the words of Cardinal Alfrink: "Conjugal love," he argued, "is an element of marriage itself and not just a result of marriage. . . . Conjugal love belongs to marriage, at least if marriage be not considered as merely a juridical contract."[99] Much of the debate was opposed to the juridical way of looking at marriage and marital love as exemplified by Gasparri and the Code. Alfrink, a biblical scholar, pointed out that "the Hebrew verb *dabaq*, in Greek *kollao*, does suggest physical, bodily, sexual union, but it suggests above all spiritual union which exists in conjugal love. Sacred scripture itself insinuates this when it compares conjugal union to the union between parents and children which is spiritual and presupposes love."[100] This, he continued, is the way modern women and men think, more spiritually, more humanly, and indeed more biblically and theologically. Cardinal Dopfner agreed. "It is not enough to propose conjugal love as a virtue, or as an extraneous subjective end of marriage, and to exclude it from the very structure of marriage itself."[101] The battle lines were already clearly drawn in the Preparatory Commission: either Gasparri's juridical approach to marriage or a renewed interpersonal approach in which conjugal love is of the essence of marriage. The latter approach began to win in the Commission and won, finally, in the Council itself.[102]

Gaudium et spes, into which a section on marriage was inserted in its preliminary stage, describes marriage as a "communion of love," an "intimate partnership of conjugal life and love."[103] The position of the majority of the Council Fathers could not be clearer. In the face of strident demands to relegate the conjugal love of the spouses to its customary secondary place in marriage, they declared conjugal love to be of the very essence of marriage, a clear rejection of an exclusively juridical approach. There was another explicit rejection of Gasparri. Marriage, the Council declares, is founded in a "conjugal covenant of irrevocable personal consent."[104] Gasparri's word *contract* is replaced by the biblical word *covenant*, which has the same legal outcomes as *contract* but also situates marriage in a biblical-theological and *interpersonal* context, rather than in an exclusively *legal* one. The Council declares that the spouses "mutually gift and accept one another," rejecting the material biological notion that they gift merely the right to the use of one another's bodies.[105] In their mutual personal covenanting and gifting, a man and a woman create an interpersonal communion of love that is permanent and is to last for the whole of life.

The Council also teaches that "by its very nature the institution of *marriage* and *married love* is ordered to the procreation and education of children, and it is in them that it finds its crowning glory."[106] We have added emphasis to this citation to underscore the teaching not only of the Council but also of the entire Catholic tradition prior to Paul VI's *Humanae vitae*, namely, that *marriage*, not *each and every marriage act* as Paul VI taught, is to be open to the procreation of children.[107] Once procreation has been mentioned, one would expect a recitation of the hierarchical ends of marriage, but, again despite insistent voices to the contrary, the Council Fathers rejected the primary end–secondary end dichotomy. To make sure that its rejection was understood, the Preparatory Commission was careful to explain that the text just cited "does not suggest [a hierarchy of ends] in any way."[108] Marriage and sexual love "are by their very nature ordained to the generation and education of children," but that "does not make the other ends of marriage of less account," and marriage "is not instituted solely for procreation."[109] The intense debate that took place both in the Preparatory Commission and in the Council itself makes it impossible to claim that the refusal to speak of a hierarchy of ends in marriage was the result of oversight or, as some traditionalists argue, a mere avoidance of the primary–secondary terminology, leaving the concept in place.[110] It was the result of a deliberated, intentional, and explicit choice of the Catholic Church meeting in Council.

Any doubt was definitively removed in 1983 by the appearance of the revised Code of Canon Law, frequently called the last Council document. "The *matrimonial covenant,* by which a man and a woman establish between themselves a partnership of the whole of life, is by its nature ordered toward the good of the spouses and the procreation and education of offspring" (Can 1055, 1). Notice three things: first, it is the *matrimonial covenant* and not *each and every act of intercourse* that is ordered toward procreation; second, there is no specification of either of these ends being primary or secondary; third, as in *Gaudium et spes,* the good of the spouses or *conjugal love* is discussed before procreation and education of children or the fruitfulness of marriage. The Catholic Church changed its canon law to be in line with its renewed theology of marriage, moving beyond the narrow legal essence to embrace in the very essence of marriage the mutual love and communion of the spouses. Toward the end of the twentieth century, the Church had come a long way from the negative approach to sexuality and marriage bequeathed to it in a long tradition going back to the struggles of the Fathers against dualistic Gnostics, and Manicheans. It would be naive, and a complete ignorance of past conciliar history, to assume that the debate ended with the Council.

PAPAL BIRTH CONTROL COMMISSION

Two theoretical models are available in the modern Catholic tradition for thinking about marriage, and each offers insight into the morality of sexual activity. One is an ancient one, a model of marriage as a procreative institution and of sexual intercourse within marriage as a primarily procreative action; the other is a modern model of marriage as an interpersonal union and of sexual intercourse within marriage as a primarily unitive action.[111] The model of marriage as procreative institution was thrust onto center stage in the 1960s in a great debate about artificial contraception.

At the instigation of Cardinal Suenens, archbishop of Malines, Belgium, whose ultimate intent was that an adequate document on Christian marriage be brought before the Second Vatican Council for debate, Pope John XXIII established a commission to study the issue of birth control. The commission was confirmed and enlarged by Pope Paul VI until it ultimately had seventy-one members, not all of whom attended its meetings or voted.[112] The final Episcopal vote took place in answer to three questions. In answer to the question "Is contraception intrinsically evil?" nine bishops voted no, three voted yes, and three abstained. In answer to the question "Is contraception, as defined by the Majority Report, in basic continuity with tradition and the declarations of the Magisterium?" nine bishops voted yes, five voted no, and one abstained. In answer to the question, "Should the Magisterium speak on this question as soon as possible?" fourteen answered yes, and one answered no.[113] A preliminary vote of the theologians who were advisors to the Commission, in response to the question "Is artificial contraception an intrinsically evil violation of the natural law?" had resulted in a count of fifteen no and four yes answers.[114] Both a majority report and a minority report were then submitted to Paul VI, who, professing himself unconvinced by the arguments of the majority, and probably also sharing the concern of the minority report that the Church could not repudiate its long-standing teaching on contraception without undergoing a serious blow to its overall moral authority, approved the minority report in his encyclical letter *Humanae vitae*.[115] The difference between the two groups is easily categorized.

The minority report, which became the controverted part of the encyclical, argued that "each and every marriage act must remain open to the transmission of life."[116] As we have already noted, Paul VI was the first to state the Church's teaching in this way. The tradition had always been that it is *marriage* itself, and not each and every act of intercourse in marriage, that is to be open to procreation, and that is what the majority report argued. It asserted that "human intervention in the process of the marriage act *for reasons drawn from the end of marriage itself* should not always be excluded, provided that the criteria of morality are always safeguarded."[117] The difference in the two positions was precisely the difference created by adherence to two different models of marriage, the minority report being based on the traditional procreative institution model, the majority report being based on the emerging interpersonal union model that had its origins in the 1930s and was embraced by the Council. Richard McCormick commented in 1968 that "the documents of the Papal Commission represent a rather full summary of two points of view. . . . The majority report, particularly the analysis in its 'rebuttal,' strikes this reader as much the more satisfactory statement."[118] That judgment continues to be the judgment of the majority of Catholic theologians and the vast majority of Catholic couples, because they adhere to the same interpersonal model on which the majority report was based—so much so that in 2006 Margaret Farley can offer the judgment, "In much of Catholic moral theology and ethics, the procreative norm as the sole or primary justification of sexual intercourse is gone."[119] More than four decades after *Humanae vitae*, despite a concerted minority effort to make adherence to *Humanae vitae* a test case of genuine Catholicity, the debate between the procreative and interpersonal models perdures in the Church and is far from resolved, as we will see in the chapters that follow.

A summary of the approach to marriage and sexual activity in the modern period of Catholic theology and teaching is easy to present.

The modern period represents yet one more development in Catholic theology and, to a lesser extent, in magisterial teaching. The major development in the Catholic theological approach to marriage is the recovery of the two purposes of marriage and sexual intercourse articulated in Genesis, the relational and procreational, and a rearranging of their relative priorities. Since Clement, Augustine, and Aquinas, the procreational became established in Catholic teaching as the *primary* purpose of marriage and the relational became relegated to a *secondary* purpose. Beginning with Pius XI's *Casti connubii* and culminating in the Second Vatican Council's *Gaudium et spes*, these two purposes of marriage have been equalized, so that neither is prior to the other. Pope Paul VI's *Humanae vitae* tried to change the terms of the debate over marriage and sexual intercourse by teaching for the first time in Catholic history that "each and every marriage *act* must remain open to the transmission of life,"[120] but that judgment is controverted by the vast majority of Catholic believers, and, "in much of Catholic theology and ethics, the procreative norm as the sole or primary justification of sexual intercourse is gone."[121] With the reestablishing of the relational purpose for marriage and sexual intercourse, the judgment about the morality of any sexual act is now made by Catholic ethicists not on the basis of the *act* alone but on the basis of the place of the act within its *relational* context. We shall see as we proceed what difference that development makes to moral judgments.

CONCLUSION

This chapter does two things. First, it documents the origins and correctness of the claim we make at its beginning, namely, that traditional Catholic sexual morality is essentially *marital* morality. That morality is encoded in two magisterial statements: "Each and every act [of sexual intercourse] must remain open to the transmission of life;" and "any human genital act whatsoever may be placed only within the framework of marriage."[122] We trace the origins of those two claims from the ancient Stoic philosophy, through the early, medieval, and modern

Catholic tradition, down to the present day when they are being reevaluated. That reevaluation, which has taken place in both theological and magisterial circles, is the second thing we document. It was provoked by the historical-critical approach, approved by the Magisterium, and applied first to the sacred scriptures and then to the teaching of the Magisterium itself.

Pope Pius XII, in his encyclical *Divino afflante spiritu*, approved the historical-critical approach to the study of the Bible and instructed Catholic exegetes that their prime concern was "to arrive at a deeper and fuller knowledge of the mind of [the author]."[123] In 1994, the CDF's Pontifical Biblical Commission made the same claim about the importance of the literal meaning of the biblical text and related it to the exigencies of a double hermeneutic. "The Bible itself and the history of its interpretation point to the need for a hermeneutics . . . . On the one hand, all events reported in the Bible are interpreted events. On the other, all exegesis of the accounts of these events necessarily involves the exegete's own subjectivity."[124] Meaning is always sociohistorically constructed, and if an interpreter is to arrive at the meaning intended by an author, then he or she has to be aware of the objective sociohistorical situation of both the ancient writer and the contemporary interpreter. This means in the concrete, for our present concern, that the Bible is not a moral manual to be followed slavishly without careful consideration of the situation of the text and of the situation of the human subject seeking to arrive at a moral judgment on the basis of the text. If this is true of the biblical text, the meanings of which found the Christian religion in general, it is even more true of the patristic, medieval, and modern texts of the later ecclesiastical tradition. Textual historicity demands not unquestioning obedience but careful attention, understanding, judgment, and decision.

As the Bible is not a manual of morality, neither is it a manual of sexual morality. It is concerned not with sexuality as such, but with living a life according to the will of God. Neither biblical Hebrew and Greek nor medieval Latin had words for the modern concepts of sexuality and sex. There are allusions to sexual acts, some of them frank and explicit but none of them constituting laws to be followed without question. All of them, to repeat, suffer the limitations introduced by their sociohistorical context; some of them also suffer from a seriously inaccurate understanding of human "nature" and a deficient sexual anthropology. This latter is particularly true of what the Bible and the early Fathers of the Church understand about human biology and, for example, about "spilling the male seed."[125] This seriously colors what the tradition has to say about human sexuality in general and about male homosexual activity in particular. It has almost nothing to say about female homosexual activity, but we withhold detailed discussion of this until a later chapter.

QUESTIONS FOR REFLECTION

1. What do you understand by *historicity*? What are its theoretical foundations? What important difference does it make to your understanding of any formulation of truth, including theological, moral truth?

2. How do you understand the statement that "Catholic sexual morality is essentially *marital* morality?" How did the Catholic Church come to such a theoretical position?

3. How important is it for you to learn that sexual questions play a relatively small role in both the Old and the New Testaments? Does that fact make any difference to the formation of your own conscience on issues relating to sexuality? What other sources are available in the Catholic tradition to form your conscience on this issue?

4. What did the Catholic Church learn about sexual morality from the early Stoic philosophers, from St. Augustine, and from St. Thomas Aquinas? Why does Joseph Fuchs argue that "one cannot take what Augustine or the philosophers of the Middle Ages knew about sexuality as the exclusive basis of a moral reflection?" Can you name one very important fact about male and female sexuality that neither Augustine nor Aquinas knew? What are the moral implications of this fact for how we think about sexual persons?

5. What developments happened in the modern age within Catholic teaching about sexual behavior, culminating especially in the teaching of the Second Vatican Council?
6. What other questions arise for you from reading this chapter?

NOTES

1. Bernard J. F. Lonergan, *Method in Theology* (New York: Herder and Herder, 1972), 325.
2. Joseph Fuchs, *Moral Demands and Personal Obligations* (Washington, DC: Georgetown University Press, 1993), 36.
3. Ibid.
4. Lonergan, *Method*, xi.
5. Fuchs, *Moral Demands*, 39.
6. CCC, 2423. Emphasis added.
7. Paul VI, *Octogesima adveniens*, 4, *AAS* 63 (1971), 401–41.
8. CDF, *Instruction on Christian Freedom and Liberation*, 72, *AAS* 79 (1987), 586.
9. John Paul II, *SRS*, 1, emphasis added.
10. Ibid., 41.
11. In her *Just Love: A Framework for Christian Sexual Ethics* (New York: Continuum, 2006), 211–15, Margaret Farley argues that "*autonomy* and *relationality*" are two basic features of human personhood that must be factored into every contemporary discussion of morality.
12. This notion of individual responsibility is brilliantly analyzed by Jean-Yves Calvez in "Morale sociale et morale sexuelle," *Etudes* 378 (1993), 642–44.
13. *SRS*, 3.
14. Calvez, "Morale sociale et morale sexuelle," 648, emphasis added.
15. See, for instance, David Cohen, *Law, Sexuality, and Society: The Enforcement of Morality in Ancient Athens* (New York: Cambridge University Press, 1991); Kenneth J. Dover, *Greek Popular Morality in the Time of Plato and Aristotle* (Berkeley and Los Angeles: University of California Press, 1974); Michel Foucault, *The History of Sexuality*, 3 vols., especially vols. 2 and 3 (New York: Pantheon Books, 1978–86); Otto Kiefer, *Sexual Life in Ancient Rome* (New York: AMS Press, 1975); Ross S. Kraemer and Mary Rose D'Angelo, *Women and Christian Origins* (New York: Oxford University Press, 1999); Martha C. Nussbaum and Juha Sihvola, eds., *The Sleep of Reason: Erotic Experience and Sexual Ethics in Ancient Greece and Rome* (Chicago: University of Chicago Press, 2002); Sarah Pomeroy, *Goddesses, Whores, Wives, and Slaves: Women in Classical Antiquity* (New York: Schocken Books, 1975); Aline Rousselle, *On Desire and the Body in Antiquity* (Oxford: Blackwell, 1988); Marilyn B. Skinner, *Sexuality in Greek and Roman Culture* (Oxford: Blackwell, 2005); various entries in Alan Soble, ed., *Sex*

from Plato to Paglia: A Philosophical Encyclopedia (Westport, CT: Greenwood, 2006). That not all these sources agree about everything is eloquent testimony to the difficulty inherent in historical interpretation.

16. Judith P. Hallett, "Women's Lives in the Ancient Mediterranean," in Kraemer and D'Angelo, eds., *Women and Christian Origins*, 13–34.

17. Demosthenes, *Against Neaera*, 122, in William Rennie, *Demosthenis Orationes* (Oxford: Clarendon, 1931), 1385.

18. See John Boswell, *Christianity, Social Tolerance, and Homosexuality: Gay People in Western Europe from the Beginning of the Christian Era to the Fourteenth Century* (Chicago: University of Chicago Press, 1980); Kenneth Dover, *Greek Homosexuality* (Cambridge: Harvard University Press, 1978); Pomeroy, *Goddesses, Whores, Wives, and Slaves*; Martti Nissenen, *Homoeroticism in the Biblical World: A Historical Perspective*, trans. Kirsi Stjerna (Minneapolis: Fortress, 1998); Bernadette Brooten, *Love between Women: Early Christian Responses to Female Homoeroticism* (Chicago: University of Chicago Press, 1996).

19. See Boswell, *Christianity, Social Tolerance, and Homosexuality*, 74–82; Foucault, *History of Sexuality*, 2: 193–97.

20. Plato, *Republic, IX*; Aristole, *Nichomachean Ethics, III*, 10.

21. *HV*, 11.

22. *PH*, 7.

23. See James F. Keenan, "Catholicism, History of" in *Sex from Plato to Paglia*, ed. Alan Soble, 143–52.

24. *DV*, 8.

25. Pontifical Biblical Commission, "Interpretation of the Bible in the Church," *Origins* (January 6, 1994), 500.

26. Ibid., 506.

27. Ibid., 519.

28. We mean by this word construal "to interpret," "to place a certain meaning on." We use it here to insinuate two connected meanings: first, the character of the theologian as construction worker within the Church; second, the character of theology as social construction, both that theology which preceded writings that came to be called scripture as well as that theology which succeeded them.

29. See *DV*, 19.

30. Ibid.

31. *DV*, 12; emphasis added.

32. Shere Hite, *The Hite Report: Women and Love* (London: Penguin, 1988), 532.

33. Bryan S. Turner, *The Body and Society* (Oxford: Blackwell, 1984), 119.

34. There are many good treatments of Jewish approaches to sexuality and sexual ethics, though, as with the Greco-Roman histories we saw, they do not all necessarily agree on everything. We recommend the following: David Biale, *Eros and the Jews: From Biblical Israel to Contemporary America* (New York: Basic Books, 1992); Louis M. Epstein, *Sex, Laws, and Customs in Judaism* (New York: Block, 1948); Michael Kaufman, *Love, Marriage, and Family in Jewish*

Law and Tradition (Northvale, NJ: Aronson, 1992); David Novak, *Jewish Social Ethics* (New York: Oxford University Press, 1992); Judith Plaskow, *Standing Again at Sinai: Judaism from a Feminist Perspective* (San Francisco: Harper and Row, 1990).

35. For a different interpretation of the creation texts, see Ronald A. Simkins, "Marriage and Gender in the Old Testament," in Todd A. Salzman, Thomas A. Kelly, and John J. O'Keefe, eds., *Marriage in the Catholic Tradition: Scripture, Tradition, and Experience* (New York: Crossroad, 2004), 21–29.

36. Edward Schillebeeckx, *Marriage: Secular Reality and Saving Mystery* (New York: Sheed and Ward, 1965), 15.

37. F. R. Barry, *A Philosophy from Prison* (London: SCM, 1926), 151.

38. *Acta et Documenta Concilio Vaticano II Apparando. Series II (Praeparatoria)* (Roma: Typis Polyglottis Vaticanis, 1968), vol. 2, pars III, 961.

39. Raymond F. Collins, *Christian Morality: Biblical Foundations* (Notre Dame, IN: University of Notre Dame Press, 1986), 176.

40. Schillebeeckx, *Marriage*, 29.

41. The Revised Standard translation modestly translates *sorerek* as "navel." But its location in the poem between thighs and belly suggests "vulva," as also the Arabic cognate of *sorerek* suggests. Marcia Falk translates it as "hips" in her *Love Lyrics from the Bible: A Translation and Literary Study of the Song of Songs* (Sheffield: Almond Press, 1982), 41. See her explanation, 127–28.

42. Karl Barth, *Church Dogmatics* (Edinburgh: T. and T. Clark, 1958–61), 3, 1, 312.

43. Ibid., 3, 2, 294.

44. Marvin Pope, *Song of Songs: A New Translation with Introduction and Commentary* (New York: Doubleday, 1977); Helmut Gollwitzer, *Song of Love: A Biblical Understanding of Sex* (Philadelphia: Fortress, 1979); Falk, *Love Lyrics from the Bible*; Roland E. Murphy, *The Song of Songs: A Commentary on the Book of Canticles or Song of Songs* (Minneapolis: Fortress, 1990); Diane Bergant, *Song of Songs: The Love Poetry of Scripture* (Hyde Park, NY: New City Press, 1998).

45. Phyllis Trible, "Depatriarchalizing in Biblical Interpretation," *Journal of the American Society of Religion* 41 (1973): 45. Her argument in 42–45 leads her to this conclusion.

46. Lisa Sowle Cahill, *Women and Sexuality* (New York: Paulist Press, 1992), 33. See also Raymond F. Collins, *Sexual Ethics and the New Testament: Behavior and Belief* (New York: Crossroad, 2000).

47. Theodore Mackin, *What Is Marriage?* (New York: Paulist, 1982), 56.

48. See its definition of marriage as an "intimate partnership of life and love," in GS, 48.

49. Whether that writer was the apostle Paul or not, and the common opinion among Catholic scholars is that he was not, is of no relevance to the present discussion.

50. Markus Barth, *Ephesians: Translation and Commentary on Chapters Four to Six. The Anchor Bible* (New York: Doubleday, 1974), 618.

51. Clement, *Stromatum* 3, 5, PG 8, 1143–47.

52. *Adv. Haer.* 1, 28, 1, PG 7, 690.

53. *Adv. Haer.* 2, 23, PG 8, 1086, 1090. See also *Paed.* 2, 10, PG 8, 498; ibid. 3, 12, PG 8, 1184 and 2, 23, PG 8, 1090–91.

54. Lactantius, *Divinarum Institutionum* 6, 23; PL 6, 718.

55. Tertullian, *Ad Uxorem I*, PL 1, 1278.

56. Ibid., 1287.

57. John Chrysostom, *De Virginitate* 9, PG 48, 539.

58. Basil, *Liber de Virginitate*, 38, PG 30, 746. See also Gregory of Nyssa, *De Virginitate* 7; PG 46, 354.

59. John Paul II, FC, 14.

60. Augustine, *De Nupt. et Concup.* 2, 32, 54, PL 44, 468–69. See also *De Bono Coniugali* passim, PL 40, 374–96.

61. *De Gen. ad Litt.* 9, 7, 12, PL 34, 397; also *De Bono Coniugali*, 24, 32, PL 40, 394.

62. *De Bono Coniugali*, 9, 9, PL 40, 380.

63. PL 40, 375.

64. *Contra Julianum* 3, 23, 53, PL 44, 729–30.

65. *De Bono Coniugali*, 6, 6, PL 40, 377–78; 10, 11, PL 40, 381.

66. Ibid., 6, 5, PL 40, 377.

67. Gregory the Great, *Epistolarum Liber IX Epist.* 64, PL 77, 1196.

68. Pierre J. Payer, *The Bridling of Desire: Views of Sex in the Later Middle Ages* (Toronto: University of Toronto Press, 1993), 14.

69. Pierre J. Payer, *Sex and the Penitentials: The Development of a Sexual Code 550–1150* (Toronto: University of Toronto Press, 1984), 165.

70. Ibid., 29.

71. John McNeill and Helena M. Gamer, *Medieval Handbooks of Penance* (New York: Columbia University Press, 1990), 253.

72. Ibid., 185. Columban imposes a more severe penance. "If one commits fornication as the Sodomites did, he shall do penance for ten years, the first three on bread and water; but in the other seven years he shall abstain from wine and meat, and [he shall] not be housed with another person forever" (ibid., 252).

73. McNeill and Gamer, *Medieval Handbooks*, 94. For adultery Theodore prescribes a penance of "fast for three years, two days a week, and in the three forty-day periods" and no intercourse with one's own wife (see ibid., 196). Payer explains that the three forty-day periods are the forty days before Christmas, before Easter, and after Pentecost (*Sex and the Penitentials*, 24).

74. Ibid. See also the canons in the Penitential of Theodore. "Those who are married shall abstain from intercourse for three nights before they communicate," and "A man shall abstain from his wife for forty days before Easter until the week of Easter" (ibid., 208).

75. See the figure on the sexual decision-making process according to the Penitentials in James A. Brundage, *Law, Sex, and Christian Society in Medieval Europe* (Chicago: University of Chicago Press, 1987), 162.

76. Richard M. Gula, *Reason Informed by Faith: Foundations of Catholic Morality* (New York: Paulist, 1989), 26.

77. See, for example, the negative and act-avoiding definition of chastity offered by Henry Davis in his influential *Moral and Pastoral Theology* (London: Sheed and Ward, 1936), vol. 2, 172; H. Noldin, *Theologiae Moralis* (Vienna: 1922), especially the treatment of "De Sexto Praecepto et de Usu Matrimonii"; Arturus Vermeersch, *Theologiae Moralis* (Rome: Pontificia Universitas Gregoriana, 1933), vol. 4, *De Castitate et Vitiis Oppositis*; Gerald Kelly, *Modern Youth and Chastity* (St. Louis: Queen's Work, 1941).

78. Aquinas, *ST*, III (suppl.), 65, 1, c.

79. Ibid., ad 1.

80. *ST*, III (suppl.), 41, 4; ibid., 49, 5; *ST*, II-II, 142, 1.

81. Albert the Great, *Comment in Libros Sententiarum*, 4, d. 26, a. 14, q. 2 ad 1.

82. Aquinas, *Comment in Quartum Librum Sent.*, d. 26, q. 2, a. 3; repeated in Suppl. 42, 3c.

83. *Contra gentiles*, 4, 78.

84. *ST*, II-II, 26, 11; also *Summa contra Gentiles*, 3, II, 123, 6.

85. Aquinas in *Summa contra Gentiles*, III, 24; Bonaventure in *In Quart. Sent.*, 33, 1, 1.

86. For a discussion of this point, see Michael G. Lawler, "Faith, Contract, and Sacrament in Christian Marriage: A Theological Approach," *TS* 52 (1991): 712–31.

87. David E. Fellhauer, "The *Consortium Omnis Vitae* as a Juridical Element of Marriage," *Studia Canonica* 13 (1979): 82.

88. Urban Navarrette, "Structura Juridica Matrimonii Secundum Concilium Vaticanum II," *Periodica* 56 (1967): 366.

89. Gerald C. Treacy, ed., *Five Great Encyclicals* (New York: Paulist, 1939), 83–84.

90. Ibid.

91. Dietrich von Hildebrand, *Marriage* (London: Longman's, 1939), v.

92. Ibid., 4, vi.

93. Ibid., 6.

94. Ibid., 25; emphasis in original.

95. Heribert Doms, *The Meaning of Marriage*, trans. George Sayer (London: Sheed and Ward, 1939), 94–95.

96. See, for instance, Sara S. McLanahan and Gary Sandefur, *Growing Up with a Single Parent: What Hurts, What Helps* (Cambridge: Harvard University Press, 1994); Paul R. Amato and Alan Booth, *A Generation at Risk: Growing Up in an Era of Family Upheaval* (Cambridge: Harvard University Press, 1997); Judith Wallerstein, Julia Lewis, and Sandra Blakeslee, *The Unexpected Legacy of Divorce* (New York: Hyperion, 2000).

97. *AAS* 36 (1944), 103.

98. *AAS* 43 (1951), 848–49.

99. *Acta et Documenta Concilio Vaticano II Apparando. Series II (Praeparatoria)*, Vol. 2, 961.

100. Ibid.

101. Ibid., 952.

102. See the votes recorded in the Commission "according to the comments of Dopfner, Alfrink, and Suenens." *Acta et Documenta Concilio Vaticano II Apparando. Series II (Praeparatoria)*, 971–85.
103. *GS*, 47, 48.
104. Ibid.
105. Ibid.
106. Ibid.; emphasis added.
107. Paul VI, *HV*, 11.
108. See Bernard Haring, *Commentary on the Documents of Vatican II* (New York: Herder, 1969), 5:234.
109. *GS*, 50.
110. Germain Grisez, *The Way of the Lord Jesus*, vol. 2, *Living a Christian Life* (Quincy, IL: Franciscan Herald Press, 1993), 565, n. 35.
111. Michael G. Lawler, *Marriage in the Catholic Church: Disputed Questions* (Collegeville, MN: Liturgical Press, 2002), 27–42.
112. Clifford Longley, *The Worlock Archive* (London: Chapman, 2000), 232.
113. Robert McClory, *Turning Point: The Inside Story of the Papal Birth Control Commission, and How* Humanae Vitae *Changed the Life of Patty Crowley and the Future of the Church* (New York: Crossroad, 1995), 127.
114. Ibid., 99.
115. For details on this, see Janet E. Smith, *Humanae Vitae: A Generation Later* (Washington, DC: Catholic University of America Press, 1991), 11–33.
116. *HV*, 11.
117. Cited in Robert Blair Kaiser, *The Politics of Sex and Religion* (Kansas City, MO: Leaven Press, 1985), 260–61. See also Longley, *Worlock Archive*, 233; emphasis added.
118. Richard McCormick, *Notes on Moral Theology 1965–1980* (Lanham, MD: University Press of America, 1981), 164.
119. Margaret A. Farley, *Just Love: A Framework for Christian Sexual Ethics* (New York: Continuum, 2006), 278.
120. *HV*, 11.
121. Farley, *Just Love*, 278.
122. *HV*, 11; *PH*, 64.
123. *AAS* 35 (1943), 307.
124. "The Interpretation of the Bible in the Church," *Origins* 23 (January 6, 1994): 511.
125. See Gen. 38:9.

CHAPTER 2

෴

Unitive Sexual Morality
A Revised Foundational Principle and Anthropology

Theologians who espouse the theology articulated in *Gaudium et spes* find in it a foundational principle for judging all human activity, including human sexual activity: the principle of the human person adequately considered. A reasonable question immediately arises: What does it mean to consider the human sexual person adequately? In response to this question, we first formulate a foundational principle of human sexuality; second, we expand on the morally significant dimensions of that principle; and third, we draw insight from these dimensions in our reconstructed definition of complementarity to formulate a comprehensive explanation of a "truly human" sexual act.

In this process we seek to offer an alternative to the primarily procreationist sexual anthropology in a more adequately considered unitive sexual anthropology. We do so with some trepidation, because sexuality is far from an unambiguous reality. Like all the human appetites, sexuality can be used for good, and then it is loving, unifying, and maybe procreative; or it can be abused for evil, and then it is unloving, divisive, and destructive of life. According to the American bishops, "the gift of human sexuality can be a great mystery at times," but the acknowledgment of mystery does not free theologians or the Magisterium from the task of attempting to penetrate the mystery and of determining the "nature," meaning, and morality of sexuality and sexual acts in the context of human relationships.[1]

Gaudium et spes articulates a fundamental principle with respect to the essential meaning of human sexuality and sexual acts.

> [Conjugal] love is uniquely expressed and perfected through the marital act. The actions within marriage by which the couple are united intimately and chastely are noble and worthy ones. Expressed in a manner which is truly human, these actions signify and promote that mutual self-giving by which spouses enrich each other with a joyful and a thankful will.[2]

Our exegesis of this principle proposes a developed theology of the unitive purpose of human sexuality and sexual acts in a marital relationship, and inquires about sexual possibilities for persons other than the married heterosexuals *Gaudium et spes* and the tradition have in mind. The context of this latter consideration is not simply the physical acts themselves but the meanings of interpersonal relationship and the sexual acts that take place within this relationship. We also ask how sexual acts reach beyond the couple to impact their extended family and community.

We note, first, an important distinction between sexuality and sexual activity. This distinction is expressed well by the United States Catholic Bishops:

> *Sexuality* refers to a fundamental component of personality in and through which we, as male or female, experience our relatedness to self, others, the world, and even God.
>
> *Sex* refers *either* to the biological aspects of being male or female (i.e., a synonym for one's gender) *or* to the expressions of sexuality, which have physical, emotional, and spiritual dimensions, particularly genital actions resulting in sexual intercourse and/or orgasm.[3]

Given our discussion in the previous chapter, we regret the implied equivalence of sex and gender, but sexuality is correctly described as intrinsic to the human person in whom there is no division between the physical and spiritual. This is an important recognition that banishes the dualism that has plagued the Christian tradition regarding human sexuality. Humans are created by God as sexual beings, embodied subjects whose spiritual and physical dimensions merge in a single being that expresses itself in a profound and holy manner in intimate human relationship and sexual acts. *Sexual* is an adjective that describes not only acts that human beings do but also the essential reality that human beings are. We can and may renounce sexual activity; we can never renounce our intrinsic sexual being.

The sexual drive has three personal meanings: it is pleasurable, relational, and potentially procreative. Scientific research has demonstrated that sexuality influences our personality, our brain activity, our understandings of self and other, and our relationships.[4] It also provides us with a means of personal communication that is carried out intimately and bodily in sexual acts. For the past one thousand years, the Catholic tradition has insisted that just and loving marital relationships and the sexual acts that both express and nourish them are sacraments, symbols of the loving relationships between God and God's people and Christ and Christ's Church. A group commissioned by the National Conference of Catholic Bishops boldly asserts, indeed, that mutually pleasurable marital sexual acts are possibly the human experiences that most fully symbolize the loving communication among the divine Trinity, a statement that affirms the goodness of both human sexuality and fully human sexual acts.[5]

CONJUGAL LOVE AND SEXUAL INTERCOURSE

The foundational principle we have advanced needs explication. First, sexual intercourse is a unique expression and perfection of conjugal love. An individual's sexuality is expressed in and through daily interactions with other human beings, not just spouses. Humans naturally relate as sexual beings. The term *intercourse*, frequently used as a euphemism for sex, literally means "communication or dealings between or among people." In this sense we have human intercourse with many people throughout the day. Sexual intercourse, however, is a unique and particular expression of the communication-intercourse of our very being with a special loved one.

While Western culture and churches tend to give the sexual aspect of the marital relationship a disproportionate focus, studies show the following relationship between age and frequency per year of sexual intercourse of a married couple: age 18–29, 110.2 times; age 30–39, 86.2 times; age 40–49, 70.6 times; age 50–59, 54.5 times; age 60–69, 33.4 times; age 70+, 17.6 times.[6] As these statistics make clear, even at a couple's sexual peak, the time spent in sexual intercourse is proportionately minimal. This data is noted not to diminish the importance of sexual intercourse for the marital relationship, but to situate it in a more realistic context. As *Gaudium et spes* teaches, the act of intercourse is the perfection of conjugal love. It expresses and strengthens the interpersonal union between a couple, which is why, going back to St. Paul, the Church has recognized that abstaining from sexual relations for too long can be detrimental to the marital union.[7] The marital relationship finds an essentially nurturing component in just and loving sexual acts that *procreate*, occasionally in a biological sense, always in the sense of creating life for the couple, their bonded relationship, their family, and their wider community. Just and loving sexual union creates and nurtures love, the very essence of Christian discipleship; it *makes love*, as we say in everyday language.

MULTIPLE DIMENSIONS OF HUMAN SEXUALITY

The sexual science of the twentieth century has taught us that human sexuality is multidimensioned. We deal now with its physical, emotional, psychological, spiritual, and relational dimensions.

Physical

We deal first with physical union, the obvious joining of bodies. In their treatment of human sexuality, Masters and Johnson explain four phases in the process of sexual intercourse. Phase one is the excitement phase, in which, for the man, the penis becomes erect due to the flow of blood into the penile tissues, and, for the woman, there is moistening of the vagina, enlargement of the breasts, and tensing of the muscles with increased breathing and heart rate. Phase two is the plateau phase, the entry of the penis into the vagina, further quickening of the heart rate and breathing, mounting erotic pleasure, and the appearance of a flush on both bodies. Frequently noted in this phase is the penetration of the female by the male; not so frequently noted, but true in every just and loving intercourse, is the welcoming envelopment of the male by the female. The male penetrates the female, not only physically but also psychologically and emotionally, and is physically enveloped by her; she, in turn, enters emotionally and psychologically into the male. In their intercourse they become, in very deed, a two-in-one-bodiness.[8]

Phase three, the climax, discharge of semen by the male and a number of orgasmic muscle spasms by the female, is the moment of greatest pleasure and ecstasy. This pleasure is, of course, quite individual, and it is part of the ambiguity of sexuality and sexual intercourse that in the climactic moments of orgasm, the act intended to be the giving of one person to the other throws each back on herself and himself in a solitude of pleasure. The act that is intended to be and is fully unitive is, at its peak moment, actually also divisive. Michel Foucault reminds us of the similarity the ancients saw between sexual orgasm and epilepsy, both moments of being most alone and vulnerable.[9] This is but one instance of the essential ambiguity of sexuality and sexual activity; we call attention to others as this chapter unfolds. Phase four is the resolution phase, in which the couple relaxes and blood pressure and respiration return to normal.[10] Though these four phases are not to be "used as a 'check list' against which to measure sexual performance," every sexually active couple can, at least sometimes, identify them in their intercourse, a natural fact that offers profound evidence for sexual "nature" as God intended it and for the "natural" pleasure of the sexual act that has been so suspect in Christian history.[11]

A unifying component of these various physical stages of the sexual act is pleasure. Sexual pleasure has always been morally suspect in the Catholic tradition, even though it is a natural and intrinsic part of sexual intercourse. Sexual pleasure is a good created by God and given as gift to humans. Like all gifts, it can be used for good or evil, and the abuses of pleasure and a morality based purely on pleasure, hedonism, are fully evident in the sociohistorical past and present. Such abuses, however, cannot and do not diminish the valuable and essential role of integrating pleasure as a natural component of human sexual morality. An essential component of a revised sexual ethical principle, then, we suggest, must be a deeper understanding of pleasure and its function in human sexuality, and the development of parameters for its responsible and moral expression. Such an investigation will discuss foreplay and other types of sexual intimacy leading to orgasm as legitimate moral expressions of sexual intimacy, and expand the parameters of traditional teaching that limits orgasm to heterosexual and vaginal intercourse.[12]

Emotional

A theology of the unitive must include the emotional dimension of human sexuality. Emotions, strong, generalized feelings with both physical and psychological manifestations, apprehend value and disvalue for each individual. They are forms of evaluative judgments, Martha Nussbaum argues, "that ascribe to certain things and persons outside a person's own control great importance for the person's own flourishing."[13] The evaluative judgment carried out by an emotion, we caution, is not yet the judgment of conscience we talked about in our prologue. In partial agreement with Nussbaum, therefore, we prefer to say that emotions are *proto-judgments*, preliminary apprehensions of value or disvalue, that become part of the data to be considered by conscience/2 before any final conscience/3 judgment is made. Emotions may be either positive or negative. Positive emotions include love, joy, hope, humor, trust, happiness, and passion; negative emotions include hatred, sadness, despair, anxiety, distrust, anger, resentment, hurt, and dissatisfaction. In the act of just and loving sexual intercourse, there is a complex combination and expression of emotions that unite two separate persons into one coupled person, the *one body* of Genesis, in an act that can express love, vulnerability, healing, and comfort, and create wholeness or, on occasion, heal woundedness, neediness, anxiety, or brokenness. Either way, the sexual act reveals a wide spectrum of human emotions and brings out total vulnerability in both the positive and negative emotions. Analyzing human sexuality and the act of intercourse in terms of its emotional dimension entails reading the mystery of the wounded human in his or her ongoing search for flourishing and wholeness in intimate relationship.

Psychological

Emotions are a unique and particular expression of a person's basic and stable human identity, and the emotional and psychological dimensions of human sexuality are intimately related. Psychiatrist Jack Dominian presents an excellent synthesis of six psychological dimensions that illustrate the sexual act between a loving couple.[14] First, through sexual intercourse a couple affirms each other's identity. The sexual act is symbolic in that when we become naked in front of another human person, we become totally and completely vulnerable. To make love in "a truly human manner" is both a mutual affirmation and a mutual unconditional acceptance of the other with all her and his physical, emotional, psychological, and spiritual blessings and flaws. This affirmation and acceptance progresses through various stages. As we have indicated above, sexual intercourse is more frequent early in a marriage, and perhaps it is also more passionate. As the relationship develops and deepens over the years, the routine of sexual affirmation and acceptance may lose its novelty, attraction, and excitement, but this is not to be interpreted to mean that affirmation and acceptance cease. In reality, they increase as the couple comes to know and accept each other more profoundly and intimately over time. While the novelty and excitement of sexual intercourse may diminish, the affirmation and acceptance of the person, a unique self created in the image and likeness of God and affirmed, accepted, and loved unconditionally, becomes more profound. Repetition may breed familiarity and a sense of routine, but it also deepens unconditional appreciation and acceptance of the other as he or she is.

Second, the sexual act reflects, affirms, and creates gender identity, a fundamental dimension of sexual identity. Gender is concerned with the socially constructed meanings of femininity or masculinity. It is determined not only by individual sexuality but also by culture, ethnicity, and rearing experience, and is expressed in actions, interactions, and social roles. Dominian describes this gender expression as a liturgy of exchange, a divine language, in which a couple communicates with each other through sexual desire.[15] In the formation and development of sexual identity through a recognition and embodiment of gender roles, it is crucial that sexual activity be a form of loving, open, honest, and authentic human communication. If it is, then the act becomes humanly communicative at the deepest level; if it is not, then the same act can stagnate or even block future possibilities for communication and formation of healthy sexual identity. This is yet one more example of the essential ambiguity of human sexual activity.

Self-esteem is the third psychological dimension of human sexuality. Psychological studies indicate that one of the greatest threats to healthy human development, including sexual development, is poor self-esteem.[16] The Christian tradition has not always done a good job of emphasizing healthy self-love. Jesus's great commandment is well known: "'You shall love the Lord your God with all your heart, with all your soul, with all your mind, and with all your strength.' The second is this: 'You shall love your neighbor as yourself'" (Mark 12:28–34; Matt. 22:34–40, 46b; and Luke 10:25–28). Not so well known is the fact that there are *three* commandments in this latter text: love God, love neighbor, *and* love self. Typically, the Christian tradition has interpreted neighbor love as altruistic and agapaic, and self-love as egocentric and antithetical to the love of the gospel. This certainly *can* be the case, and the cultures of those countries that emphasize radical individualism encourage egocentric love, but egocentric love is not the healthy self-love demanded by the gospel. Authentic self-love first affirms oneself as a self-in-God, good, valuable, and lovable, and then, in alliance with neighbor-love, turns toward the other and gives this good, valuable, and lovable self-in-God unconditionally to the other. As Aquinas might argue: no one gives what he does not have. If a man does not truly and fully accept himself, in both his wholeness and his brokenness, he can neither give himself fully to an other person nor fully accept the other person. So it is, too, with a woman.

Fourth, sexual intercourse is therapeutic and relieves distress. The human person is a psychosomatic unity, an intrinsic union of body and spirit. There is distinction between body and spirit in the human being, but there is no separation, and there is ongoing and constant dialogue between them. When a couple makes love, each person brings to that experience all the psychological burdens that accompany daily life, including worries about the relationship, possible conception, work, finances, and children. The act of sexual intercourse makes possible the suspension of those anxieties and worries, at least for the moment, and has a healing effect on the individual. This relief of distress, however, depends on the nature of the relationship. If the relationship is just, loving, committed, and honest, relief of distress is often an intrinsic component of sexual activity. If, however, the relationship is promiscuous, inauthentic, or dishonest, while the physical act can still suspend distress for the moment, the after-effects of that experience can cause greater distress, in the form of guilt, a sense of inauthentic or dishonest intimate communication, or objectification of the other.

Fifth, sexual intercourse is reconciling. There are no conflict-free relationships, not even in the most just and loving of marriages. Frictions, disagreements, and misunderstandings are all inevitable aspects of any human relationship, and any and all of these experiences can create hurt, distress, and general distrust of the other in the relationship. One is not likely to find couples who desire sexual intimacy at the peak of such quarrels, but intimacy comes after the resolution of the quarrel and may be an intrinsic component of the resolution. Some couples claim that the best sex they have is after an argument. This is because sexual intimacy heals the wounds caused by the quarrel and reaffirms the bond and commitment that may have been threatened by it.

Finally, sexual intercourse is a profound act of thanksgiving or eucharist. The embodied nature of the human person binds him or her to bodily expression which is best exemplified, though by no means limited to, verbal language. Beyond verbal language there is body language, and beyond body language there is ritual language, symbolic actions with socially approved meanings. Couples can say to each other "I love you," or "I thank you," or "I forgive you," and in the spoken words they are reaching to meanings far beyond the words. They can say the same things in socially approved actions, by looks, by touches, by gifts, and in all of these actions they are similarly reaching far beyond the actions to express love, forgiveness, reconciliation, affirmation, thanksgiving. In the physical action of sexual intercourse, an action as symbolic in the West as any spoken word, they express all these things in the most profound and total way available to an embodied human being, namely, through the completely unmasked and therefore totally vulnerable body. They say to each other, in the words of the ancient Anglican wedding ritual, "with this *body* I thee worship." They say, that is, in the etymological meaning of the word *worship*, I ascribe worth to you and to us, and for this worth I give thanks.

Couples who are Catholic cannot help but link this moment of sexual thanksgiving for human relationship with that liturgical thanksgiving for divine relationship they call Eucharist.[17] "This is my body which is given for you," Jesus says to his disciples at the Supper."[18] "This is my body given for and to you," lovers say to each other in the act of intercourse. In both the Supper and the sex, the body and the person synonymous with it are vulnerable, even broken, but both body and person are given in love to the other, trusting that they will be received in love and handled with care. In the Supper, both past and present, the Body of Christ is given to be eaten; so too are the bodies of the truly human lovers in sexual intercourse. Adrian Thatcher points out, legitimately, that "many of the intimacies of love-making are fairly literally an eating of the body of the person one loves. Kissing, especially deep kissing; the use of the tongue in caressing and stimulating; biting, sucking, and nibbling; these are all patently ways in which we eat the bodies of our lovers."[19] The central theological point here is a very Catholic one. The God incarnate in the Christ who gives his body in the Supper for the salvation of all is the same God incarnate in the lovers and their act of mutual self- and body-giving for the salvation of their relationship. In Catholic theology, the one ritual is as sacramental of God as the other, which is why both Eucharist and marriage are listed among the Catholic sacraments.

Spiritual

The relationship of communion between the three persons of the Trinity provides the model for every genuine human communion, and the grace of the Spirit enables each and every believer to share this communion with a loved other through a multitude of actions, including sexual actions. *The* characteristic of marriage, distinguishing it from other forms of friendship, is that it is expected to be an exclusive sexual relationship. From what we have explained in this section, it is not difficult to conclude that the communion between spouses expressed in the sexual intercourse that characterizes marriage is also a sacrament of the divine communion. That is precisely what the Catholic Church intends when it teaches that marriage is a sacrament.

The act of sexual intercourse allows humans a unique insight into the love shared within the Trinity. In intercourse there is the unconditional gift of self to the other and the unconditional reception of the other's gift of self in return. Such mutuality, reciprocity, and unconditional acceptance reflect the total self-surrender within the Trinity. "It is our capacity to love and be loved," Gallagher notes, "that *makes us most God-like.*"[20] The love, including the sexual love, shared by a couple in relationship draws them together into communion, and this shared communion reflects the communion of the Trinity, draws them closer to God, strengthens their relationship, and overflows into all their other relationships. Most profoundly, this sexual communion always procreates new life, just as the loving communion between the Father and Son yields the Spirit. Even in cases where biological procreation is neither possible nor desired for legitimate reasons, their sexual union procreates and enhances the couple's life in communion in imitation, and as sacrament, of the divine Trinity, the infinite source of gracious and loving communion.

Relational

Spirituality is all about relationship. So, too, is human sexuality, grounded in relationship with God, with neighbor, and with self. Human sexuality is a gift from God that draws us toward interpersonal communion. It is an intrinsic, mysterious dimension of human beings that draws individuals out of self and toward another. "Sexuality is a dimension of one's restless heart, which continually yearns for interpersonal communion, glimpsed and experienced to varying degrees in this life, ultimately finding full oneness only in God, here and hereafter."[21] In and through human sexuality and relationships humans seek to become whole and holy. This relational gift is at the core of human identity and allows humans to enter into communion with God and one another.

Relationship with the gospel "neighbor" takes several forms. First, and primarily, neighbor is the spouse or intimate other. Sexual acts are the most intimate communion between two people; in them two individuals become physically and personally a coupled one. Catholic tradition refers to this relationship in terms of a covenant and a communion of persons and limits this covenantal communion to marriage between a man and a woman.[22] A second close neighbor is family. God's gift of sexuality provides women and men with the desire to unite as a couple and to create, nurture, and educate new life out of their union, thereby creating family. The Catholic Church correctly describes family as the "original cell of social life" and the "domestic church," a relational community of partnered life and love.[23]

Neighbor also extends to the human family and community beyond the domestic church. Discipleship is an all-encompassing relational reality, embracing even enemies.[24] Too often in history Catholic moral theology has focused on the individual's acts and their impact on the individual's relationship with God, while neglecting the broader social implications of those acts. For instance, whereas magisterial teaching has focused on the separation of the unitive and procreative dimensions of the sexual act as the basis for condemning artificial reproduction, some moral theologians have focused more on the social justice issues of using such technology in terms of cost and the use of limited medical resources.[25] (We develop this point in chapter 6.) This shift in focus is especially relevant in sexual ethics. Too often, sexual and social ethics are seen in isolation from each other, each utilizing its own methodology and having its own point of reference. Whereas the Magisterium's sexual ethics tends to focus on acts and absolute norms that guide individuals and married couples, its social ethics tends to focus on the complex network of interrelationships that constitute a community and general principles to guide these interrelationships toward the common good. Sexuality as a relational concept challenges us to more fully integrate its individual and communal moral dimensions.

Finally, human sexuality is a unique gift to each individual that summons everyone to recognize, accept, appreciate, and integrate the gift in the Christian task of drawing closer to God in Christ and neighbor. History demonstrates beyond doubt that, with the exception of an intellectual and abstract acknowledgment that sexuality and sex are good because they are created by a good God, much of the Christian tradition has not appreciated the goodness of this gift practically and concretely. This lack of appreciation for the gift of human sexuality in its various forms has created a great deal of guilt and self-loathing, with the unfortunate consequence that people sometimes live out their sexuality in unhealthy ways. Perhaps this is truer nowhere than in the case of men and women with a homosexual orientation who feel personally rejected by the Church in what Jordan refers to as the "rhetoric of moral management."[26] This rhetoric is grounded in exclusion and is evidenced in the Magisterium's designation of homosexual inclination as "objectively disordered," a designation that inhibits many gay and lesbian Catholics from revealing their sexual orientation.[27] Negatively labeling them as "objectively disordered" does not facilitate homosexuals' integration of their sexuality. Sexuality is intimately related to our attraction to other persons, to love, and to committed relationships. For this natural attraction to be nurtured and manifested in responsible relationships, it must be accepted and integrated in a healthy manner. It may be true that no human person has fully integrated his or her human sexuality, but Christians still need to be conscious of and critically reflect upon perspectives that, consciously or unconsciously, frustrate the personal acceptance and integration of sexuality.

These dimensions of the sexual person—physical, emotional, psychological, spiritual, and relational—explain the foundational principle for human sexuality contained in *Gaudium et spes* and reflect a holistic sexual anthropology. Our final task in this chapter is to draw out the logical implications of this principle for morally evaluating *Gaudium et spes*'s "truly human" sexual act. To do so, we will have recourse to the concept of complementarity and the virtues of chastity, love, and justice. Combined, our foundational principle, truly human sexual acts, complementarity, and the just-mentioned virtues expand the possibility of moral sexual acts, which is currently limited in magisterial teaching to reproductive acts between married heterosexuals, to include nonreproductive homosexual and heterosexual acts.

We begin our excursus on the truly human sexual act with a look at the virtue of chastity, the central virtue guiding human sexuality throughout Christian tradition. We complete it with the virtues of justice and charity.

CHASTITY

Chastity is a virtue that facilitates the attainment and integration of authentic human sexuality. The *Catechism of the Catholic Church* provides a succinct definition. Chastity is "the successful integration of sexuality within the person and thus the inner unity of [the hu]man in his [and her] bodily and spiritual being. Sexuality, in which [the hu]man's belonging to the bodily and biological world is expressed, becomes personal and truly human when it is integrated into the relationship of one person to another."[28]

Chastity, then, is the authentic integration of a person's sexuality into human relationship and the practical living out of that relationship in fidelity and commitment to another person. In our citation of the *Catechism's* definition of chastity, we intentionally left out the final clause of that definition. As stated, the focus is on integrating one's sexuality bodily and spiritually, but the final clause limits this integration to heterosexual relationships: "in the complete and lifelong mutual gift of a man and a woman." There is a tension between this final clause and the opening clauses. As is now accepted in the scientific community and stated in the Catechism and other magisterial documents, homosexuals do not choose their condition or orientation; it is a result of physiological (nature) and social (nurture) factors.[29] As such, what does it mean for a homosexual person to integrate his or her sexuality? Does it require celibacy, or is there the possibility of a moral expression of sexual activity between two people of the same sex given the criteria for a theology of the unitive that we are developing? The *Catechism* does not equate chastity for the homosexual person with celibacy.[30] On the basis of our theological principle, persons of a homosexual orientation may live a life of chastity within a monogamous, just, loving, committed relationship subject to the same moral guidelines used to morally evaluate a heterosexual nonfecund relationship. We will expand on this in chapter 5.

The above definition of chastity has profound implications for what it means to express our sexuality and sexual acts in a manner that is truly human. Sexuality is a gift from the creator God to facilitate men's and women's task of becoming fully human in and through interpersonal relationship. Humans seek both wholeness, sometimes called human flourishing, and holiness in their journey toward becoming fully integrated, relational, loving persons. This requires them to embrace their sexuality, to seek to develop and perfect those dimensions that facilitate its authentic development, and to resist whatever frustrates this development. In a world of original, personal, and social sin, this is not an easy project. The world humans inhabit, however, is not only a world of sin; it is also a world of abounding grace. It is a world into which the Father of all has sent his Son to be incarnated, making it thereby essentially holy. It is a world into which the Son has sent the Spirit-Paraclete to lead it into all truth. It is a world in which that Spirit roams freely, bestowing gifts of all kinds on all men and women of goodwill.[31] It is a world in which the search for full humanity, and therefore also for God, is pursued sexually by both heterosexuals and homosexuals, and therefore any search for the truly human must include both these groups.

TRULY HUMAN AND COMPLEMENTARITY

The rest of this chapter focuses on two important and related terms, "truly human" and "complementarity," that have recently been introduced into the discussion of sexual morality in the Catholic tradition.[32] *Gaudium et spes* declared that the sexual intercourse in and through which spouses symbolize their mutual gift to each other is to be "in a manner which is *truly human*."[33] The sexual act, the Council intended, is to be a deliberated and intentional act, not just an act that a person does without any responsible discernment. Unfortunately, the Council offered no definition of what it meant by "truly human."

The CDF's *Considerations regarding Proposals to Give Legal Recognition to Unions between Homosexual Persons* (CRP) has recently sought to clarify the meaning of "truly human sexual acts." It first states that homosexual unions lack "the conjugal dimension which represents the human and ordered form of sexuality," and then articulates the principle that "sexual relations are human when and insofar as they express and promote the mutual assistance of the sexes in marriage and are open to the transmission of new life."[34] This is the unitive-procreative principle that, in the twentieth century, became the foundational principle for all Catholic sexual teaching. According to this principle, truly human sexual acts are acts within marriage that are simultaneously unitive of the spouses and open to procreation, and only such acts are judged to be truly human. CRP uses the term *sexual complementarity* in relation to this principle, which includes parenting and the education of children and, on this foundation, defends heterosexual marriage and condemns homosexual unions. The term *complementarity* has appeared only relatively recently in magisterial sexual teaching, in Pope John Paul II's *Familiaris consortio* (1981).[35] Its types and implications for defining truly human sexual acts have yet to be fully explored. In the next section we investigate and critique several types of complementarity to advance its understanding and its implications for the "truly human" sexual act. Before proceeding to that discussion, however, we must first confront a common feminist argument against the very use of the word *complementarity*.

Feminist theologian Barbara Hilkert Andolsen, for instance, opposes the word because it is tainted "by its close association with justifications for [patriarchal] gender inequality." Such gender inequality, she points out, has been shown to be "part of the gender ideology of the [European] bourgeois family since the seventeenth or eighteenth century."[36] We are in complete agreement with Andolsen that the idea of complementarity has been used to perpetuate gender inequality to the detriment of women, not only in the European tradition of the past two hundred years but also in the John Paul II–inspired Roman Catholic tradition of the twentieth century. For that reason, we would like to abandon both the idea and the word. That, however, would leave both idea and word in the Catholic tradition unchallenged and unreconstructed. We prefer to accept both idea and word from the Catholic tradition and seek to purge it of every suggestion of either gender or sexual inequality. That we do in the following sections with our idea of sexual orientation complementarity.

Sexual Complementarity: Biological and Personal

There are two general types of sexual complementarity in the CDF's document, biological and personal, with subtypes within each (table 2.1). The definition of what constitutes truly human sexual acts depends on how biological and personal complementarity are defined in themselves and in relation to each other. We will consider each definition in turn.

BIOLOGICAL COMPLEMENTARITY: HETEROGENITAL AND REPRODUCTIVE

Biological complementarity is divided into what we label *heterogenital* and *reproductive complementarity*. The CDF describes heterogenital

TABLE 2.1   Types of Sexual Complementarity in Magisterial Teaching

I. Biological Complementarity

Title	Definition
Heterogenital Complementarity	The physically functioning male and female sexual organs (penis and vagina)
Reproductive Complementarity	The physically functioning male and female reproductive organs (testes and sperm, ovaries and ova) used in sexual acts to biologically reproduce

II. Personal Complementarity

Title	Definition
Communion Complementarity	The two-in-oneness within a heterogenital complementary marital relationship created and sustained by truly human sexual acts
Affective Complementarity	The integrated psychoaffective, social, relational, and spiritual elements of the human person grounded in heterogenital complementarity
Parental Complementarity	Heterogenitally complementary parents who fulfill the second dimension of reproductive complementarity, namely, the education of children

complementarity this way: "Men and women are equal as persons and complementary as male and female. Sexuality is something that pertains to the physical-biological realm."³⁷ Heterogenital complementarity pertains to the biological, genital distinction between male and female. The mere possession of male or female genitals, however, is insufficient to constitute heterogenital complementarity; genitals must also function properly. If they cannot function complementarily, as they cannot in either male or female impotence, neither heterogenital nor reproductive complementarity is possible, and in that case canon law prescribes that a valid marriage and sacrament are also not possible.³⁸ Though heterogenital complementarity is the foundation for reproductive complementarity, the two are to be carefully distinguished, for while the Magisterium teaches that a couple must complement each other heterogenitally, it also teaches that, "for serious reasons and observing moral precepts," it is not necessary that they biologically reproduce.³⁹ Infertile couples and couples who choose for serious reasons not to reproduce for the duration of the marriage can still enter into a valid marital and sacramental relationship. In light of this teaching, Pope Paul VI's statement that "each and every marriage act must remain open to the transmission of life" is *morally* ambiguous in the cases of infertile couples, couples in which the wife is postmenopausal, and couples who practice permitted natural family planning with the specific intention of avoiding the transmission of life.⁴⁰ Gareth Moore correctly notes that "vaginal intercourse which we know to be sterile is a different type of act from vaginal intercourse which, as far as we know, might result in conception."⁴¹

Potentially reproductive and permanently or temporarily nonreproductive heterosexual acts, then, are essentially different kinds of acts. What about heterosexual nonreproductive acts and homosexual acts, if anything, distinguishes them? Since both are nonreproductive, it cannot be their nonreproductivity. It can be only that the former exhibit heterogenital complementarity and the latter do not. Grounding potentially reproductive and permanently or temporarily nonreproductive heterosexual acts in heterogenital, rather than reproductive, complementarity raises two sets of questions. First, it raises questions about the morality of other types of nonreproductive heterosexual acts, such as oral or anal sex, which are permanently nonreproductive even though heterogenital complementarity is present. Second, the Magisterium's claim that homosexual acts are intrinsically disordered because they are closed to the transmission of life can be challenged, for permanently nonreproductive heterosexual acts are as biologically closed to the transmission of life as are homosexual acts. From a strictly reproductive point of view, nonreproductive heterosexual acts *may* have more in common with homosexual acts in terms of personal complementarity and relationality than with reproductive heterosexual acts. There is no doubt that homosexual acts do not exhibit heterogenital or reproductive complementarity, but it still remains to be seen whether they exhibit personal complementarity.

PERSONAL COMPLEMENTARITY: COMMUNION,
AFFECTIVE, AND PARENTAL

The CDF also refers to sexuality on the "personal level—where nature and spirit are united." We refer to the personal level of sexuality as *personal complementarity*, which can be divided into several subcategories.

Communion Complementarity

Communion complementarity in the marital relationship is "a communion of persons is realized involving the use of the sexual faculty."[42] The male and female genitals, penis and vagina, contribute to the realization of a communion of persons in marriage expressed in truly human sexual acts. The CDF implies, however, that without heterogenital complementarity, communion complementarity is not possible. "There are absolutely no grounds for considering homosexual unions to be in any way similar or even remotely analogous to God's plan for marriage and family. Marriage is holy, while homosexual acts go against the natural moral law. Homosexual acts close the sexual act to the gift of life. They do not proceed from a genuine affective and sexual complementarity. Under no circumstances can they be approved.'"[43] Such assertions are made with no supporting scientific evidence. We set forth abundant evidence to the contrary in chapter 5.

Affective Complementarity

This type of complementarity is at the crux of magisterial teaching on sexual complementarity, because it intrinsically links biological and personal complementarity. Citing the *Catechism of the Catholic Church*, the CDF asserts, without adducing any proof, that affective complementarity is lacking in homosexual acts. It does not clarify here what it means by affective complementarity, but we can glean some insight from another magisterial source. The CCE teaches that, "in the Christian anthropological perspective, affective-sex education must consider the totality of the person and insist therefore on the integration of the biological, psycho-affective, social and spiritual elements."[44] Since affective sex education seeks to integrate all the elements of the human person, affective complementarity must similarly seek to integrate them in a truly human sexual act. Important questions for magisterial understanding of affective complementarity are how it understands these elements in the individual person, in the person in relationship, and in a truly human sexual act.

Pope John Paul II claims that "even though man and woman are made for each other, this does not mean that God created them incomplete."[45] Each individual has the potential to be complete by integrating the biological, psychoaffective, social, and spiritual elements of affective complementarity. Claiming that men and women are complete in themselves seems to respond to the concerns expressed by some theologians that the idea of complementarity implies that celibate religious or single people are somehow not complete and lack something in their humanity.[46] Second, when he moves from individual to couple, even though man and woman are "complete" in themselves, John Paul argues that "for forming a couple they are incomplete."[47] He further notes that "woman complements man, just as man complements woman. . . . Womanhood expresses the 'human' as much as manhood does, but in a different and complementary way."[48] We must ask, however, where the incompleteness and the need for complementarity reside in an individual that is complete in himself or herself but is incomplete for forming a couple. Where in the human person does this incompleteness exist that needs complementing by the opposite sex? John Paul responds, "Womanhood and manhood are complementary *not only from the physical and psychological points of view*, but also from the *ontological*. It is only through the duality of the 'masculine' and the 'feminine' that the 'human' finds full realization."[49]

Kevin Kelly accurately notes that "ontological complementarity maintains that the distinction between men and women has been so designed by God that they complement each other, not just in their genital sexual faculties but also in their minds and hearts and in the particular qualities and skills they bring to life, and specifically to family life."[50] The masculine and feminine complement each other to create a "unity of the two," a "psychophysical completion," not only in sexual acts but also in marital life.[51] Finally, beyond heterogenital complementarity for the purpose of reproduction, John Paul's claim of affective complementarity leaves ambiguous and undeveloped *how* these elements are integrated in a truly human sexual act. To summarize: in magisterial teaching on affective complementarity, the affective (biological, psychoaffective, social, and spiritual) elements are strictly divided according to gender and comprise essential male and female human natures; only when they are brought together in marriage and sexual acts is the human couple complete.

There are two important points to note in John Paul II's and the Magisterium's explanations of affective complementarity. First, there is an intrinsic relationship between heterogenital and personal complementarity, between body and person (heart, intelligence, will, soul).[52] Second, given the Magisterium's teaching on the immorality of homosexual acts, it is clear it regards heterogenital complementarity as a sine qua non for personal complementarity in truly human sexual acts. Without heterogenital complementarity, the other elements of affective complementarity in the sexual act cannot be realized.

Several points need to be made regarding the claims that God created individuals complete in themselves but incomplete when they come to form a couple and that this incompleteness is made complete through the (biological, psychoaffective, social, and spiritual) affective complementarity of male and female. First, to claim that a person is complete in himself or herself indicates that the person is complete biologically, psychoaffectively, socially, and spiritually, at least when the person is in relationship with God and neighbor. Second, while it is clear that male and female complete one another biologically in terms of genitalia for reproduction, it is not clear how they are incomplete and complete each other psychoaffectively, socially, and spiritually. John Paul II claims, "It is only in the union of two sexually different persons that the individual can achieve perfection in a synthesis of unity and mutual psychophysical completion."[53] Biological, psychoaffective, social, and spiritual elements of the human person are ontologically, that is essentially, divided along masculine and feminine lines, however, without justification, save that they are said to be God-given from the very beginning.[54] It is reasonable to question, however, whether the psychoaffective, social, and spiritual elements are essentially divided along gendered masculine and feminine lines and find completion only in male–female unity.[55] Besides genitalia, what are the "feminine" affective elements a man lacks, and what are the "masculine" affective elements a woman lacks?

There are gender stereotypes in magisterial documents. Femaleness is defined primarily in terms of motherhood, receptivity, and nurturing, and maleness is defined primarily in terms of fatherhood, initiation, and activity.[56] With the exception of biological maternity and paternity, the claim of ontologically or essentially gendered psychological traits does not seem to recognize the culturally conditioned and socially constructed "nature" of gender and does not adequately reflect the complexity of the human person and relationships. Within individuals and relationships, psychoaffective, social, and spiritual elements are not exclusively "natural" to either gender per se but may be found in either gender, may vary within a relationship, and may express themselves differently depending on the relational contexts.[57] Psychoaffective, social, and spiritual traits are variously distributed among males and females and are not intrinsic to either's "nature" prior to socialization. For instance, some males are more nurturing than some females, and some females more dominant and analytical than some males. These traits also vary within relationships in which there may be two dominant people or two nurturing people. Do we want to claim in these cases that these two people do not complement each other? The "masculinity" and "femininity" of the nonbiological elements are largely conditioned and defined by culture and are not essential components of masculine and feminine human nature mysteriously creating a "unity of the two."[58] The further claim of essential difference between male and female whereby the male and female find psychoaffective, social, and spiritual completion in one another only in marriage is entirely unsubstantiated by any scientific evidence.

Since there are reasonable grounds for questioning the Magisterium's claim that affective complementarity entails certain psychoaffective, social, and spiritual elements essential to the male and female and strictly divided on gender lines and, further, that these can be realized only in heterosexual marriage and heterosexual acts, the absolute claim prohibiting homosexual acts because they lack affective complementarity is substantially weakened. While homosexual persons cannot realize the biological element of affective complementarity (heterogenital and reproductive complementarity), it remains a question whether or not they can realize its personal elements. Granted, there is an important sense in which affective complementarity integrates the biological and personal elements in a truly human sexual act. We believe, however, that the Magisterium's account relies primarily on heterogenital complementarity, entails an incomplete, if not distorted, vision of gender, and neglects an adequate consideration of the experiential and relational dimensions of human sexuality.[59]

Parental Complementarity

Parental complementarity argues against same-sex unions based on the claim that, "as experience has shown, the absence of sexual complementarity in these unions creates obstacles in the normal development of children who would be placed in the care of such persons. . . . Allowing children to be adopted by persons living in such unions would actually mean doing violence to these children."[60] The Congregation provides no scientific evidence, here or elsewhere, to substantiate its claim that homosexual unions are an obstacle to the normal development of children. There is, however, abundant evidence to the contrary, as we shall elaborate in chapter 5. This social-scientific data supports the established claim that communion and affective complementarity between the parents greatly facilitate both parental complementarity and the positive nurture of children.[61] Given this evidence, the question of whether parental complementarity is as essentially linked to heterogenital complementarity as the CDF claims is unavoidable. Parental complementarity, however, does serve to remind us that truly human sexual acts have public implications beyond the couple's private act of sexual intercourse, and that intercourse that leads to conception and adoption both demand long-term caring, nurturing, and authentic familial and social relationships.

INTERRELATIONSHIP BETWEEN HETEROGENITAL AND PERSONAL COMPLEMENTARITY

Though heterogenital complementarity is necessary in magisterial teaching to realize a truly human sexual act, it is not sufficient. Heterosexual rape and incest take place in a heterogenitally complementary way, but no one would claim they are also personally complementary. Truly human complementarity is not either/or—either heterogenital complementarity or personal complementarity—but both/and, heterogenital and personal complementarity together. The magisterium correctly posits an essential relationship between biological (heterogenital and possibly reproductive) and personal (communion, affective, and parental) complementarity, but there is a misplaced prioritization of heterogenital over personal complementarity in the absolute moral prohibition of homosexual acts. In addition, there is a misplaced emphasis on reproductive complementarity in the prohibition of nonreproductive sexual acts between heterosexuals.

Important questions for the theological understanding of truly human sexual acts are whether or not there can be such acts without heterogenital complementarity and whether or not there can be such acts that are nonreproductive sexual acts. First, is heterogenital complementarity the primary, foundational, and sine qua non component of truly human sexual acts, or must genital and personal complementarity be more thoroughly integrated to found a truly human sexual act? If the latter is the case, then might a just and loving homosexual act fulfill the criteria for a truly human sexual act? Second, even though nonreproductive heterosexual acts may not fulfill reproductive complementarity, does that mean that, ipso facto, they violate personal complementarity, cannot fulfill the criteria for truly human sexual acts, and are thus morally wrong? We approach these questions via what we call *sexual orientation complementarity* and *holistic complementarity*.

SEXUAL ORIENTATION COMPLEMENTARITY AND TRULY HUMAN SEXUAL ACTS: A RECONSTRUCTED COMPLEMENTARITY

An important psychosocial dimension of the human person, and therefore of the sexual human person, is the person's integrated relationship to self. To be truly human, a sexual act must be integrated with the whole self. The CCE asserts what is widely taken for granted today, namely, that sexuality "is a fundamental component of personality, one of its modes of being, of manifestation, of communicating with others, of feeling, of expressing and of living human love. Therefore it is an integral part of the development of the personality and of its educative process."[62] The Congregation goes on to cite the CDF's *Persona Humana* and its teaching that it is "from sex that the human person receives the characteristics which, on the biological, psychological, and spiritual levels, make that person a man or a woman, and thereby *largely condition his or her progress towards maturity and insertion into society*."[63] If it is true that a person's sexuality and sexual characteristics largely condition her or his insertion into society, and we agree that it is true, then the question naturally arises about the "nature" and meaning of what is called today sexual orientation, that dimension of human sexuality that directs a person's sexual desires and energies and draws him or her into deeper and more sexually intimate human relationships. To define "truly human" sexual acts, we must first understand sexual orientation.

The meaning of the phrase "sexual orientation" is complex and not universally agreed upon, but the Magisterium offers a description. It distinguishes between "a homosexual 'tendency,' which proves to be 'transitory,' and 'homosexuals who are definitively such because of some kind of innate instinct.'" It goes on to declare that "it seems appropriate to understand sexual orientation as a *deep-seated* dimension of one's personality and to recognize its *relative stability* in a person. A homosexual orientation produces a stronger emotional and sexual attraction toward individuals of the same sex, rather than toward those of the opposite sex."[64] Guided by Robert Nugent, we define sexual orientation as a "psychosexual attraction (erotic, emotional, and affective) toward particular individual *persons*"[65] of the opposite or same sex, depending on whether the orientation is heterosexual or homosexual. Sexual orientation is produced by a mix of genetic, hormonal, psychological, and social "loading."[66]

Concerning the genesis of homosexual and heterosexual orientations, the bishops note what is agreed on in the scientific community, namely, that there is as yet no single isolated cause of a homosexual orientation. The experts point to a variety of loading factors—genetic, hormonal, psychological, and social—from which with high probability the orientation derives and develops. There is a growing agreement also in the scientific community that sexual orientation, heterosexual or homosexual, is a psychosexual attraction that the person does not choose and that she or he cannot change.[67] In addition, since homosexual orientation is experienced as a given and not as something freely chosen, it cannot be considered sinful, for morality presumes the freedom to choose. This judgment is not to be understood as a claim that, according to the Magisterium, a homosexual orientation is morally good or even that it is morally neutral, for elsewhere it teaches that "this inclination . . . is objectively disordered," that it "is a more or less strong tendency ordered toward an intrinsic moral evil"; that is, homosexual acts that flow from the orientation are always immoral or intrinsically disordered.[68] The Magisterium teaches that homosexual acts are intrinsically disordered because "they are contrary to the natural law. They close the sexual act to the gift of life. They do not proceed from a genuine affective and sexual complementarity."[69] Heterosexuality is the norm against which all sexual acts are to be judged.

The Magisterium condemns homosexual acts because they do not exhibit heterogenital and reproductive complementarities, and, because they do not exhibit these biological complementarities, it further notes, they are incapable of realizing personal complementarity, regardless of the *meaning* of the act for a homosexual couple. Since the sexual act is frequently closed to reproductive complementarity, sometimes permanently in the case of infertile couples and postmenopausal women and sometimes temporarily for fertile heterosexual couples, heterogenital complementarity is established as *the* litmus test for determining whether or not a sexual act can fulfill personal complementarity and thus be "truly human." There is no doubt that truly human sexual acts necessarily include personal complementarity, but, for the Magisterium, personal complementarity is not sufficient for a truly human sexual act. Heterogenital complementarity is the primary, foundational, sine qua non condition for what defines a truly human sexual act. Since homosexual acts lack heterogenital complementarity, they can never be truly human.

We suggest that the needed complementarity for a truly human sexual act is *holistic* complementarity that unites people bodily, affectively, spiritually, and personally under the umbrella of a person's sexual orientation. Heterogenital complementarity is needed for possible reproduction, but it is not needed for the sexual, affective, spiritual, and personal connection between two people that the recent Catholic tradition acknowledges as an end of marriage equal to procreation.[70] Though they cannot exhibit heterogenital complementarity, there is extensive anecdotal and empirical evidence that homosexual individuals can exhibit this holistic complementarity. We shall explore this evidence in detail in chapter 5.

Orientation complementarity reconstructs the Magisterium's definitions of affective and genital complementarity and situates genital complementarity under the umbrella of personal complementarity. First, orientation complementarity cannot espouse the Magisterium's hetero-genital point of departure for affective and personal complementarity, for sexual orientation underlies and is more foundational anthropologically than heterogenitality. As we have seen, for the Magisterium the point of departure for affective complementarity is an essential unity between the biological (heterogenital) and the personal that can find completion only in heterosexual marriage and conjugal acts. The definition of affective and personal complementarity is the "unity of the two," in which the mascu-line and feminine affective elements (biological, psychoaffective, social, and spiritual), which for forming a couple are incomplete, find completion in heterogenitally complementary reproductive type sexual acts. In our model, the point of departure for affective complementarity is not the *genital* but the *sexual human person* of either a homosexual or a hetero-sexual orientation. The definition of affective complementarity in truly human sexual acts is not John Paul's the "unity of the two," that is, the male and the female, but the unity of two *persons*, in whom the affective elements (biological, psychoaffective, social, and spiritual) complement one another.[71] In the case of persons with a homosexual orientation, these acts will be male–male or female–female; in the case of persons with a heterosexual orientation, these acts will be male–female.[72]

Orientation complementarity also requires us to redefine heterogeni-tal complementarity in relation to affective complementarity. Severing the male–female essential complementarity of the affective elements includes the genitals. No longer is heterogenital complementarity the foundational sine qua non for personal complementarity. In a truly human sexual act, the genitals are at the service of personal complementarity, and they may be male–male, female–female, or male–female, depending on whether the individual person's orientation is homosexual or heterosexual. Our principle of holistic complementarity, which includes sexual orientation complementarity as one of its types, embraces the entirety and complex-ity of the human person and reconstructs genital complementarity to be in dialogue with, and totally at the service of, personal and orienta-tion complementarity. The genitals may be said to be complementary when they are used in a truly human sexual act that realizes personal, psychoaffective, social, and spiritual complementarity.

Truly human sexual acts are to be morally evaluated, not simply as isolated acts, but only in the context of this complex orientation, personal, and genital interrelationship. When we shift the foundation for a truly human sexual act from heterogenital complementarity to holistic complementarity—an integrated orientation, and personal and genital complementarity—the principle for what constitutes a truly human sexual act can be formulated as follows.

A truly human sexual act is an act in accord with a person's sexual orientation that facilitates a deeper appreciation, integration, and sharing of a person's embodied self with another embodied self. Genital complementarity as understood within the context of orientation and personal complementarity is always a dimension of the truly human sexual act, and reproductive complementarity *may* be a part of it in the case of fertile, heterosexual couples who choose to reproduce. Reproductive complementarity will not be a possibility in the case of homosexual couples (or temporarily or permanently infertile heterosexual couples), but genital complementarity, understood in an integrated, embodied, personal, orientation sense, and not just in a biological, physical sense, will be. This personalist interpretation of genital complementarity, which contextualizes the physical genitals as organs of the whole person, allows us to expand the definition of a truly human sexual act to embrace both heterosexual and homosexual nonreproductive acts.

The Magisterium teaches that only marital, reproductive sexual acts are truly human sexual acts. In explaining its condemnation of masturbation, for example, it notes the following: ". . . the deliberate use of the sexual faculty outside normal conjugal relations essentially contradicts the finality of the faculty. For it lacks the sexual relationship called for by the moral order, namely the relationship which realizes 'the full sense of mutual self-giving and human procreation in the context of true love.' All deliberate exercise of sexuality must be reserved to this regular relationship."[73] Mutual masturbation, anal sex, and oral sex all lie outside the parameters of this definition, do not realize the finality of the sexual faculties, and therefore cannot be truly human or moral. This statement invites comment and critique, and, on the basis of this critique, we expand the concept of a truly human sexual act to include nonreproductive sexual acts, both heterosexual and homosexual.

First, masturbation, both individual and mutual couple masturbation, and other nonreproductive sexual acts "[contradict] the finality of the faculty." In this statement there is a clear parallel with Aquinas, who comments that some external acts are disordered in themselves, "as happens in every use of the genital organs outside the marriage act." "The end of the use of the genital organs," he continues, "is the generation and education of offspring, and therefore every use of the aforementioned organs which is not proportioned to the generation of offspring and its due education is disordered in itself."[74] What are we to make of Aquinas's and magisterial statements on the finality or end of the genital organs? Aquinas's emphasis on the primary end of the genital organs for the procreation and education of children, since the promulgation of *Gaudium et spes*, no longer holds true. The procreation and education of children *and* the union between the spouses are equal ends of marriage; there is no longer a Catholic hierarchy of ends. The magisterium now defines the "finality of the faculty" of the sexual organs in terms of *both* the procreation and education of children *and* the union between the spouses in every sexual act.

We must also note Aquinas's limited understanding of human biology in relation to human sexuality and reproduction. The female ovum was not discovered until the 1850s. Prior to its discovery, the commonly held belief was that the male seed was solely responsible for generation; the female merely provided the fertile ground or field for the male seed, a true homunculus, or little man, to develop into a fully fledged human being.[75] To spill the seed, or little man, anywhere it could not develop properly—on the earth, in a mouth, or in an anal orifice—for instance, was regarded as murder, and murder was always judged to be a serious moral evil. As we know now from contemporary biology, both the male sperm and the female ovum are necessary to provide the forty-six chromosomes that make up the human genome. The tradition's erroneous understanding of human biology and reproduction allowed it to make innacurate claims about what is "natural." While magisterial teaching now recognizes the facts of human reproductive biology, it still continues to assert exclusively the natural finality of the sexual organs.

Is it the case, however, that reproduction is the natural finality of the sexual organs? Reproduction may be achieved via a human act of sexual intercourse, but the act of reproduction itself is not a human act; it is achieved through a determined biological process. If reproduction were inescapably the natural purpose of the sexual act, then all reproductive-type sexual acts would have the possibility of realizing this purpose. Infertile women and men continue to have sexual intercourse, but their act is inescapably nonreproductive. All human beings have *sexual* organs, but not all human beings have *reproductive* organs; that an organ is sexual does not necessarily mean that it is also reproductive. Clearly, with permanently infertile couples, the term "open to the transmission of life" is morally ambiguous at best, morally meaningless at worst. It is far from clear, therefore, that the sexual organs have the "natural finality" assigned to them.

There are three senses in which one could claim a natural finality for the sexual organs. The first is the purpose given them by "nature"; the second is the purpose given them by human beings' use of those organs; the third is the purpose given them by the "moral order" or divine law. The first purpose we have already addressed. While "nature" can be interpreted in a purely biological sense, in the sense of Aquinas, tradition, and current magisterial teaching, it is more accurately under-stood in terms of what facilitates overall human well-being or human flourishing. To claim that nonreproductive sexual acts are "unnatural" or "against nature," one must prove that such acts, by definition, frus-trate human well-being or human flourishing. This leads to the second claim of the finality of the sexual organs, the meaning human beings give to this finality. Sexual organs do not have a single purpose; they have many purposes. The penis, for example, is responsible for both the evacuation of liquid waste and sexual intercourse that may or may not achieve reproduction. In sexual acts, it may also serve other purposes, the giving of pleasure, for instance, the relieving of tension, the celebration and enhancement of intimacy between two lovers, whether or not the particular sexual activity is capable of achieving reproduction. All of these purposes have meaning for human beings and may or may not facilitate human flourishing, depending on the meaning of this particular sexual act for this particular couple.

To counter these humanly assigned finalities of the sexual organs, one may respond with the third argument for finality; namely, even if people attach different meanings to sexual acts, there is an order established by God that determines the correct finality of the sexual organs, and this finality is reproduction. Reproductive complementarity, therefore, is an intrinsic meaning of the sexual act. Numerous questions may be posed to this claim. Why do we need to claim that God created a particular body part for a particular purpose? Cannot a particular body part have multiple purposes, as indicated above? If we do accept a God-given purpose, what are the reasons we may not act against it? Is to act against a God-given finality always morally wrong, or simply less than ideal? If it is simply less than ideal, is it accurate to claim that although reproductive sexual acts are ideal sexual acts, nonreproductive sexual acts cannot facilitate human flourishing? There are many acts we do that are less than ideal, such as eating, sleeping, or exercising too much or too little, but we do not, on that account alone, judge them immoral.

Is a "truly human" sexual act synonymous with an ideal sexual act? This would seem to set an unreasonably high standard for any act of sexual intercourse that must necessarily entail a reciprocal "total personal self-giving" between the couple.[76] This total self-giving would entail in each and every sexual act all those dimensions of human sexuality explored above—biological, emotional, psychological, relational, and spiritual—and any experienced married couple will tell you that the requirement of "total personal self-giving" in each and every sexual act is simply not real. It is nothing but ideology posing as reality. Is it possible that what was judged traditionally to be the single God-given purpose of sexual organs be expanded to include other God-given purposes discerned on the basis of human experience and conscientious and faithful reflection on that experience?[77]

All of these are important questions that need to be investigated. If after such an investigation, however, we were to come to the (unlikely) conclusion that there is undoubtedly a single God-given purpose for sexual organs, would we then have to conclude logically that the God-given purpose is exclusive of all other sexual activity, or could it be inclusive of other sexual activity? Could we not, in other words, claim that on occasion the sexual organs could still be used for other purposes? Indeed, the organs are frequently used for other purposes deemed perfectly moral, for instance, among infertile couples. There is no possibility of achieving the reproductive finality of the organs in these infertile sexual acts, but the acts always have the potentiality to affirm and enhance personal complementarity and human flourishing. The same is true with regard to nonreproductive acts. Though they cannot realize reproductive complementarity, nothing precludes them per se from realizing personal complementarity. Marital experience shows that such sexual acts, rather than being destructive of human flourishing, may actually facilitate it. The experience of the married shows beyond doubt that it is never a question of either successful reproduction and therefore human flourishing or nonreproduction and therefore human diminishment. The judgment of whether or not a particular sexual act is moral is to be determined, as all moral judgments are to be determined, on the basis of its impact on human flourishing within the context of a particular interpersonal relationship. We have outlined this basis as a truly human sexual act that evinces holistic complementarity.

The foundation for our definition of a truly human sexual act and its moral evaluation rest, then, not primarily on heterogenital or reproductive complementarity, but on the integrated relationship between orientation, personal, and genital complementarity. Given that complex dialogical relationship, it remains to ask whether or not a particular sexual act facilitates or frustrates the partners' human flourishing, their becoming more affectively and interpersonally human and Christian. We agree with Stephen Pope: "Interpersonal love is here the locus of human flourishing," and we are now able to offer a definition of complementarity.[78] Complementarity is a multifaceted quality—orientational, physical, affective, personal, and spiritual—possessed by every person, that draws him or her into relationship with another human being, including into the lifelong relationship of marriage, so that both may grow, individually and as a couple, into human well-being and human flourishing.

HOLISTIC COMPLEMENTARITY, TRULY HUMAN SEXUAL ACTS, AND SEXUAL NORMS

In light of the various types of complementarity explored in the foregoing, a truly human sexual act must be an authentic integration and expression of holistic complementarity as set forth in the following diagram.

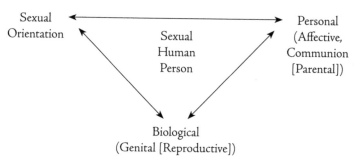

FIGURE 2.1   Holistic Complementarity

Holistic complementarity includes orientation, personal, and biological complementarity, and the integration and manifestation of all three in just and loving, committed sexual acts that facilitate a person's ability to love God, neighbor, and self in a more profound and holy way.

Just and Loving Truly Human Sexual Acts

The careful reader will have noticed our consistent specification that to be truly human, sexual activity, heterosexual or homosexual, must be not only in accord with holistic complementarity but also *just and loving*. The words "just and loving" must be explained. The search for moral judgment in sexual matters today frequently ends with the vapid claim that sexual activity is moral when it is loving. That judgment is vapid because it is usually devoid of content. We agree with Farley that "love is the problem in ethics, not the solution," and it is the problem to the extent that it is contentless.[79] Our task here is to give it content. We begin with an ancient definition: to love is to will the good of another.[80] Love is an activity of the will, a decision to will and to seek the good of another human being. True love, as every lover knows, is ec-static; that is, in love a person goes out of herself or himself to another self who is absolute and unique in herself or himself. That there are two absolutely unique and yet like selves in any loving relationship introduces the cardinal virtue of justice, "the virtue according to which, with constant and perpetual will, someone renders to someone else her or his due rights."[81] If asked what justice has to do with sexual acts, we respond that, since sexual acts are between two, equal personal selves, justice has everything to do with them.[82]

One characteristic, perhaps the greatest characteristic, of a modern person is her or his equality with every other person. For Christians, that equality takes on a deeply religious character, because it is believed to be the very plan of the God who created 'adam male and female, blessed them, and named them together 'adam.[83] A sexual act that is just and loving will seek the good of equality for, and will render all the rights flowing from equality to, both partners. Any sexual act that involves inequities—of power, social or economic status, or level of maturity, for example—will be ipso facto not truly human. Flowing from the personal character of equality is the related personal character of freedom. A sexual act that is just and loving will render the rights associated with freedom to the other partner and will seek the good of freedom for both partners in the act. That will mean, in the concrete, that a just and loving sexual act will require the free consent of both partners and that any sexual act that subverts free consent will be, by that very fact, not truly human. The use of power, violence, rape against an unwilling partner will, therefore, never be truly human. With the modern "discovery" that woman is as free as man, free consent may be seriously interfered with, or even precluded entirely, by any sexual activity that is marked by socially constructed male domination or female subordination. The same reasoning applies to anyone of diminished capacity—the immature, the dependent, the drugged, the drunk, for example—for diminished capacity will automatically mean diminished consent.

A consistently recognized end of sexual activity, heterosexual or homosexual, is both the expression and enhancement of interpersonal relationship, love, or friendship; sexual activity is, in the common phrase, a way to make love. To express and enhance relationality, however, sexual activity must be *mutual*; it must be wanted by and participated in freely by both partners. True love, truly willing the good of another, is never one-sided; there is no true love until love is mutual. It is the mutual love between lovers that creates between them the communion that characterizes lovers. That leads us to a further specification of the mutuality between lovers, namely, mutual, long-term commitment. The Christian tradition has always required some form of long-term commitment, some kind of solemn promise or covenant, from the partners for sexual intercourse to be moral. That this covenant always was linked to marriage, and that marriage was primarily linked to procreation, is no reason not to retain commitment as a reasonable and moral norm for sexual activity, heterosexual or homosexual. We believe long-term commitment is required for a just and loving relationship, including truly human sexual acts, to mature into fruitfulness for both marital and common good. That fruitfulness, which may include the love and communion between the partners, children, and the common good of the community in which the partners and any children live, requires a long-term commitment to be nourished into maturity.[84] To be loving and just, therefore, any sexual act requires commitment to be truly human.

Normative Implications for Catholic Sexual Ethics

Three implications for Catholic sexual ethics follow if we espouse holistic complementarity, irradiated with the virtues of justice and love, as our foundational principle for truly human sexual acts. The first is that the Magisterium's absolute moral norm prohibiting all homosexual acts must, at least, be reexamined. Without a prior consideration of one's sexual orientation, a sexual act that violates heterogenital complementarity can no longer be considered, from this fact alone, absolutely immoral. Genital complementarity is relevant in determining the morality of truly human sexual acts, but it is not the primary factor. The morality of the use of the genitals in sexual acts must be determined primarily in light of orientation and personal complementarity.

The second implication for Catholic sexual ethics follows from the first; the foundation for sexual moral norms may need to be redefined. Current magisterial teaching posits, for both homosexuals and heterosexuals, an intrinsic relationship between biological and personal complementarity in which heterogenital complementarity is primary and foundational. On this foundation, certain sexual acts are ipso facto immoral because they violate heterogenital complementarity, regardless of sexual orientation and the relational meaning of the act for personal complementarity. In holistic complementarity, there is an integrated relationship between orientation, personal, and biological complementarity that serves as the foundation for sexual norms. In this relationship, for both heterosexuals and homosexuals, orientation and personal complementarity are primary, and they determine what constitutes authentic genital complementarity in a particular sexual act. If orientation complementarity indicates that a person is of heterosexual orientation, then personal complementarity would indicate that authentic genital complementarity would be male–female. If orientation complementarity indicates that a person is of homosexual orientation, then personal complementarity would indicate that authentic genital complementarity would be male–male or female–female. In current magisterial teaching, heterogenital complementarity is the primary foundational dimension for the essential relationship between biological and personal complementarity. In our holistic complementarity model, orientation and personal complementarity are the foundational dimensions for the integrated relationship between orientation, personal, and biological complementarity.

The third implication is that nonreproductive sexual acts cannot be absolutely morally prohibited. Although such acts violate reproductive complementarity, they do not ipso facto violate personal complementarity and diminish human flourishing. The truly human sexual act in our sexual anthropology is a sexual act that facilitates holistic complementarity, which may or may not include reproductive complementarity in any given sexual act. One may reasonably argue that reproductive sexual acts are the ideal expression of human sexuality, but this does not logically justify the judgment that any sexual act that does not attain that ideal, an infertile or homosexual act, for instance, is morally wrong. Other types of sexual acts that lead to orgasm but are nonreproductive demonstrably facilitate personal complementarity and human flourishing, and may also realize reproductive complementarity in the case of reproductive technologies, as we will see in chapter 6.

In light of these three considerations, we advance the following with regard to sexual moral norms and truly human sexual acts. Sexual moral norms must be formulated and truly human sexual acts must be defined in light of a revised theological anthropology grounded in holistic, not heterogenital, complementarity. A person's sexual orientation is a fundamental dimension of the concretely and normatively human dimension of her or his being, and sexual norms that prescribe or proscribe specific sexual acts must be formulated and applied in light of that orientation. Sexual moral norms must seek to facilitate the integration of holistic complementarity—orientation, personal, and biological complementarity. This integration does not allow for the absolute condemnation of particular sexual acts without due consideration of a person's sexual orientation and the meaning of this sexual act for these persons in relationship—that is, in personal complementarity—which is expressed in and through genital complementarity. The Magisterium's model posits absolute norms forbidding homosexual acts and all nonreproductive-type sexual acts. Our model cannot justify these absolute norms, but it does posit a formally absolute norm in relation to truly human sexual acts.

Formal absolutes are norms that emphasize character and/or virtue in relation to acts. A formal absolute norm, for instance, might state the following: a not-truly-human, abusive, dishonest, uncommitted, unjust, unloving sexual act, heterosexual or homosexual, is morally wrong; a truly human, caring, honest, committed, just, loving, sexual act, heterosexual or homosexual, is morally right.[85] The integration of holistic complementarity, that is, the integration of orientation, personal, and biological complementarity, determines whether a sexual act is moral or immoral. In the case of a person with a homosexual orientation, a truly human, caring, honest, committed, just, loving, sexual act will be expressed personally with male–male or female–female genitalia. In the case of a person with a heterosexual orientation, a truly human, caring, honest, committed, just, loving, sexual act will be expressed personally with male–female genitalia. Some theorists have proposed this shift to formal absolutes in terms of a virtue-based sexual ethic in which the cardinal virtues of prudence, justice, fortitude, and temperance, always allied with the theological virtues of faith, hope, and charity, would be the guiding "norms" for what constitutes truly human sexual acts.[86]

CONCLUSION

For any sexual act to be truly human, it must exhibit holistic complementarity, equality between the partners, equal freedom for both partners, free mutuality between the partners, and the mutual commitment of both partners. The Christian tradition will add that those characteristics are all to be informed by the love of God and neighbor enjoined by Jesus. That neighbor-love is concretized by willing and seeking the good of the neighbor, compassion, mercy, forgiveness, and reconciliation, extending even to those neighbors who may be characterized as "enemies."[87] Considerations like these lead Farley to a conclusion with which we are comfortable and with which we will conclude this chapter.

Sex between two persons of the same sex (just as two persons
of the opposite sex) should not be used in a way that exploits,
objectifies, or dominates; homosexual (like heterosexual) rape,
violence, or any harmful use of power against unwilling victims (or those incapacitated by reason of age, etc.) is never
justified; freedom, integrity, privacy are values to be affirmed
in every homosexual (as heterosexual) relationship; all in all,
individuals are not to be harmed, and the common good is to
be promoted.[88]

That sums up nicely what we have been arguing, and it leads us to
our ultimate conclusion. On the basis of our revised foundational sexual
ethical principle, *some* homosexual and heterosexual acts, those that meet
the requirements for holistically complementary, just, and loving sexual
acts, are truly human; and *some* homosexual and heterosexual acts, those
that do not meet the requirements for holistically complementary, just,
and loving sexual acts, are not truly human. Whether any given sexual
act, heterosexual or homosexual, is truly human is determined, as every
moral judgment in the Catholic tradition is determined, not by the naked
application of abstract moral principles, but by a careful, hermeneutical
analysis of how those principles apply in real, concrete, particular human
relationships.

QUESTIONS FOR REFLECTION

1. How do you understand the sexual person? Does this chapter confirm or challenge that understanding? Explain.
2. The sexual drive has three personal meanings: it is pleasurable; it is
   relational; it is potentially procreative. How do you see these meanings contributing to Gallagher's Catholic judgment that "mutually
   pleasurable marital sexual acts are possibly the human experiences
   that most fully symbolize the loving communication between the
   divine Trinity?"

3. Human sexuality has been demonstrated to be multidimensional. How do you integrate in your life the physical, emotional, psychological, spiritual, and relational dimensions of your sexuality? Does this integration cause you any difficulty?

4. How do you understand the word *complementarity* and the terms *sexual orientation complementarity* and *holistic complementarity* as used in this chapter? Are the terms in any way meaningful to you?

5. There are three common senses in which one could claim a natural purpose for the sexual organs. The first is the purpose given them by "nature"; the second is the purpose given them by humans; the third is the purpose given them by God. How do you think these purposes could be identified accurately and distinguished from one another? If they could be identified and distinguished, how would that help you in establishing sexual moral norms?

6. What do you think of the principle that, to be truly human and moral, sexual acts must be both in accord with holistic complementarity and just and loving? How does or will this principle manifest itself in your life?

7. What other questions arise for you from reading this chapter?

NOTES

1. United States Conference of Catholic Bishops (USCCB), *Always Our Children* (Washington, DC: USCCB, 1997), 3.

2. GS, 49.

3. USCCB, *Human Sexuality: A Catholic Perspective for Education and Lifelong Learning* (Washington, DC: USCCB, 1991), 9.

4. Simon LeVay and Sharon M. Valente, *Human Sexuality* (Sunderland, MA: Sinauer Associates, 2006); Simon LeVay and Curt Freed, *Healing the Brain* (New York: Times Books, 2002); Simon LeVay, *The Sexual Brain* (Cambridge: MIT Press, 1995). See also *PH*, 1.

5. See Charles A. Gallagher, *Embodied in Love: Sacramental Spirituality and Sexual Intimacy* (New York: Crossroad, 1985), 21–37.

6. Tom W. Smith, *American Sexual Behavior: Trends, Socio-Demographic Differences, and Risk Behavior* (Chicago: National Opinion Research Center, University of Chicago), 74. This document can be accessed at www.norc.uchicago.edu/issues/American_Sexual_Behavior_2003.

7. I Cor. 7:3–5; GS, 51.

8. These thoughts on Genesis 2:24 are developed from the section "Penetrer-Etre Penetrer," in Xavier Lacroix, *Le corps de chair: Les dimensions éthiques, esthétiques, et spirituelles de l'amour* (Paris: Cerf, 1992), 111–14.

9. Michel Foucault, *L'usage des plaisirs* (Paris: Gallimard, 1984), 142.

10. W. H. Masters and Virginia E. Johnson, *Human Sexual Response* (Boston: Little, Brown, 1966), 3–8.

11. June M. Reinisch and Ruth Beasley, *The Kinsey Institute New Report on Sex: What You Must Know to Be Sexually Literate* (New York: St. Martin's Press, 1990), 84.

12. For an investigation of pleasure as an essential component of human sexuality, see Christine E. Gudorf, *Body, Sex, and Pleasure: Reconstructing Christian Sexual Ethics* (Cleveland: Pilgrim Press, 1995).

13. Martha C. Nussbaum, *The Upheavals of Thought: The Intelligence of Emotions* (New York: Cambridge University Press, 2003), 22.

14. We are indebted to Jack Dominian's excellent "Sexuality and Interpersonal Relationships," in Joseph A. Selling, ed., *Embracing Sexuality: Authority and Experience in the Catholic Church* (Burlington, VT: Ashgate, 2001), 12–15.

15. Ibid., 20.

16. Ibid., 13.

17. The connection of marriage and Eucharist is beautifully developed in Germain Martinez, *Worship: Wedding to Marriage* (Washington, DC: Pastoral Press, 1993).

18. Luke 22:19.

19. Adrian Thatcher, *Liberating Sex: A Christian Sexual Theology* (London: SPCK, 1993), 89.

20. Gallagher, *Embodied in Love*, 108; emphasis in original.

21. USCCB, *Human Sexuality*, 9.

22. See Can 1055, 1.

23. CCC, 2207; Pope John Paul II, *FC*, 21.

24. Matt. 5:43–48.

25. See Maura Ryan, *Ethics and Economics of Assisted Reproduction: The Cost of Longing* (Washington, DC: Georgetown University Press, 2001), 134.

26. Mark D. Jordan, *The Silence of Sodom: Homosexuality in Modern Catholicism* (Chicago: University of Chicago Press, 2000), 74.

27. CCC, 2538; James F. Keenan, "The Open Debate: Moral Theology and the Lives of Gay and Lesbian Persons," *TS* 1/64 (2003), 146.

28. CCC, 2337.

29. CCC, 2358; *Always Our Children*, 5.

30. CCC, 2359.

31. See *LG*, 12 and 34. See also Leo J. O'Donovan, *A World of Grace: An Introduction to the Themes and Foundations of Karl Rahner's Theology* (New York: Seabury, 1980); and Thomas F. O'Meara, *Loose in the World* (New York: Paulist, 1974).

32. For a more fully developed explanation of these terms, see Todd A. Salzman and Michael G. Lawler, "*Quaestio Disputata*. Catholic Sexual Ethics: Complementarity and the Truly Human," *TS* 67, no. 3 (September 2006): 625–52.

33. *GS*, 49; emphasis added.

34. *CRP*, 7.

35. *FC*, 19. The pope speaks of a "natural complementarity."

36. Barbara Hilkert Andolsen, "Review of *The Sexual Person: Toward a Renewed Catholic Anthropology*, Todd A. Salzman and Michael G. Lawler" in *Conversations in Religion & Theology* 8 (2010): 87.

37. *CRP*, 3.

38. Can 1084, 1.

39. *HV*, 10; see also Pope Pius XII, "The Apostolate of the Midwife," in *The Major Addresses of Pope Pius XII*, ed. Vincent A. Yzermans, vol. 1, *Selected Addresses* (St. Paul: North Central, 1961), 169.

40. *HV*, 11.

41. Gareth Moore, *The Body in Context: Sex and Catholicism*, Contemporary Christian Insights (New York: Continuum, 2001), 162.

42. *CRP*, 3.

43. Ibid., 4; *CCC*, 2357.

44. CCE, *EGHL*, 35.

45. John Paul II, *Women: Teachers of Peace*, 3, Message of His Holiness Pope John Paul II for the XXVIII World Day of Peace (January 1, 1995), www.vatican.va/holy_father/john_paul_ii/messages/peace/documents/hf_jp-ii_mes_08121994_xxviii-world-day-for-peace_en.html (accessed May 20, 2006).

46. Christine E. Gudorf, "Encountering the Other: The Modern Papacy on Women," in *Feminist Ethics and the Catholic Moral Tradition, Readings in Moral Theology No. 9*, ed. Charles E. Curran, Margaret A. Farley, and Richard A. McCormick (New York: Paulist, 1996), 75; and Charles E. Curran, *The Moral Theology of Pope John Paul II* (Washington, DC: Georgetown University Press, 2005), 192–93.

47. Edward Collins Vacek, "Feminism and the Vatican," *TS* 66 (2005), 173–74, referring to John Paul II, "Authentic Concept of Conjugal Love," *Origins* 28 (March 4, 1999): 655.

48. John Paul II, "Letter to Women," 7.

49. Ibid.; emphasis in original; *FC*, 19.

50. Kevin Kelly, *New Directions in Sexual Ethics* (London: Cassell, 1999), 51–52. He critiques ontological complementarity as ultimately "oppressive and deterministic."

51. John Paul II, "Letter to Women," 8; *MD*, 6; John Paul II, "Authentic Concept of Conjugal Love," 5.

52. *FC*, 19.

53. John Paul II, "Authentic Concept of Conjugal Love," 5.

54. John Paul II, "Letter to Women," 7–8.

55. Moore, *Body in Context*, 121–27.

56. See *FC*, 23; John Paul II, "Letter to Women," 9; *MD*, 18; and *Women: Teachers of Peace*.

57. Cristina L. H. Traina, "Papal Ideals, Marital Realities: One View from the Ground," in *Sexual Diversity and Catholicism: Toward the Development of Moral Theology*, ed. Patricia Beattie Jung with Joseph Andrew Coray (Collegeville, MN: Liturgical Press, 2001), 280–82.

58. See Elaine L. Graham, *Making the Difference: Gender, Personhood, and Theology* (Minneapolis: Fortress, 1996); Margaret A. Farley, *Just Love: A Framework for Christian Sexual Ethics* (New York: Continuum, 2006), 156–57.

59. Traina, "Papal Ideals," 282.

60. *CRP*, 7.

61. For a review of this data, see Osnat Erel and Bonnie Burman, "Interrelatedness of Marital Relations and Parent–Child Relations: A Meta-Analytic Review," *Psychological Bulletin* 118 (1995), 108–32; Paul R. Amato and Alan Booth, *A Generation at Risk: Growing Up in an Era of Family Upheaval* (Cambridge: Harvard University Press, 1997), 67–83; Stacy J. Rogers and Lynn K. White, "Satisfaction with Parenting: The Role of Marital Happiness, Family Structure, and Parents' Gender," *Journal of Marriage and Family* 60 (1998), 293–316; David H. Demo and Martha J. Cox, "Families with Young Children: A Review of the Research in the 1990s," *Journal of Marriage and Family* 62 (2000): 876–900.

62. CCE, *EGHL*, 4.

63. *PH*, 1; emphasis added.

64. USCCB, *Always Our Children*, 4–5; emphasis added. See also *PH*, 8.

65. Robert Nugent, "Sexual Orientation in Vatican Thinking," in *The Vatican and Homosexuality: Reactions to the "Letter to the Bishops of the Catholic Church on the Pastoral Care of Homosexual Persons*," ed. Jeannine Gramick and Pat Furey (New York: Crossroad, 1988), 55.

66. This terminology is borrowed from John E. Perito, *Contemporary Catholic Sexuality: What Is Taught and What Is Practiced* (New York: Crossroad, 2003), 96.

67. See William Paul, et al., eds., *Homosexuality: Social, Psychological, and Biological Issues* (Beverly Hills: Sage, 1982); Pim Pronk, *Against Nature? Types of Moral Argumentation regarding Homosexuality* (Grand Rapids, MI: Eerdmans, 1993); Richard C. Pillard and J. Michael Bailey, "A Biological Perspective on Sexual Orientation," *Clinical Sexuality* 18 (1995): 1–14; Lee Ellis and Linda Ebertz, *Sexual Orientation: Toward Biological Understanding* (Westport, CT: Praeger, 1997); Richard C. Friedman and Jennifer I. Downey, *Sexual Orientation and Psychoanalysis: Sexual Science and Clinical Practice* (New York: Columbia University Press, 2002). Robert L. Spitzer ("Can Some Gay Men and Lesbians Change Their Sexual Orientation? 200 Participants Reporting a Change from Homosexual to Heterosexual Orientation," *Archives of Sexual Behavior* 32 [2003]: 403–17) presents a contrary and minority perspective.

68. CDF, "Vatican List of Catechism Changes," *Origins* 27 (September 25, 1997):

257; CDF, "Letter to the Bishops of the Catholic Church on the Pastoral Care of Homosexual Persons," www.vatican.va/roman_curia/congregations/cfaith/documents/rc_con_cfaith_doc_19861001_homosexual_persons_en.html, 3 (accessed January 4, 2012).

69. CCC, 2357; CRP, 4.

70. See GS, 48–50; Code of Canon Law, Can 1055, 1; Lawler, *Marriage in the Catholic Church: Disputed Questions* (Collegeville, MN: Liturgical Press, 2002), 27–42.

71. Though it is beyond the scope of this chapter, as in the Magisterium's model, *how* these elements complement one another in a "truly human sexual act," heterosexual or homosexual, needs to be more fully developed.

72. We recognize the reality of bisexual persons, but focus and space do not allow us to address this orientation in detail.

73. *PH*, 9.

74. Aquinas, *De Malo*, 15.1c.

75. See Aristotle, *Generation of Animals*, I, 21, 729b. For greater detail, see also Paige duBois, *Sowing the Body: Psychoanalysis and Ancient Representations of Women* (Chicago: University of Chicago Press, 1988), 39–85; Sirach 26:19; *Mishna*, Ketuboth, 1, 6; Carol Delaney, *The Seed and the Soil: Gender and Cosmology in Turkish Village Society* (Berkeley and Los Angeles: University of California Press, 1991).

76. *FC*, 11.

77. For a discussion of the role and function of experience in Catholic ethical method, see Todd A. Salzman, "The Basic Goods Theory and Revisionism: A Methodological Comparison on the Use of Reason and Experience as Sources of Moral Knowledge," *Heythrop Journal* 42 (October 2001): 423–50; and *What Are They Saying about Roman Catholic Ethical Method?* (Mahwah, NJ: Paulist Press, 2003), ch. 2; and Michael G. Lawler and Todd A. Salzman, "Human Experience and Catholic Moral Theology," *Irish Theological Quarterly* 76 (2011): 35–56.

78. Stephen J. Pope, "Scientific and Natural Law Analyses of Homosexuality: A Methodological Study," *Journal of Religious Ethics* 25 (1997): 111.

79. Margaret Farley, "Ethic for Same-Sex Relations," 100.

80. See *ST*, I-II, 28, 1c.

81. *ST*, II-II, 58, 1.

82. We advise the reader that the original draft for this chapter was completed before Margaret Farley's beautiful book *Just Love* became available to us. We are affirmed that both the importance we assign to just love and our analysis of it are matched in general and independently by Farley. See *Just Love*, especially 200–206.

83. See Gen. 5:1.

84. For a fuller development of this point, see Michael G. Lawler, *Family: American and Christian* (Chicago: Loyola Press, 1998), 166–74.

85. The formal criteria listed for what constitutes a morally right or wrong truly human sexual act, though not the specific acts themselves, are common in magisterial and moral theological discourse.

86. See Alasdair MacIntyre, *After Virtue: A Study in Moral Theory* (Notre Dame, IN: University of Notre Dame Press, 1981); Martha Nussbaum, *The Fragility of Goodness: Luck and Ethics in Greek Tragedy and Philosophy* (New York: Cambridge University, 1988); "Non-Relative Virtues: An Aristotelian Approach," in *Ethical Theory: Character and Virtue*, ed. Peter A. French, Theodore E. Uehling Jr., and Howard K. Wettstein (Notre Dame, IN: University of Notre Dame Press, 1988), 32–53; James F. Keenan, "Proposing Cardinal Virtues," *TS* 56 (1995), 709–29; Keenan, *Virtues for Ordinary Christians* (Kansas City, MO: Sheed and Ward, 1996); and Keenan, "Virtue Ethics and Sexual Ethics," *Louvain Studies* 30 (2005): 180–97.
87. See Matt. 5:43–48.
88. Farley, "An Ethic for Same-Sex Relations," 105.

CHAPTER 3

Marital Morality

In the previous chapter we advanced a theoretical foundational principle for making judgments about the morality of sexual actions. That principle was articulated as follows: Sexual actions within marriage by which a couple is united intimately and chastely are noble and worthy. Expressed in a manner that is truly human and justly loving, these actions signify and promote that mutual self-giving by which spouses enrich each other, their family, and their community with a joyful and thankful will.

We also reconstructed the idea of complementarity, initiated by Pope John Paul II, into holistic complementarity, comprised of orientation, personal, and genital complementarity. In this and the following chapters, we apply the theoretical discussion of the previous chapter to clarify the morality of the practical sexual questions about heterosexual marriage and contraception (chapter 3), cohabitation and premarital sexuality (chapter 4), homosexuality (chapter 5), and artificial reproductive technologies (chapter 6).

MODERN CATHOLIC THOUGHT AND MARITAL MORALITY

We provided in chapter 1 a detailed exposition of the development of this ends-of-marriage element of the Catholic tradition from Pope Pius

XI to the Second Vatican Council, and we need not repeat it here. There is need, however, to examine the specific development of this element in the Council. The Council debate, both the preliminary one in the Preparatory Commission and the definitive one in the Council itself, centered on the hierarchy of ends, specifically on the relative values of conjugal love and the procreation of children. We do not need to detail that debate here, but only its outcome in *Gaudium et spes*.[1] The Council described marriage as "a communion of love," an "intimate partnership of conjugal life and love."[2] In the face of loud demands to consign the conjugal love of the spouses to a secondary end, it declared it to be of the essence of marriage. Both marriage and conjugal love "are ordained for the procreation and education of children and find in them their ultimate crown," but again there is no primary end–secondary end hierarchy.[3] Indeed, lest this latter text be misrepresented in a hierarchical way, the Preparatory Commission specifically explained that it "does not suggest [a hierarchy of ends] in any way."[4] In spite of this clear statement that there is no hierarchy of the ends of marriage, magisterial teaching on the absolute prohibition of artificial contraception in *Humanae vitae* is implicitly based on a procreative model of marriage and reflects such a hierarchy.

MARITAL MORALITY AND CONTRACEPTION

We began to confront the lengthy and passionate debate occasioned by Pope Paul VI's encyclical letter *Humanae vitae* in chapter 1. Leslie Woodcock Tentler has recently and comprehensively examined the history of this debate, and Julie Rubio has recently pleaded for the transcendence of the divide created by the debate.[5] We agree with Rubio that the divide is "unnecessary and unhelpful."[6] She complains, however, of the silence of Catholic theologians on the topic of contraception since *Humanae vitae* in 1968, and Tentler shows that the silence has been progressively deafening since Pius XI's *Casti connubii* in 1930. Therefore, though we agree with Margaret Farley that for the vast majority of Catholic moral theologians "the procreative norm as the sole or primary justification of sexual intercourse is gone," we judge continuing silence unhelpful to both the Church-People of God and the Church-Magisterium, and grossly unfaithful to the theologian's task of "interpreting the documents of the past and present magisterium, of putting them in the context of the whole of revealed truth, and of finding a better understanding of them by the use of hermeneutics."[7] In this section, therefore, we raise again the question of contraception within marriage.

CONTRACEPTION AND HISTORICAL CONTEXTS

We use *contexts* in the plural because there have been, at least, three different historical contexts in which the Church's theoretical teaching on marriage has been fashioned, and different consequences for *praxis* may be drawn from each of these different contexts. In the 1960s, the Second Vatican Council sought to discern the "signs of the times" with respect to Catholic reality, including the reality of marriage and family. One outcome of the Council, achieved by diocesan bishops and theologians over the insistent objections of Vatican functionaries, was a changed reception of the Catholic theology of marriage that altered the Church's teaching on marriage.[8] An examination of the historical path to that re-reception is illuminating.

The Procreative Model of Marriage

One model of marriage dominated the Catholic theological tradition from the second to the twentieth century. That model presented marriage as a *procreative institution,* a stable structure of meanings in which a man and a woman become husband and wife in order to procreate children. That model has its origin in the Genesis command to "be fruitful and multiply" (Gen. 1:22), and it was solidified, as we noted in chapter 1, in the early Christian struggle to legitimate marriage as something good against Greek dualist theories, which viewed reproduction negatively.

The dominance in the early Church of the procreative argument as a primary purpose of marriage was not, however, without contrary voices.

Orthodox Theologian Paul Evdokimov shows that both Saints John Chrysostom and Basil offered contrary arguments. Chrysostom argued that marriage was instituted for two reasons, "to lead a man to be contented with one wife and to give him children, but it is the first which is the principal reason"; marriage does not absolutely include procreation, "the proof of which is in the number of marriages that cannot have children." Basil offers an interesting comparison. The creation of the world adds nothing to God's plenitude, and so it is too with marriage. It has its own plenitude, and children add nothing to that plenitude, except that they make the spouses father and mother. Children are added to marriage as "a *possible* not an *indispensable* consequence of marriage."[9] Even Augustine, who prioritized procreation in marriage, hinted at another good of marriage, which "does not seem to me to be good *only* because of the procreation of children, but also because of the natural companionship of the sexes. Otherwise, we could not speak of marriage in the case of old people, especially if they had either lost their children or had begotten none at all."[10] All of these examples clearly link marriage, sexual intercourse, and the relationship of the spouses apart from procreation.

In the thirteenth century, Thomas Aquinas gave the priority of procreation its most reasoned argument. "Marriage has its principal end in the procreation and education of offspring." It has also "a secondary end in man alone, the sharing of tasks which are necessary in life, and from this point of view husband and wife owe each other faithfulness.... The first end is found in marriage insofar as man is animal, the second insofar as he is man."[11] This is a tightly reasoned argument, as is customary in Aquinas, and its *primary end–secondary end* terminology dominated the Catholic understanding of marriage for the next seven hundred years. But Aquinas's authority should not obscure the fact that his argument is a curious one, since the primary end of specifically *human* marriage as a faithful relationship is dictated by the human's generically *animal* nature as occasional procreator. It was on that basis that his argument was challenged in the twentieth century. Before that challenge, however, it had been enshrined for the first time in an official Catholic document in the Code of Canon Law in 1917.[12] "The primary end of *marriage* is the procreation and nurture of children; its secondary end is mutual help and the remedying of concupiscence" (Can 1013, 1). Note here something that is generally overlooked, namely, that in Aquinas and the 1917 Code procreation is the primary end of *marriage*, not of *sexual intercourse*, as it would become in twentieth-century Catholic debate. This theological fact will be important in a later context.

The procreative institution is the result of a contract in which, according to the 1917 Code of Canon Law, "each party gives and accepts a perpetual and exclusive right over the body for acts which are of themselves suitable for the generation of children" (Can 1081, 2). Notice that the procreative marital contract was about *bodies* and their *acts*, and the procreative institution was only secondarily and reluctantly about persons and their mutual love. At the beginning of the third millennium, sociological research shows sexual intercourse is no longer viewed exclusively as being for biological procreation: 82 percent of young adult Americans now see it as for *making love*, not necessarily for making babies.[13] That meaning is replicated by another research datum: 75–85 percent of American Catholics, who consider themselves good Catholics, approve a form of contraception forbidden by the Church.[14] The situation is the same elsewhere. Speaking of the situation in England, for example, sociologist Michael Hornsby-Smith notes that "the evidence we have reviewed suggests . . . that lay people . . . have largely made up their own minds on this matter, and now regard it as none of the business of the clerical leadership of the Church."[15] A 2010 survey of English Catholics reveals that "just 4 per cent of Catholics believe the use of artificial contraception is wrong."[16] The theologian seeking factual judgment founded in experience has to ask whether or not such data tells us anything about, if not the truth of human experience, at least its relevance for Catholic theory and practice.

Humanae vitae *and Contraception:*
Challenges to the Procreative Model

The debate on contraception was definitively focused in 1968 with the publication of Pope Paul VI's encyclical *Humanae vitae*. This document emerged from the traditional procreative model of marriage and prescribed that "each and every marriage act must remain open to the transmission of life."[17] Pope John XXIII established a commission to study the issue of birth control, and the final vote in the commission was in response to three questions. In answer to the first question, "Is contraception intrinsically evil?" nine bishops responded no, three responded yes, and three abstained. In answer to the second question, "Is contraception, as defined by the Majority Report, in basic continuity with tradition and the declarations of the Magisterium?" nine bishops responded yes, five responded no, and one abstained. In answer to the third question, "Should the Magisterium speak on this question as soon as possible?," fourteen responded yes, and one responded no.[18] A preliminary vote of the theologians who were advisors to the Commission, in answer to the question "Is artificial contraception an intrinsically evil violation of the natural law?" resulted in a count of fifteen no and four yes.[19] Both an official majority report and an unofficial minority report from the four dissenters were then submitted to Paul VI who, professing himself unconvinced by the arguments of the majority and sharing the concern of the minority that the Church could not repudiate its long-standing teaching on contraception without undergoing a serious blow to its overall moral authority, approved the minority report in his encyclical letter *Humanae vitae*.[20] The fundamental difference between the two groups is easily categorized.

The minority report argued that "each and every marriage act . . . must remain open to the transmission of life."[21] The majority report argued that it is *marriage* itself, not "each and every *marriage act*," that is to be open to the transmission of life. It asserted that "human intervention in the process of the marriage act *for reasons drawn from the end of marriage itself* should not always be excluded, provided that the criteria of morality are always safeguarded."[22] The fundamental difference in the two positions was caused by adherence to two different models of marriage. The minority report was based on the traditional procreative institution model that focused on the "natural" meaning of the *act* of sexual intercourse; the majority report was based on the new interpersonal union model that emerged from the Council that focused on the total meaning of *marriage* and of sexual intercourse within marriage. Richard McCormick's judgment that "the documents of the Papal Commission represent a rather full summary of two points of view . . . the majority report, particularly the analysis of its rebuttal, strikes this reader as much the more satisfactory statement," continues to be the documented judgment of the vast majority of Catholic theologians and the vast majority of Catholic couples, because they adhere to the same interpersonal model on which the majority report was based.[23]

The Majority Report can serve as an exemplar of the problem that ensues from only partial discussion of a problem. Attached to it was a long "Pastoral Introduction" that set out what the majority thought the new approach to contraception should be and how it was to be resolved with what had been consistently taught before. The introduction explains:

> What has been condemned in the past and remains so today is the *unjustified refusal of life, arbitrary* human intervention for the sake of moments of egotistical pleasure; in short the rejection of *procreation as a specific task of marriage.* In the past the Church could not speak other than she did, because the problem of birth control did not confront human consciousness in the same way. Today, having clearly recognized the legitimacy and even the duty of regulating births, she recognizes too that human intervention in the process of the marriage act *for reasons drawn from the end of marriage itself* should not always be excluded, provided that the criteria of morality are always safeguarded.[24]

The theological problem here is only half the story. The other half, the half that swayed both the minority of the Papal Commission and Pope

Paul VI, is that this suggestion seems so contrary to the traditional position of the Magisterium that it might undermine the Magisterium's entire moral tradition and authority. The inability or simple refusal to recognize this problem, we believe, is at the root of the divide that continues to separate minority and majority today.

The Personal Procreative-Union Model of Marriage

The unprecedented horrors of the First World War transformed the context of human affairs in Europe, where the horrors were localized. This period of "bereavement" and "national trauma" gave birth to a variety of philosophical movements, including the movement that came to be known as personalism.[25] This personalism gradually affected theology and made its first, tentative Catholic appearance in December 1930, in Pope Pius XI's *Casti connubii*, his response to the Anglican Lambeth Conference's approval of the morality of artificial contraception. That encyclical initiated the expansion of the procreative model of marriage into a more personal model of conjugal love and intimacy. *Casti connubii* began timidly to give way to an *interpersonal union model*, in which procreation remained an important facet of marriage but did not encompass all that marriage is. Pius insisted that marriage had as its primary end procreation but also that the mutual love and life of the spouses was an important end.

This mutual love, expressed by loving acts, has "as its primary purpose that husband and wife help each other day by day in forming and perfecting themselves in the interior life . . . and above all that they may grow in true love toward God and their neighbor." So important is the mutual love and life of the spouses, Pius argued, drawing on the *Catechism of the Council of Trent*, that "it can, in a very real sense, be said to be *the chief reason and purpose of marriage*, if marriage be looked at not in the restricted sense as instituted for the proper conception and education of the child but more widely as the blending of life as a whole and the mutual interchange and sharing thereof."[26] If we do not focus in a limited way on procreation, Pius taught, but broaden the scope of the model to embrace also the marital life and love of the spouses, then that life and love is the primary reason for marriage. With this authoritative teaching, Pius introduced a new, transitional model of marriage, a *procreative union model*, which, after thirty-five years of growing pains, eventually blossomed into an entirely new and previously unheard-of Catholic model of marriage, a model of *interpersonal union*.

Pius XI suggested there is more to marriage than the biologically rooted, act-focused, procreative institution model can explain. He suggested a personal procreative-union model, a suggestion that was taken up by European theologians. In marriage, spouses enter an interpersonal relationship in which they confront one another as "I" and "Thou" and initiate a mysterious union of their very beings. This union of their personal beings, and not merely the physical union of their bodies, is what the oft-quoted "one body" of Genesis 2:24 intends. It is this interpersonal union that the bodily union of sexual intercourse both signifies and instrumentally causes, and intercourse achieves its primary end when it actually does signify and cause interpersonal union. "Every marriage in which conjugal love is thus realized bears spiritual fruit, becomes *fruitful*—even though there are no children."[27] The resonance of this interpersonal description of marriage and marital lovemaking with the lived experience of modern married couples is clear.

In this interpersonal model, the primary end of sexual intercourse in marriage is the marital union between the spouses, and this primary end is achieved in every just and loving act of intercourse in and through which the spouses actually enter into intimate communion. Even in childless marriages, marriage and sexual intercourse achieve their primary end in the marital union of the spouses. "The immediate purpose of marriage is the realization of its meaning, the conjugal two-in-oneness. . . . This two-in-oneness of husband and wife is a living reality, and the immediate object of the marriage ceremony and their legal union." The union and love of the spouses tends naturally to the creation of a new person, their child, who fulfills both parents individually and as a two-in-oneness. "Society is more interested in the child than in the natural fulfillment of the parents, and it is this which gives the child primacy among the natural results of marriage."[28] Contemporary social scientific data, however, demonstrates the fallacy in assigning primacy to the child, for the relational well-being of the parents is the key to the well-being of their child.[29]

The Catholic Church's reaction to these new ideas was, as so often in theological history, a blanket condemnation that made no effort to sift truth from error. In 1944, the Holy Office (once the Inquisition and now the CDF) condemned "the opinion of some more recent authors, who either deny that the primary end of marriage is the generation and nurture of children, or teach that the secondary ends are not essentially subordinate to the primary end, but are equally primary and independent."[30] In 1951, after yet another world war of even greater horror, as personalism gained more adherents, Pius XII felt obliged to intervene again. "Marriage," he taught, "as a natural institution in virtue of the will of the Creator, does not have as a primary and intimate end the personal perfection of the spouses, but the procreation and nurture of new life. The other ends, inasmuch as they are intended by nature, are not on the same level as the primary end, and still less are they superior to it, but they are essentially subordinate to it."[31] The terms of the question of the ends of marriage could not have been made more precise. Another question, however, was seriously clouded.

For twenty years after *Casti connubii*, the Catholic Church struggled with a paradox. Since, on the basis of its reading of natural law whose author was assumed to be God, the primary end of sexual intercourse in marriage is procreation, every act of intercourse should be open to procreation. But a moral question arose. Is it moral for a couple to practice periodic continence with the explicit intention of avoiding conception; that is, is it moral for a couple intentionally to limit their sexual intercourse to the wife's monthly period of infertility? This question raged for twenty years until Pius XII, in a speech to Italian midwives in 1951, ruled that such action was moral as long as there are "serious reasons" of a "medical, eugenic, economic, or social kind," with no specification of what such serious reasons might be.[32] The obligation to procreate, the Pope argued, rests not on individual couples but on the entire human race. An individual couple can be excused from adhering to this obligation, even for the lifetime of a marriage, if they have sufficient reason.

This ruling, later validated by Paul VI in *Humanae vitae*, introduced a strange paradox into Catholic teaching about sexuality and marriage. On the one hand, God, the presumed author of natural law, determined that the end of each and every act of sexual intercourse is to be open to procreation; on the other hand, the Catholic Church determined that a couple may be sexually active and intentionally avoid this end if they have sufficient reason. Selling's comment is insightful: "Although it has never been admitted by the Magisterium, with the teaching on periodic continence the natural law approach to sexual morality had reached a cul-de-sac."[33] The Second Vatican Council would attempt to resolve this and other paradoxes in ecclesial doctrine about marriage by rejecting the model in which this papal argument is based.

Though the Council did not deal in any detail with marriage and the sacrament of marriage, *Gaudium et spes* did provide material intimately related to our present discussion. Marriage, it taught, is a "communion of love . . . an intimate partnership of life and love."[34] In spite of insistent demands from a small Vatican minority to repeat the centuries-old tradition of marriage as procreative institution, thus consigning spousal love to its traditional secondary end, the Council declared the mutual love of the spouses to be of the very essence of marriage, founded in "a conjugal covenant of irrevocable personal consent."[35] *Covenant* is a biblical word, saturated with overtones of divine, personal, steadfast love, characteristics now applied to the marriage between a man and a woman. The description of the object of the marital covenant places the interpersonal character of marriage beyond doubt. The spouses, the Council teaches, "mutually *gift and accept one another*," the focus on animal bodies and their acts replaced by a focus on persons.[36] In their marital covenant, spouses create, not a procreative institution, but a loving interpersonal union that, since covenanted love is steadfast, is to last as long as life lasts, and may or not be procreative.[37]

The intense and well-documented debate that took place in the Council makes it impossible to claim, as Germain Grisez wishes to, that the refusal to sustain the received marital tradition was the result of a simple avoidance of the language.[38] It was the result of deliberate and hotly deliberated choice, a choice replicated and given canonical formulation twenty years later in the revised Code of Canon Law in 1983, often called the Second Vatican Council's final document. Marriage "is ordered to the well-being of the spouses and to the procreation and upbringing of children" (Can 1055, 1), with no suggestion that either end is superior to the other. Notice that once again in the Catholic tradition, it is *marriage* and not *sexual intercourse* that is ordered to procreation. Marriage is "brought into being by the lawfully manifested consent of persons who are legally capable" (Can 1057, 1), and that consent "is an act of the will by which a man and a woman by irrevocable covenant mutually give and accept *one another* for the purpose of establishing a marriage" (Can 1057, 2). The Catholic Church revised its laws about marriage in the twentieth century to bring them into line with a newly received and developing theology of marriage, moving beyond the model of marriage as an exclusively procreative institution to embrace a model of interpersonal union in which the mutual love and communion of the spouses is as important as procreation. It did not, however, revise its norms guiding sexual acts in marriage in light of these theological developments.

As we have already shown, the judgment of the majority on the papal commission continues to be the judgment of the majority of Catholic theologians and Catholic couples. They do not receive the prescription that every act of sexual intercourse must be open to new life, because they do not receive the biologically procreative model of sexuality and marriage on which it is based. Rather, they re-receive the procreative model as an interpersonal procreative model on which the majority report was based. The sociologically documented nonreception of *Humanae vitae* and the nuanced re-reception of the procreative model in its interpersonal form, among both those expert in theology and those expert in marriage, suggest a contemporary example of re-reception and dramatic development of doctrine in the Church, in line with the developments that took place in the doctrines on usury, slavery, religious freedom, and membership in the Body of Christ.[39] Sociological research suggests that dramatic development is now well under way. It shows that the assertion "The Church believes that each and every marriage act must be open to the transmission of new life" is not true today for the vast majority of Catholics who make up the Church-People of God on whom the Second Vatican Council placed such emphasis.[40] At the very least, the social scientific data suggests a development that the whole Church, "from the Bishops to the last of the faithful," is called to discern in order to judge whether it is or is not an authentic example of re-reception of the apostolic truth toward which the Spirit of truth is constantly impelling the Church.[41]

A RENEWED PRINCIPLE OF HUMAN SEXUALITY AND CONTRACEPTION

We turn now to our renewed principle and its concomitant further principle to ask what light they may throw on the debate over contraception. The renewed principle, to refresh your memory, is articulated as follows:

> [Conjugal] love is uniquely expressed and perfected through the marital act. The actions within marriage by which the couple are united intimately and chastely are noble and worthy ones. Expressed in a manner which is truly human, these actions signify and promote that mutual self-giving by which spouses enrich each other with a joyful and thankful will.

The further principle is that, to be moral, sexual acts must be holistically complementary, just and loving. The consideration of both principles leads to the conclusion that *some* heterosexual and *some* homosexual acts, those that are holistically complementary, just, and loving, are moral; and *some* heterosexual and *some* homosexual acts, those that are not holistically complementary, just, and loving, are immoral. The question here is whether these principles can contribute to the discussion of the morality of artificially contraceptive acts. We shall argue that they do.

The love relationship between a man and a woman is transformed into a marriage, an "intimate partnership of life and love," by the valid legal ritual of their wedding.[42] The wedding transforms the man and the woman into husband and wife. If their shared love is matched by their shared faith in the God revealed in Christ, their wedding can also be a religious ritual that transforms their relationship into a sacrament of the relationship between Christ and Christ's Church.[43] The root relationship or bond of these three, the relationship or bond that requires constant nurture for the support of the other two, is not the legal bond arising from wedding or the religious bond arising from sacrament. It is the relationship or bond arising from the mutual love in which the spouses affirm one another as good and equal selves, the very love that leads them in the first instance to commit to join their love and their life for as long as life lasts in marriage.[44] Though "*marriage* and *married love* are by nature ordered to the procreation and education of children . . . , [m]arriage is not merely for the procreation of children. Its nature as an indissoluble covenant between two people and the good of the children demand that the mutual love of the spouses be properly shown, that it should grow and mature."[45]

In the contemporary Catholic tradition, marriage has two equal, nonhierarchical ends, the mutual love of the spouses and the procreation of children. Any doubt about the Second Vatican Council's intentions with respect to the equality of the ends of marriage, and we have already demonstrated that there is no possibility of legitimate doubt, was removed by the revised Code of Canon Law.[46] Marriage has two equal ends: the mutual love of the spouses and the procreation of children, with no hierarchical distinction between them. The equality of the ends in *Gaudium et spes* and in the Code necessarily changes the traditional argument about the morality of contraception. Our principle for discerning the meaning of sexual acts in marriage is focused on these two equal ends.

When a man and a woman are wedded, their human "nature" is transformed by the ritual; it is specified as definitively wedded. The partners are no longer the merely individual man and individual woman they were prior to the ritual; they have been made, rather, ritually and definitively coupled spouses, the biblical two-in-one-flesh.[47] Spouses are humans who have given themselves in love to each other, have taken mutual responsibility for their separate and communal lives, and have promised to be permanently faithful to the covenant responsibilities they have pledged one to the other for the whole of life. It is in the context of that mutual, covenantal, spousal, just, and loving self-gift that the morality of their marital acts, including the act of sexual intercourse, has meaning.

In their real historical, as distinct from some ideal and ahistorical, experience, human beings are fallible, are prone to sin, and live their lives within variously sinful structures. Their actual nature, the Catholic tradition teaches in its doctrine of original sin, is a sinful, wounded nature, always in need of salvation. Though spouses can *intend* their love and mutual self-gift to be total and indissoluble, in the concrete reality of their woundedness they cannot *make* them total and indissoluble at any given moment of their life, for love and self-gift reach out into the unknown, unpredictable, and uncontrollable future. All they can do, in Margaret Farley's wise words, is "initiate in the present a new form of relationship that will endure in the form of fidelity or betrayal"; this they do by their ritual consent at their wedding, and their covenantal commitment to each other "is [their] love's way of being whole while it still grows into wholeness."[48] In Catholic theological language, marital love, like love of God and love of neighbor, is essentially eschatological; that is, it reaches its totality only in the *eschaton*, or end, of marital life, not during and certainly not at the beginning of it. This eschatological quality of human love, allied to the sinful human structures that constantly threaten it, makes marital love "naturally" unfinished, imperfect, and fragile.

TOTALITY AND THE CONJUGAL ACT

All of this raises a question about the position on totality adopted, for instance, by Pope John Paul II and the traditionalists who uncritically follow him. The pope writes that

Sexuality, by means of which man and woman give themselves to one another through the acts which are proper and exclusive to spouses, is by no means something purely biological, but concerns the innermost being of the human person as such. It is realized in a truly human way *only* if it is an integral part of the love by which a man and a woman commit themselves *totally* to one another until death. The *total* physical self-giving would be *a lie* if it were not the sign and fruit of a *total* personal self-giving. . . . This *totality* which is required by conjugal love also corresponds to the demands of responsible fertility.[49]

We agree with Lisa Cahill that "the cumulative effect of such rhetoric is to hit married couples over the head with an unattainable norm for their conduct—one which, moreover, is hardly left at the level of ideal, being translated into rules for action of the most concrete and absolute sort."[50] There is no problem offering a moral ideal to spouses; there is a major problem offering absolute, concrete rules that take no account of historical circumstances that can modify the ideal.

Cahill is correct in identifying the problem with this papal and traditionalist argument. It is not conducted on the level of abstract principle to be interpreted and specified according to concrete circumstance, as the abstract principle "Thou shall not kill," for example, is interpreted in the Catholic moral tradition. The tradition interprets "Thou shall not kill" to mean "Thou shall not directly kill an *innocent* person," but you can morally kill an aggressor in proportionate self-defense or in a just war. The pope's traditionalist argument about the meaning of sexual intercourse is conducted not on the level of principle but on the level of absolute concrete rule that applies in each and every circumstance and admits of no exception. We agree with Cahill that, in keeping with their interpretation of human "nature" as "pure nature" and their total ignoring of concrete human experience, traditionalists read human experience "through the lens of the advocated teaching, and assume an ideal and abstract character little reflective of the give-and-take of enduring sexual relationships, especially marriage."[51] Our approach interprets human "nature" as the empirical, socially constructed "nature" persons share in the less-than-ideal and frequently wounded and messy circumstances of their real, historical lives. In the concrete "nature" of love and marriage, Cahill's "give-and-take of enduring sexual relationships," the "nature" of human love, and of the marriage that is intended to serve its growth to fullness, is unfinished, imperfect, fragile, and far from total.

Although it is not possible for humans to emulate fully the total love of God and to love totally, there is a totality involved when that love is covenanted between two free and equal human beings in marriage. That totality is the totality of the couple's relationship as it is personalized, legalized, and covenanted in marriage and the totality of the family they create together. The totality of the marriage embraces the good of each partner, the good of their relationship, and the good of any children that may be born from their marital intercourse. Any decision about the morality of any marital act, including but not restricted to the act of marital intercourse, has to consider not only the specific act but also how and where that act fits in the totality of the marriage, and how it contributes to the flourishing of the various marital goods. Once it is conceded, as *Gaudium et spes* and the Code of Canon Law concede, that marital love and relationship and procreation are equal ends of marriage, then the judgment about the morality of artificial contraception cannot be made on the exclusive basis of pure "nature" and the interpretation of its relatively rare reproductive outcome.

THE INSEPARABILITY PRINCIPLE REVISITED

Paul VI argues in *Humanae vitae* that God has established an inseparable connection between "the unitive significance and the procreative significance which are both inherent to the marriage act."[52] John Paul II approves this claim with no further elaboration.[53] No proof is offered by either pope in support of this claim, Paul VI simply opining that "we believe our contemporaries are particularly capable of seeing that this teaching is in harmony with human reason."[54] This lack of proof or reason and the fact that the majority of our contemporaries do not see this teaching in harmony with human reason has been a major cause of the debate over Paul VI's claims. It can be argued that Paul himself pro-moted the debate via an apparent internal contradiction in his argument. In the paragraph immediately preceding his claim of the inseparable connection between the unitive and procreative significances of marital intercourse, he appears to have argued the contrary. Marital intercourse does not cease to be "legitimate even when, for reasons independent of their will, it is foreseen to be infertile. For its natural adaptation to the expression and strengthening [signifying and causing] of the union of husband and wife is not thereby suppressed."[55] Here, Paul is approving the act of intercourse even when it is known that there is no possibility of procreation, and the basis of his approval seems to be precisely that the act is still directed toward signifying and causing marital love and union.

In these infertile acts, the unitive and procreative aspects are not only separable but also actually separated by the pope. The encyclical, at this point, seems to imply a factual separation of the unitive and procre-ative aspects of individual acts of sexual intercourse during the infertile period. Paul VI even ascribes this separation of unitive and procreative significance to the wise plan of God. "God has wisely disposed natural laws and times of fertility in order that, by themselves, they might sepa-rate subsequent births." Vincent Genovesi judges that the pope might just as well have written that "God has wisely disposed natural laws and rhythms of fertility that, by themselves, cause a separation in *the two meanings of the conjugal act as procreative and unitive*."[56] With such evidence in support, and lack of compelling proof in nonsupport, it is no wonder that the claim of the inseparable connection between unitive and procreative meanings of marital sexual intercourse has been widely and convincingly challenged.

It appears that by "nature" and the wise design of God, verified in worldwide human experience, there are two kinds of natural sexual inter-course, one that is conceptive and one that is nonconceptive. We deny the truth of the proposition that the unitive meaning of sexual intercourse is a universally natural meaning of the sexual act. The unitive meaning is "natural" only as socially interpreted in Western culture. We have no doubt that the procreative and unitive dimensions of marital intercourse are intimately related, particularly in the sense that they are both good for children, the one to procreate a new child, the other to ensure the successful nurture and education of that child. That they are absolutely inseparable, however, is far from demonstrated, especially since it can be argued legitimately that procreation is a "natural" *physiological* outcome of only *some* intercourse and that union of the spouses is a "natural" *cultural* outcome of *every* just and loving intercourse.

Accepting without debate Paul VI's unproven assertion of the insep-arable connection between the two ends of marriage and the two intrinsic meanings of sexual intercourse in marriage, John Paul II judges "natural" and artificial birth control on the basis of his "totality" argument.

> When couples, by means of recourse to contraception, separate these two meanings that God the Creator has inscribed in the being of man and woman and in the dynamism of their sexual communion, they act as arbiters of the divine plan and they manipulate and degrade human sexuality—and with it them-selves and their married partner—by altering its value of *total* self-giving. Thus the innate language that expresses the *total* reciprocal self-giving of husband and wife is overlaid, through contraception, by an objectively contradictory language, namely, that of not giving oneself *totally* to the other. This leads not only to a positive refusal to be open to life but also to a falsification of the inner truth of conjugal love, which is called upon to give itself in personal *totality*.[57]

Again, that totality argument, which we would not challenge as an *ideal* for couples, founders on the rock of concrete circumstances where ideals get concretized as absolute norms. The argument John Paul offers here against contraception is equally applicable to natural family planning, in which couples clearly act as "arbiters" of their marital

intercourse and "alter" its value of total self-giving by *intentionally* deciding to have intercourse at a time when they judge that the wife is infertile. Indeed, in the face of the evidence, both scientific and experiential,
that women in general experience the peak of their sexual desire and
responsiveness immediately before, during, and after ovulation, it is
arguable that the decision not to have intercourse at that time is acting
against total self-giving and nature, at least as much as any act of artificial
contraception.[58]

Moral judgment on contraception, whether natural or artificial, has
to be made on a basis that includes what is good for the flourishing of
the couple, their marriage, and any children already born to their family.
Adhering to the Catholic tradition that the generation of children and
parenthood are defining characteristics of marriage that deserve to be
both respected and preserved, our argument is that it is *marriage itself*
and not *each and every marital act* that is to be open to the transmission
of life and parenthood. That argument is akin to the judgment already
convincingly advanced by the majority of the Papal Commission in 1967,
though we offer a different foundation for it. Human intervention in the
process of the marriage act *for reasons drawn from the end of marriage itself,*
that is from the good of the spouses, their marital relationship, and any
children born of their marital intercourse, should not always be excluded,
provided that the Catholic criteria of morality are always safeguarded. The
two phrases we have underscored are at the heart of this principle.

Our argument is clear. Procreation is undoubtedly a good of *marriage,* but, in the Catholic tradition advanced by Pius XII and Paul VI,
it is not an essential good without which marriage could not exist. It
can be avoided for "serious reasons," "just reasons," "worthy and weighty
reasons," even "probable reasons."[59] The covenanted union of life and
love that is the very essence of marriage and that is scientifically documented as necessary for the education and nurture part of procreation
to be successful is, on the other hand, a necessary good of marriage. The
loving and just union of the spouses is a necessary good of marriage, for
the spouses, their children, and the communities, civil and religious, in

which they live. It is not difficult to see why the not-necessary marital good of procreation can, on occasion and in the proper moral circumstances, give way to the necessary good of marriage itself, not because it is a lesser good but because, on this specific occasion and for these just, serious, and weighty reasons, it is for the good of the spouses and their children. We argue that, to be moral, both conceptive and natural and artificial contraceptive intercourse must take place within the context of these various marital and familial goods. The demands of the good of marriage, the good not only of the couple but also of their existent children, can on occasion take priority over the good of procreation. A compromise may be needed between the good of the spouses and the good of procreation, the now-equal goods of marriage according to Catholic teaching. Not every married couple need procreate, or even be open to procreation, every time they have intercourse; indeed, as Pius XII taught, not every couple need procreate at all.

There is virtually no debate among Catholic theologians about the foregoing. The debate is about the *means* that may be taken to prevent procreation. The Catholic moral tradition is unanimous: Not only a chosen end must be moral but also the means chosen to achieve that end. The end of supporting my family is a perfectly moral end; working as an accountant for a construction company is a perfectly moral means to achieve that end; stealing from the construction company is not a moral means to achieve that end. Our question here is what means may be used to achieve the perfectly moral end of preventing procreation? Our answer is that, when spouses have a serious, just, and weighty marital or familial reason to prevent procreation in a specific concrete circumstance, procreation can be prevented by any means that does not damage their complementary, just, loving marital or parental relationship, and is not otherwise immoral. The rational basis for such a judgment, to repeat, is the nature of both the marital and familial relationship and the necessary goods associated with them that, when a serious, just, and weighty reason is present, take precedence, as we have explained, over the good of procreation.

CONCLUSION

This chapter is about marital morality and, of necessity in contemporary Catholicism, about birth control as an important issue in that morality. It situates marital morality within our foundational principle, namely, that sexual acts within marriage by which a couple is united intimately and chastely are noble and worthy and, when expressed in a truly human and justly loving manner, signify and promote that mutual self-giving by which spouses enrich each other, their family, and their community with a joyful and thankful will. It situates marital morality, therefore, in a context not of individual marital *acts* but of the overall marital *relationship*. In this context, we argue and conclude that *some* intentionally conceptive and *some* intentionally nonconceptive marital acts, whether achieved "naturally" or artificially, are moral, namely, those that promote the complementary, just, and loving marital relationship between the spouses and/or the just and loving relationship between parents and their children. We argue further that *some* intentionally conceptive and *some* intentionally nonconceptive acts, whether achieved "naturally" or artificially, are immoral, namely, those that damage the complementary, just, and loving relationship between the spouses and/or the just and loving relationship between parental spouses and their children. The morality of any act of marital intercourse is determined, as it is always determined in the Catholic moral tradition, not only by the act itself but also by the *intention* of the spouses following their well-informed consciences, which includes a conscientious and integral examination of the marital and familial circumstances in which the act is performed. We earlier concluded similarly regarding homosexual and nonreproductive heterosexual sexual acts.

QUESTIONS FOR REFLECTION

1. The model of marriage as a procreative institution has dominated Catholic thinking about marriage and sexuality for eighteen hundred years. How did that model come into the Catholic tradition, and how did it achieve such a level of dominance? Do you think that model has to be dominant in the future just because it was dominant in the past?

2. Pope Paul VI's encyclical *Humanae vitae* taught that "each and every marriage act must remain open to the transmission of life." A large majority of the Birth Control Commission that Popes John XXIII and Paul VI appointed to study the question of contraception judged, and recommended to Pope Paul VI, that "human intervention in the process of the marriage act for reasons drawn from the ends of marriage itself should not always be excluded." What is the origin of these two different points of view? Which of them is more compelling for you? Why?

3. Paul VI also argued in *Humanae vitae* that God has established an inseparable connection between the personal, unitive meaning of sexual intercourse and its biological procreative meaning. He argued that "our contemporaries are particularly capable of seeing that this teaching is in harmony with human reason." Do you see this teaching in harmony with your reason? Do you see any biological reason(s) that suggest that it is not in harmony with contemporary scientific reason?

4. What is the origin of the personal procreative-union model of *marriage* now available in the Catholic tradition? What official Catholic documents gave impetus to this new model of marriage in the twentieth century? What is the importance of the Second Vatican Council's teaching that marriage is "a communion of love . . . and intimate partnership of life and love"? What difference, if any, do you judge that makes for thinking about marriage and the norms guiding sexual acts within marriage?

5. Procreation is undoubtedly an important Catholic good of marriage, but Popes Pius XII and Paul VI taught that it was not an *essential* or necessary good. The vowed union of life and love of the spouses, on the other hand, is an essential good, necessary for the marriage and family to flourish. What do you see as the implications for marriage and the norms guiding sexual acts within marriage of these two Catholic doctrinal statements? Can Catholics act on their different interpretations of these two statements and still remain good Catholics?
6. What other questions arise for you from reading this chapter?

NOTES

1. Those who desire to read the detail of the convoluted debate can consult Giovanni Turbanti, *Un concilio per il mondo moderno: La redazione della costituzione pastorale "Gaudium et spes" del Vaticano II* (Bologna: Editrice Il Mulino, 2000); Charles Moeller, "History of the Constitution," in *Commentary on the Documents of Vatican II*, ed. Herbert Vorgrimler (New York: Herder, 1969) vol. 5, 1–76; Mackin, *What Is Marriage?* (New York: Paulist, 1982), 249–74.
2. GS, 47, 48.
3. Ibid.
4. See Bernard Häring, in *Commentary on the Documents of Vatican II*, vol. 5, 234. Häring, of course, played an active role on the subcommission that established the definitive text of *Gaudium et spes*. See Turbanti, *Concilio per il mondo moderno*.
5. Leslie Woodcock Tentler, *Catholics and Contraception: An American History* (Ithaca, NY: Cornell University Press, 2004); Julie Hanlon Rubio, "Beyond the Liberal/Conservative Divide on Contraception," *Horizons* 32 (2005): 270–94.
6. Rubio, "Beyond the Liberal/Conservative Divide," 271.
7. Margaret A. Farley, *Just Love: A Framework for Christian Sexual Ethics* (New York: Continuum, 2006), 278; International Theological Commission, *Theses on the Relationship between the Ecclesiastical Magisterium and Theology* (Washington, DC: USCCB, 1977), 6.
8. See *History of Vatican II*, 3 vols., ed. Giuseppe Alberigo, English version edited by Joseph A. Komonchak (Maryknoll, NY: Orbis, 2000).
9. Paul Evdokimov, "Le sacerdoce conjugal," in *Le Mariage*, eds. Georges Crespy, Paul Evdokimov, and Christian Duquoc, (Paris: Maison Mame, 1966), 94–95; emphasis added.
10. *De Bono Coniugio*, 3, 3; *PL* 40, 375; emphasis added.
11. *ST*, 3 (Suppl.), 65, 1, c.

12. See Urban Navarette, "Structura Juridica Matrimonii Secundum Concilium Vaticanum II," *Periodica* 56 (1967): 366.

13. William V. D'Antonio, James D. Davidson, Dean R. Hoge, and Ruth A. Wallace, *Laity: American and Catholic: Transforming the Church* (Kansas City, MO: Sheed and Ward, 1996), 79. Corroborating evidence is supplied by James D. Davidson, Patricia Wittberg, William J. Whalen, Kathleen Mass Weigert, Andrea S. Williams, Richard A. Lamanna, and Jan Stentfnagel, *Search for Common Ground: What Unites and Divides Catholic Americans* (Huntington, IN: Our Sunday Visitor, 1997), 47.

14. See Andrew M. Greeley, William C. McCready, and Kathleen McCourt, *Catholic Schools in a Declining Church* (Kansas City, MO: Sheed and Ward, 1976), 35; D'Antonio et al., *Laity: American and Catholic*, 140; Davidson et al., *Search for Common Ground*, 131.

15. Michael Hornsby-Smith, *Roman Catholicism in England: Customary Catholicism and Transformation of Religious Authority* (Cambridge: Cambridge University Press, 1991), 177.

16. See *The Tablet* (September 18, 2010), 45.

17. *HV*, 11. The encyclical was written in Italian (see Lucio Brunelli, "The Pill That Divided the Church," *Thirty Days* 4 [July–August 1988], 66), probably because its main editor was the Franciscan padre Ermenegildo Lio, of the Pontifical Athenaeum Antonianum, who made such *sustained* efforts to reintroduce Ottaviani's rejected schema, *De Castitate, Virginitate, Matrimonio, Familia*, into Schema XIII which became *Gaudium et spes*. (See Turbanti, *Concilio per il mundo moderno*.) Janet Smith references several English translations and offers her own translation "based on the Latin, though on a few occasions, when the Latin seemed irrecoverably obscure, recourse was made to the Italian" (Janet Smith, *Humanae vitae: A Generation Later* [Washington, DC: Catholic University of America Press, 1991], 269). She does not tell us why or where the Latin is "irrecoverably obscure" or how the Italian is any less obscure, but when compared to the official Latin text and official English translation, the translation she offers is rather free.

18. See Robert McClory, *Turning Point: The Inside Story of the Papal Birth Control Commission and How* Humanae Vitae *Changed the Life of Patty Crowley and the Future of the Church* (New York: Crossroad, 1995), 127.

19. Ibid., 99.

20. Some of the majority theologians and the four of the minority are named in *The Catholic Case for Contraception*, ed. Daniel Callahan (London: Macmillan, 1969), 149 and 174. Tentler writes that the Minority Report was "largely written by Germain Grisez, then a Georgetown University theologian, and the Jesuit John Ford" (*Catholics and Contraception*, 227). For details on this, see Smith, *Humanae vitae*, 11–33.

21. *HV*, 11.

22. Cited in Longley, *Worlock Archive*, 233; emphasis added.

23. Richard McCormick, *Notes on Moral Theology 1965–1980* (Lanham, MD: University Press of America, 1981), 164.

24. See Robert Blair Kaiser, *The Politics of Sex and Religion* (Kansas City, MO: Leaven Press, 1985), 260–61; emphasis added. Also in Longley, *Worlock Archive*, 233. Both Kaiser and Longley translate the French word *finalité* as *finality*; we prefer the more traditional theological word *end*, which is, in fact, what the French *finalité* intends.

25. The words are from Stephen Sloesser, *Jazz Age Catholicism: Mystic Modernism in Postwar Paris* (Toronto: University of Toronto Press, 2005), an insightful look into this period.

26. *AAS* 22 (1930), 548–49; emphasis added.

27. Dietrich von Hildebrand, *Marriage* (London: Longmans, 1939), 25; emphasis in original.

28. Doms, *Meaning of Marriage*, 94–95.

29. See Michael Lamb and Abraham Sagi, *Fatherhood and Family Policy* (Hillsdale, NJ: Erlbaum Associates, 1983); Ronald J. Angel and Jacqueline L. Angel, *Painful Inheritance: Health and the New Generation of Fatherless Families* (Madison: University of Wisconsin Press, 1993); Jean Bethke Elshtain, "Family Matters: The Plight of America's Children," *Christian Century* 110 (1993): 710–12; Sara McLanahan and Gary Sandefur, *Growing Up with a Single Parent* (Cambridge: Harvard University Press, 1994); David Blankenhorn, *Fatherlessness in America: Confronting Our Most Urgent Social Problem* (New York: Basic Books, 1995); David Popenoe, *Life without Father* (New York: Free Press, 1996); Arlene R. Skolnick and Jerome H. Skolnick, *Family in Transition* (New York: Longman, 1999); Linda J. Waite and Maggie Gallagher, *The Case for Marriage: Why Married People Are Happier, Healthier, and Better Off Financially* (New York: Doubleday, 2000); Judith Wallerstein and Julia Lewis, *The Unexpected Legacy of Divorce: A 25 Year Landmark Study* (New York: Hyperion, 2000).

30. *AAS* 36 (1944), 103.

31. *AAS* 43 (1951), 848–49.

32. Ibid., 846.

33. Joseph A. Selling, ed., "Marriage and Sexuality in the Catholic Church," in *Embracing Sexuality: Authority and Experience in the Catholic Church* (Burlington: Ashgate, 2001), 185.

34. GS, 47–48.

35. Ibid., 48.

36. Ibid.; emphasis added.

37. For an extended analysis of covenant, see Michael G. Lawler, "Marriage as Covenant in the Catholic Tradition," in *Covenant Marriage in Comparative Perspective*, ed. John Witte Jr. and Eliza Ellison (Grand Rapids, MI: Eerdmans, 2005), 70–91.

38. Germain Grisez, *The Way of the Lord Jesus*, vol. 2, *Living a Christian Life* (Quincy, IL: Franciscan Herald Press, 1993), 565, n. 35.

39. See John T. Noonan Jr., *A Church That Can and Cannot Change* (Notre Dame, IN: University of Notre Dame Press, 2005); Michael G. Lawler, *What Is and*

What Ought to Be: The Dialectic of Experience, Theology, and Church (New York: Continuum, 2005), 119–42.

40. *LG*, 37.
41. Augustine, *De Praed. Sanct.*, 14, 27; *PL* 44, 980. See also *LG*, 12.
42. *GS*, 48.
43. See Michael G. Lawler, *Marriage and the Catholic Church: Disputed Questions* (Collegeville, MN: Liturgical Press, 2002), 1–26.
44. Ibid., 66–91.
45. *GS*, 50; emphasis added.
46. Can 1055; emphasis added.
47. See Audrey Richards, *Chisungu* (London: Faber and Faber, 1956), 120–21; Michael Lawler, *Symbol and Sacrament: A Contemporary Sacramental Theory* (Mahwah, NJ: Paulist, 1987), 5–15.
48. Margaret Farley, *Personal Commitments: Beginning, Keeping, Changing* (San Francisco: Harper and Row, 1986), 34.
49. *FC*, 11; emphasis added. John Paul repeats this argument, though in slightly different terms, in *FC*, 32. Paul M. Quay ("Contraception and Conjugal Love," *TS* 22 [1961]: 18–40) had argued in the same way twenty years prior to *FC*. Smith, in *Humanae vitae* (108–12), does not so much argue the position as cite with favor both Quay and John Paul II, allowing her to conclude that "the evil of contraception, then, is that it belies the truth that the 'language of our bodies' should be expressing: the truth that we are seeking complete union with the beloved" (112).
50. Lisa Sowle Cahill, "Human Sexuality," in *Moral Theology: Challenges for the Future*, ed. Charles E. Curran (New York: Paulist, 1990), 198.
51. Ibid., 199.
52. *HV*, 12.
53. *FC*, 32.
54. *HV*, 12.
55. Ibid., 11.
56. Vincent J. Genovesi, *In Pursuit of Love: Catholic Morality and Human Sexuality* (Collegeville, MN: Liturgical Press, 1966), 194; emphasis in original.
57. *FC*, 32; emphasis added.
58. See, for instance, John R. Cavanagh, "The Rhythm of Sexual Desire in the Human Female," *Bulletin of the Guild of Catholic Psychiatrists* 14 (1967): 87–100. Cavanagh was a member of the Papal Commission who originally was a strong advocate of periodic abstinence but, instructed by the Commission's debates, changed his opposition to artificial contraception. For more on Cavanagh, see Charles E. Curran, *Critical Concerns in Moral Theology* (Notre Dame, IN: University of Notre Dame Press, 1984), 216–24. See also June M. Reinisch and Ruth Beasley, *The Kinsey Institute New Report on Sex* (New York: St. Martin's Press, 1990), 119; Leslie Woodcock Tentler, *Catholics and Contraception: An American History* (Ithaca: Cornell University Press, 2004), 225.
59. *HV*, 10, 16.

CHAPTER 4

༄

Cohabitation and the Process of Marrying

Emmanuel Ntakarutimana expresses the Central African experience of marrying in the following words. "Where Western tradition presents marriage as a point in time at which consent is exchanged between the couple in front of witnesses approved by law, followed by consummation, the tradition here recognizes the consummation of a marriage with the birth of the first child. To that point the marriage was only being *progressively realized*."[1] Four years of field experience in East Africa taught us the same thing. We offer three points of clarification. First, the Western tradition to which Ntakarutimana refers is the Western tradition of only the past four hundred years; it goes back neither to Jesus nor to the New Testament. Second, in the received Western tradition, as in the African traditions, becoming validly and indissolubly married is a process, which begins with the exchange of consent and ends with subsequent consummation. Third, two ongoing questions arise: What are we to make of the differences between the Catholic, Western tradition of marrying and other cultural traditions, and how long can the Catholic Church continue to insist that the historically recent Western tradition is *the* universal tradition for all?

This chapter reflects on these points. In it we try, in Kevin Kelly's words, to make "faith-sense of experience and experience-sense of faith."[2] That is, we come to the contemporary experience of cohabitation with a

COHABITATION AND THE PROCESS OF MARRYING

Catholic faith, and we attempt to bring that faith into conversation with the experience of cohabitation and how that experience affects the lives of cohabiting couples. We engage in this exercise conscious of the fact that human experience is a long-established source for Catholic moral judgments. This chapter is specifically about the process of becoming married in the living Catholic tradition of past and future. As it reflects on the history of marriage in the West, it necessarily uncovers two facts about the phenomenon contemporary society calls cohabitation. First, cohabitation is nothing new in either the Western or the Catholic tradition; second, as practiced both in the past and in the present, Western cohabitation is not unlike the African marriage of which Ntakarutimana writes. The chapter develops in three cumulative sections. The first section considers the contemporary phenomenon of cohabitation; the second unfolds the Western and Christian historical tradition as it relates to cohabitation and marriage; the third formulates a moral response to this phenomenon in light of theological reflection and our foundational sexual ethical principle.

Before embarking on this exploration, however, it is important to define precisely what is meant by the term *cohabitation*. The word derives from the Latin *cohabitare*, to live together. It applies literally to all situations where one person lives with another person: marriage, family, students in a dormitory, roommates in an apartment. An added specification is necessary to distinguish the meaning of the word in contemporary usage and, therefore, in this chapter. Cohabitation names the situation of a man and a woman who, though not husband and wife, live together as husband and wife and enjoy intimate sexual relations. We offer a typology that distinguishes two types of cohabitation in relationship to marriage. The cohabitation of couples already firmly committed to marry we call *nuptial* cohabitation; all other cohabitations we call *nonnuptial* cohabitation, because there is as yet no conscious intention to marry. Since some reviewers, including the United States Conference of Catholic Bishops, have misrepresented our position in an earlier book as promoting *all* cohabitation and *all* premarital sex, it is important to be clear from the outset that everything we say about cohabitation in this chapter is said specifically and only of nuptial cohabitation and cohabitors, that is, those who are already committed to marry each other.[3]

COHABITATION IN THE CONTEMPORARY WEST: WHAT THE SCIENCES TELL US

The sharp increase in cohabitation is one of the most fundamental social changes in Western countries today. Over half of all first marriages in the United States are preceded by cohabitation.[4] Studies find a similar trend in Europe, Great Britain, Norway, Sweden, the Netherlands, France, Belgium and Germany, Canada, and Australia.[5] Two social-scientific facts about cohabitation are frequently mentioned by Catholic theologians. The first is that unmarried heterosexual cohabitation increased dramatically in the United States, and elsewhere in the Western world, in the last quarter of the twentieth century. For couples marrying in the United States in the decade between 1965 and 1974, the percentage of marriages preceded by cohabitation was 10 percent; for couples marrying between 1990 and 1994, that percentage dramatically quintupled to 50 percent.[6] In 1987, 30 percent of women in their late thirties reported they had cohabited; in 1995, 48 percent reported they had cohabited. These increases did not leave the social climate in which cohabitation flourished untouched. Rather, as cohabitation cohorts become more and more homogenized, cohabitation itself becomes more and more conventional and socially endorsed.

The second fact often mentioned is that premarital cohabitation tends to be associated with a heightened risk of divorce when the cohabitors later marry, a fact on which there is consensus from a large variety of different researchers, samples, methodologies, and measures.[7] This second fact has become beloved of Catholic commentators on unmarried heterosexual cohabitation and its implications for subsequent marriage, which leaves both them and their pastoral responses at risk of being uninformed and outdated, for more recent studies on more recent cohorts report more nuanced data about the relationship of cohabitation and marital instability.[8]

As early as 1992, Schoen showed that the inverse relationship between premarital cohabitation and subsequent marital stability was minimal for recent birth cohorts, a result which he linked to the growing prevalence of cohabitation.[9] In 1997, McRae demonstrated the common negative association between premarital cohabitation and marital stability when she analyzed her British sample in toto. When, however, she analyzed her sample by age cohort, her findings supported Schoen: "Younger generations do not show the same link between pre-marital cohabitation and marriage dissolution." She agreed with Schoen's conclusion that "as cohabitation becomes the majority pattern before marriage, this link will become progressively weaker."[10] That majority pattern, as already noted, has now arrived. When they analyzed their results in toto, Woods and Emery uncovered much the same data as McRae, but when they controlled for personal characteristics, premarital cohabitation had no predictive effect on divorce.[11] In a sophisticated study of an Australian sample, de Vaus and his colleagues found the link between cohabitation and marital instability was apparent only for older cohorts.[12] Teachman recently replicated that result, showing that when a woman has cohabited only with her husband, cohabitation is not associated with increased likelihood of divorce.[13]

Two of America's most respected marriage researchers, Scott Stanley and Linda Waite, endorse the thesis that not all cohabitors and all cohabiting relationships are equal. Stanley writes that "those who are particularly at risk from premarital cohabitation are most likely those who have not already decided, for sure, this is who they want to marry before cohabitation. . . . While not all couples are at greater risk for cohabiting prior to marriage, it's surely a very great and unwise risk for those who are not sure they have found who they want to marry."[14] Waite states that "couples who live together with no definite plans to marry are making a different bargain than couples who marry or than engaged cohabitors."[15] She adds that "those on their way to the altar look and act like already-married couples in most ways, and those with no plans to marry look and act very different. For engaged cohabiting couples, living together is a step on the path to marriage, not a different road altogether."[16] There are, then, at least two kinds of cohabitors, those already committed to marriage, perhaps even engaged, and those not so committed, and it is only uncommitted cohabitation that is linked to an increased likelihood of divorce after marriage.[17] Commenting on a 2010 US government report noting that those who cohabited prior to engagement were at greater risk for divorce after marrying than those who had not cohabited, and that those who cohabited after engagement were at no greater risk than those who had never cohabited, Stanley emphasizes what his research has consistently shown.[18] Those who cohabit with their intended spouse after they have made the decision to marry, or after they have become engaged, are at no more risk for divorce than those who have never cohabited.[19] Empirical research clearly shows two things that are relevant here: there are the two kinds of cohabitors we have noted, namely nuptial and non-nuptial cohabitors; and commitment is a distinctive determinant in relationship stability, whether that relationship be cohabitation or marriage.

THE MEANING AND NATURE OF COMMITMENT

Before we consider betrothal, we must discuss the commitment that distinguishes both nuptial cohabitors and married couples. John Paul II teaches that conjugal love "aims at a deeply personal unity, a unity that, beyond union in one flesh, leads to forming one heart and soul; it demands indissolubility and faithfulness in definitive mutual giving; and it is open to fertility."[20] Kelly contends that this describes the situation of those cohabitors who have committed to a loving relationship with one another and who later come to him to be married. He refuses to consider them as "living in sin," because that would be "a denigration of something they had experienced as sacred and from God"; they come to the Church "to celebrate the gift of their love for each other and to give it new permanence through the solemn commitment of their marriage vows to each other and to God."[21] Their growing *commitment* in love to each other and, ultimately, their developed commitment to marriage has a concrete and recognizable face. Marriage researcher Scott Stanley has brilliantly analyzed this commitment.

Stanley distinguishes two kinds of commitment: commitment as *dedication*, defined as "an internal state of devotion to a person or a project," and commitment as *constraint*, which "entails a sense of obligation."[22] Those who lose the sense of dedication and retain only the sense of constraint "will either be together but miserable . . . or come apart."[23] Applied to relationships, including marriage, commitment as dedication, which we define as "a freely chosen and faithful devotion to a person or project," is twofold: commitment to the partner and commitment to the relationship. Commitment to the partner entails those characteristics that John Paul lists or implies, namely, fidelity, loyalty, and fortitude in the vicissitudes and messiness of the relationship. Commitment to the relationship entails exclusivity, indissolubility, and possible fertility as fruitfulness.[24] Couples who share this double commitment give evidence of a strong couple identity, "a strong orientation toward 'us' and 'we.'" They "make their partner and marriage a high priority." They "protect their relationship from attraction to others." They are willing to "sacrifice for one another without resentment." They take a long-term view, "they invest themselves in building a future together."[25] Such double commitment, Stanley and others show, is the surest path to the marital intimacy that all partners and spouses seek.

Couples with such double commitment report that they feel comfortable revealing their deepest desires, failings, and hurts to each other.[26] They do not think about possible alternatives to their partner, they are more satisfied with their marital life in general and their sex life in particular, and they have no need to consider adultery.[27] They are more willing to give up things important to them for the sake of their relationship, and they report higher levels of happiness and stability than do partners who do not regularly sacrifice for the sake of their relationship.[28] These couples have a strong sense of their future together and are more likely to speak of that future and of their dreams for it than of their past conflicts, failures, and disappointments.[29] It is such commitment, we suggest, that nuptial cohabitors exhibit, albeit in seed at the beginning of their cohabitation together but in full flower when they come to be married. It is precisely the seedling, inchoate love and commitment coming to full flower that needs to be ritually realized and celebrated in the betrothal to which we now turn.

BETROTHAL AND THE CHRISTIAN TRADITION

Theology must be attentive to social change. It must also be attentive to the wealth of information provided by the social sciences because, as theological history demonstrates, human experience, which includes social change, though it does not control theological reflection, does inform and influence Christian theology.[30] Since theology is and must be rooted in reality, the relationship between the social reality of cohabitation and the theology of marriage must be carefully explored in light of and informed by all available and appropriate sources of wisdom. Contemporary Christians easily assume that the nuclear family of twentieth-century America, the so-called traditional family, is both biblical and natural. It is always a surprise to them to discover that it is neither.[31] There is a similar problem with the contemporary phenomenon of cohabitation. Again, it is easily assumed to be a new phenomenon; and, again, it is not.

HISTORICAL CONSIDERATIONS

Two imperial Roman definitions have dominated the Western discussion of marriage. The first is found in Justinian's *Digesta* (23, 2, 1): "Marriage is a union of a man and a woman, and a communion of the whole of life, a participation in divine and human law." The second is found in Justinian's *Instituta* (1, 9, 1): "Marriage is a union of a man and a woman, embracing an undivided communion of life." These two "definitions," which are no more than descriptions of marriage as culturally experienced in imperial Rome, controlled every subsequent discussion of marriage in the Western tradition. They agree on the bedrock: marriage is a union and a communion between a man and a woman embracing the whole of life.[32]

Marriage, therefore, in both the Christian theological and the Western legal traditions, is the union of a man and a woman. But how is marriage effected in the eyes of these two traditions which, up to the Reformation, were identical? Already in the sixth century, Justinian's *Digesta* (35, 1, 15) decreed the Roman tradition: the only thing required for a valid marriage was the mutual consent of both parties. The northern European custom was different; there penetrative sexual intercourse after consent made a valid marriage. This different approach to what made marriage valid provoked a widespread legal debate in Europe. Both the Roman and the northern opinion had long histories, sound rationale, and brilliant proponents in twelfth-century Europe, but the debate was ended in mid-century by Gratian, master of the Catholic University of Bologna, who proposed a compromise solution. Consent *initiates* a marriage, or makes it *ratum*; subsequent sexual intercourse completes it, or makes it *consummatum*. This compromise continues to be enshrined in the Catholic Code of Canon Law (Can 1061).

To be underscored here is the *process* character of valid, indissoluble marriage in the Catholic Church, for that process character is central to the argument presented in the third section. The present canon law requires for valid, indissoluble marriage two distinct acts, the mutual free consent of the couple and their subsequent, penetrative sexual intercourse. How the law was followed in practice is a part of the historical marital tradition of both the Catholic and the Western worlds that has been long ignored. It is grossly ahistorical to assume that the current practice and understanding of marriage is what has always been.

Gratian's compromise—mutual consent ratifies a marriage and sexual intercourse makes it ratified and consummated—ended the debate between the Romans and the northern Europeans over what effected marriage. Consent could be given in either the future or the present tense. When it was given in the future tense, the result was called betrothal, and the process from cause (consent) to effect (betrothal) was known as *sponsalia*, or spousals; that is, the couple became spouses. When consent was given in the present tense, the result was called marriage, and the process from cause (consent) to effect (marriage) was known as *nuptialia*, or nuptials. The first sexual intercourse between the spouses usually followed the betrothal, and this is a fact of the Catholic tradition that has been obscured by the now-taken-for-granted sequence of wedding, marriage, sexual intercourse. It was not, however, until the Council of Trent in the sixteenth century that the Catholic Church prescribed that sequence and decreed that marriage resulted from the nuptials or ceremonial wedding. For over half of contemporary Catholic couples in the modern West, the sequence has reverted to the pre-Tridentine sequence: cohabitation, sexual intercourse, wedding.

The pre-Tridentine sequence has been well documented in sociohistorical sources. Jean Remy describes the situation in France, where sexual relations regularly began with *sponsalia* or betrothal. "In the sixteenth century, the Churches began to lead a campaign against premarital sex. Previously the engagement or betrothal carried great weight. If the Church frowned on the unblessed marriage she did not forbid it. Very often, above all in the country, the Church marriage took place when the woman was pregnant, sometimes towards the end of her pregnancy."[33] His statement justifies the pre-Tridentine sequence against the backdrop of its cultural context. It holds equally true for African cultures today.[34] A host of commentators describe the situation in England and its empire. Lawrence Stone writes: "Before the tightening up of religious controls over society after the Reformation and the Counter-Reformation in the mid-sixteenth century, the formal betrothal ceremony seems to have been at least as important, if not more so, than the wedding." To many, the couple were from that moment "man and wife before God."[35] Alan Macfarlane emphasizes that "the engaged lovers before the nuptials were held to be legally husband and wife. It was common for them to begin living together immediately after the betrothal ceremony."[36]

Later, a celebration of the marriage, an occasion for relatives and friends to bring gifts and to feast, was held, but up to the Council of Trent in the Catholic tradition and up to the Hardwicke Act in mid-eighteenth-century England, the central event of the *sponsalia*, or betrothal was held separate from the ceremonial event of the *nuptialia*, or wedding. After the betrothal, "the couple saw themselves as man and wife, and therefore sexual intercourse was a natural consequence."[37] This meant, of course, as G. R. Quaife points out, that "for the peasant community, there was very little pre-marital sex. Most of the acts seen as such by Church and State were interpreted by the village [the cultural community] as activities within marriage—a marriage begun with the promise and irreversibly confirmed by pregnancy."[38] Neither church nor state was satisfied with this marital process, but neither had any choice but to recognize the validity of marriages thus effected. Church law, accepted by European states as binding in marital affairs, was clear. Free consent to marry, whether articulated publicly or privately, initiated marriage, and sexual intercourse after consent, with or without subsequent pregnancy, consummated marriage and made it indissoluble. In the eyes of the Church, marriages, however private and secret, that were the result of free consent and subsequent consummation had to be held as valid marriages and therefore, when the spouses were baptized, also as valid sacraments. Genuinely secret or clandestine marriages, however, became the scourge of Europe and provoked a change in both canon and civil law.

The Council of Trent's decree *Tametsi* (1563) prescribed the marriage the Catholic Church would henceforth recognize as valid and sacramental and, when consummated, indissoluble: that marriage, and only that marriage, that was publicly celebrated in the presence of a duly appointed priest and two witnesses.[39] Only if celebrated in this canonical form, as it came to be called, would a marriage between Catholics be recognized by the Church as valid and sacramental. *Tametsi* transformed the ritual of marriage, namely, the wedding, from a simple contract between families, one not circumscribed by any legal formalities, to a solemn contract, one in which certain legal formalities had to be observed for validity. In addition to transforming the contractual nature of marriage, *Tametsi* transformed also the *how* and the *when* of marriage. No longer could anyone claim that marriage was effected at betrothal; it could be effected only at a public Church ceremony called a wedding. The modern era of marriage had begun.

In England, among the upper and aspiring middle classes, betrothal lost its public character and became an internal family affair called *engagement*, a prelude to marriage that was never to be confused with marriage, and which did not confer the rights of marriage, including the right to sexual intercourse. An engaged couple could never be confused with the married couple they would become after their wedding. This development in the process of marriage, and in the success of the English upper class in imposing its practice on everyone in England, reached its apogee in 1753, when Lord Hardwicke introduced an act to prohibit clandestine marriages. The Hardwicke Act, which became law on May 1, 1754, prescribed that no marriage in England would be valid other than the one performed by an ordained clergyman, after the calling of banns for three successive weeks or the purchase from the local bishop of a license not to call banns. The present process of marriage in the West, specifically the focus on the wedding ceremony as the beginning of marriage, has been in effect since only the sixteenth century. The present practice of the English-cum-American civil law has been in effect only since the mid-eighteenth century.

SOCIOTHEOLOGICAL CONSIDERATIONS

Prior to 1564, when the papal bull prescribing compliance with the decisions of the Council of Trent became Catholic law, Catholics needed no wedding ceremony to be married. Prior to 1754, the citizens of England and its empire needed no wedding to be married. That historical reality can never be erased. That the process of becoming validly married in the Catholic and Western traditions has not always been as it currently is, that Catholic marriage practice was adapted and greatly transformed within historical memory, leads easily to the conclusion that it could adapt and change again. That *possible* change in Catholic marital practice will be the focus of this section of this chapter. We emphasize from the outset that there is nothing new in the change we will propose.[40] Rather, the change is a reversion to something old, something that was part of the Catholic tradition of marriage for centuries before Trent, which, to counter secret marriages, introduced the change that established the present received tradition. From the actual historical reality of the marital sequence, betrothal-sexual intercourse-wedding, the conclusion that it could be so again is logically legitimate. This section will show that it is also theologically legitimate.

The parallel between the premodern and modern practices is striking. Premodern betrothal led to full sexual relations and possible pregnancy, which, in turn, led to indissoluble marriage; modern nuptial cohabitation leads to full sexual relations and, in turn, to indissoluble marriage, with or without pregnancy. We underscore here, again, that in this chapter we are focused only on *nuptial cohabitation*, cohabitation premised by the intention to marry. Nothing we say refers to non-nuptial cohabitation. "The full sexual experience practiced by betrothed couples [in pre-Tridentine and pre-Victorian times] was ... *emphatically premised by the intention to marry*."[41] It is only those cohabitors with an emphatic intention to marry who are our concern.

Our proposal is straightforward: a return to the processual marital sequence of betrothal (with appropriate ritual to ensure community involvement), sexual intimacy, and ceremonial wedding to acknowledge and to mark the consummation of both valid marriage and sacrament. This is not a new proposal; it has been made with different nuances before. The first detailed proposal was made in 1977 by Canadian moral theologian André Guindon; he was followed independently in 1978 by French theologian M. Legrain.[42] Guindon seeks to respond theologically and canonically to the growing prevalence of cohabitation in Canada. He argues that the socioeconomic changes that have taken place over the past two hundred years—the new roles accorded to women; the desire, especially of women, for an adult and satisfying sexuality; and the centrality of mutual love in the marital relationship—have transformed the contemporary marital situation. He notes that the human sciences have shown that sexuality is a language to be progressively learned in an ongoing apprenticeship subject to all the laws of human development. Reflecting this social scientific data, he seeks a renewed theological understanding of consummation, founded not automatically on a first act of sexual intercourse but on the personal, spiritual, and physical union established between the partners. These historical, cultural, anthropological, and theological transformations invite a corresponding transformation of the norms guiding the sexual person in relationship. This leads Guindon to propose the consummation of a marriage before its ratification, consummated and ratified marriage rather than the traditional-since-Gratian ratified and consummated marriage.

Legrain reflects a different perspective, that of customary African marriage where "even among Christians . . . only those who have followed all the customary tribal requirements, including the performance of the required rituals, are held to be truly married."[43] He, as Guindon, is concerned with the processual character of consummated, indissoluble marriage, particularly with the Roman claim that consummation follows from the first sexual intercourse. That is not the case in African custom. Echoing Ntakarutimana, Legrain states what is obvious to all cognizant of the African context: "The marriage of Christians would never be accepted as *ratum et consummatum* until the birth of a child."[44] The birth of a child stamps a union as marital, marks the union in African eyes as a truly consummated marriage.

In Legrain's and African eyes, marriage is not just a wedding ceremony when a couple gives publicly witnessed consent—however dear such precision might be to canon lawyers—but a *process* from betrothal through human, including sexual, intercourse to the consummating birth of a child. Could African customary marital rituals be Christianized? Of course they could, just as imperial Roman and northern European tribal rituals were Christianized to yield the present received tradition. That they have not yet been Christianized is due to the imposition of a Roman canonical form based on the assumption that a compromise twelfth-century European form is *the* unique Christian model for marriage. They could be Christianized by accepting the processual character of African marriages as a human value and adapting, yet once again, legislation, liturgy, and pastoral practice to highlight human, marital, and sacramental value. If what Legrain argues is possible for an African cultural context, and we see no theological reason why it is not, it is also possible for a Western cultural context once again in the full flower of change.

What Guindon and Legrain propose is an adaptation of Christian, sacramental marriage to diverse cultural realities. They abandon the received Catholic model of marriage taking place at a moment in time, the moment of mutually given public consent, and they seek to replace it with a developmental model, in which marriage takes place in stages.[45] They agree in recognizing a real marriage from the moment of betrothal, and in recognizing a consummated and indissoluble marriage when the couple have fully expressed in their marital life the marital values of their culture. Above all—and this is to be underscored for the benefit of those, including the United States Conference of Catholic Bishops, who accuse them and us of condoning *all* premarital sex—they agree in condoning sexual intercourse *only* between couples who have seriously committed themselves to becoming married. For Legrain, those are African Christian couples living out the required customary stages of a marriage; for Guindon, and for us, those are Western Christian couples nuptially cohabiting with an already-given firm consent to marry.

The stumbling block to granting moral legitimacy to any premarital sexual activity in the Catholic tradition, and in all the Christian traditions, is the exclusive connection the traditions see between sexual intercourse and marriage. "Every genital act must be within the framework of marriage."[46] Outside of marriage genital activity always constitutes a grave sin and excludes one from sacramental communion. That teaching certainly appears to be a major stumbling block to the claim of this chapter that *some* pre-wedding sexual activity is morally legitimate. There can be no way forward until the traditional and exclusive connection between sexual activity and marriage, which is, in fact, the exclusive connection between sexual activity and procreation, is severed. To get really real about sexuality and sexual activity in the modern world, the exclusive connection between sexual intercourse and procreation has to be abandoned.[47]

We have suggested that different circumstances and different premises, perhaps learned from a close study of the contemporary social and theological situation, might lead to different conclusions. That suggestion is true for sexuality, procreation, and marriage, the connection of which has a long history in the Catholic Church. The earliest Christian theologians learned it from the ancient Stoic philosophers who, basing their explanations of sexuality on their observations of animal behavior, argued that the sexual organs were only for procreation.[48] This argument, exclusively based on physical structure, organs, and functions, might be a good argument for nonhuman animals whose sexual activity is limited by instinct and fertile periods ("heat"). Is it a good argument, however, for human animals, whose sexuality is not exclusively instinctual but is under the control of social, psychological, and personal factors? Whose fertility is restricted to a few days a month, and whose normal sexual feelings, desires, and activities occur more frequently than, and do not always coincide with, their fertile periods?[49]

Many Catholic and Christian theologians, informed by the insights of the human sciences, believe it is not. They believe that the bodily act of sexual intercourse between humans has a surplus of personal meaning beyond the physical. They see it as much more than an animal activity. They see it as an interpersonal language celebrating personal love and mutuality; a language acknowledging and enhancing the value of an other; a language in which a couple, mutually committed to each other, "make love." They acknowledge that, like any language, the language of sex must be learned with the utmost care, honesty, and ongoing fidelity. It is hardly surprising that with these changed premises, they would come to conclusions quite different from those drawn from a traditional approach.

The Stoic approach to sexual activity and its exclusive connection to marriage canonized marriage in the Western tradition as a *procreative institution*, an institution whose primary end was procreation. Other ends of marriage related to the spouses were acknowledged, but they were secondary to procreation, and the primary end–secondary end hierarchy dominated the Catholic approach to marriage for centuries. The great Protestant theologian Karl Barth once complained that the traditional Christian doctrine of marriage, both Catholic and Protestant, situated marriage in juridical rather than in theological categories.[50] The Roman Catholic Church corrected that imbalance in 1965. The history of marriage in the Catholic tradition has progressed from a model of *procreative institution*, in which procreation is everything, to a model of *interpersonal union*, in which the relationship and love between the spouses is the foundation of both the marriage and the sacrament of marriage. There is no evidence that this theological shift was in any way influenced by the human sciences, but almost forty years later the social-scientific evidence is overwhelming.

The genuine procreation of children, which always intended and continues to intend their education and nurture beyond mere biological generation, which intends human motherhood and fatherhood beyond mere biological maternity and paternity, depends on the happiness and stability of the relationship between the spouses/parents. Divorce is a result of the breakdown of the relationship between the spouses, and it is now beyond debate that divorce is bad for children.[51] For those parents who successfully progress beyond maternity and paternity to genuine motherhood and fatherhood, thus successfully nurturing children into functioning adults, in thirty years their children are grown up and they still have twenty to thirty years to live together. That living together will be successful only if the relationship between the spouses has been a loving and faithful one for the whole of life. If for no other reason than that, it is time for the Church's exclusive preoccupation with the act of intercourse and procreation to yield to interpersonal reality; it is time for the Church to preoccupy itself not with procreation but with positive marital relationship.

It is time to return our discussion to the claim that the sexual act must always take place exclusively within marriage. It is not a claim that anyone who knows the social-scientific evidence would challenge; inductive experience shows that, for most human beings, all that is expected and desired from a mutually self-giving relationship is best delivered in that stable relationship we call marriage.[52] The question arises, however, why it is that the sexual act must always take place exclusively within marriage. We submit that sexual intercourse so radically involves all the potentials of a human person that it is best expressed and safeguarded in *a stable and lasting relationship* between two people. That stable, lasting, and legally guaranteed relationship has traditionally been called marriage.

What has happened in the modern age is that those couples whom we call nuptial cohabitors are beginning their stable marital, including their sexual, relationship prior to their wedding ceremony. They are committed to each other, though they have not articulated that commitment in legal, public ritual; they fully intend to marry when the psychological and, especially, the economic restrictions modern society puts upon their right to marry are removed. Their nuptial cohabitation, perhaps even their betrothed or engaged cohabitation, is the first "little step" in their journey toward marriage.[53] In the canonical words of the received tradition, their engagement or betrothal *initiates* their marriage; their subsequent ceremonial wedding, before or after the birth of a child, *consummates* their marriage and makes it indissoluble. Since their betrothal however expressed, and we would prefer that it be expressed in a public ritual, initiates their marriage, their cohabitation is no more premarital than that of a pre-Tridentine and pre-Harwicke couple.[54] Their cohabitation and intercourse are certainly pre–wedding ceremonial, but that is not to say they are, therefore, also premarital.

A major change in the approach of Catholic ethicists to sexual sin parallels the change in the approach to marriage.[55] The majority of Catholic ethicists have agreed for years that decisions of morality or immorality in sexual ethics should be based on the context of *interpersonal relationship* and not merely on *physical acts* like masturbation, petting, and premarital, marital, and extramarital sexual intercourse, both heterosexual and homosexual.[56] Cahill argues, "A truly humane interpretation of procreation, pleasure and intimacy will set their moral implications in the context of enduring personal relationships, not merely individual sexual acts."[57] Serious immorality, what is traditionally called mortal sin, is not decided on the basis of an individual act against "nature," that is, the biological, physical, natural processes common to all animals. It is decided on the basis of human goods, human relationships built upon them, and human flourishing. Cahill suggests such human goods as "equality, intimacy, and fulfillment as moral criteria."[58] We would add the virtues of love and justice, to make more fully explicit what she clearly intends. Sexuality has three bodily meanings: intimacy of bodily contact, even bodily interpenetration; pleasure; and reproduction or procreation. Immoral or less than moral behavior is defined not exclusively by any sexual act related to these three, but rather by any act that is less than loving, just, equal, compassionate, and mutually fulfilling.

In the case of nuptial cohabitors, a man and a woman who are deeply committed to each other, and perhaps already engaged to marry, and whose pre-wedding but nuptial sexual intercourse takes place in this context of personal commitment to a future marriage, the moral theological argument proceeds along these lines. A man and a woman have a fundamental freedom to marry. Modern society has established socioeconomic structures for marriage that the couple are presently unable to achieve. These circumstances surrounding the intercourse of this couple who are deeply committed to each other, who are in right relationship to both each other and to God, and who fully intend to marry, "may render their premarital intercourse . . . not a moral evil." That such intercourse is not a moral evil would appear to be true especially, Philip Keane argues, "when the committed couple whose rights are unreasonably prejudiced by society do not experience themselves as genuinely free to take the more ideal route of abstaining from that intercourse that cannot be publicly proclaimed as part of a marriage."[59]

We accept the probative value of this argument. In the proposal we are presenting, however, the mutually committed nuptial cohabiting couple is already, if only inchoately, married, and their intercourse, therefore, is not strictly premarital but inchoately marital, as it was in the pre-Tridentine Catholic Church and pre-Hardwicke England. Our proposal envisages a marital journey that is initiated by mutual commitment and consent, and is lived in mutual love, justice, equality, intimacy, and fulfillment in a nuptial cohabitation pointed to a wedding that consummates the *process* of becoming married in a public manner. In such a process, we believe, sexual intercourse meets the legitimate Catholic and social requirement that the sexual act must take place exclusively within the confines of a stable marriage.

COMPLEMENTARITY AND NUPTIAL COHABITATION

As we have already seen, complementarity has recently emerged as a foundational concept for Catholic sexual teaching. While we critiqued John Paul II's and the Magisterium's sine qua non, foundational heterogenital complementarity, and posited an alternative "holistic complementarity"—the integration of orientation, personal, and biological complementarity—we did not explicitly comment on the evolving nature of complementarity. The issue of nuptial cohabitation and its relationship to the sacrament of marriage provides us an occasion to do so.

There is both a classicist and a historically conscious view of complementarity in the writings of John Paul II and the Magisterium. The classicist view of complementarity, which defines the essence of human "nature," is reflected in the Genesis accounts whereby God creates humans male and female from the beginning. Male and female are "two ways of being a body" that "complete each other"; they are complementary in "self-consciousness," "self-determination," and "being conscious of the meaning of the body."[60] This complementarity between male and female is labeled elsewhere "ontological complementarity," that is, "it is only through the duality of the 'masculine' and the 'feminine' that the 'human' finds full realization."[61] Kelly accurately notes that "ontological complementarity maintains that the distinction between men and women has been so designed by God that they complement each other, not just in their genital sexual faculties but also in their minds and hearts and in the particular qualities and skills they bring to life, and specifically to family life."[62] In the ontological order, John Paul II teaches, "it is only in the union of two sexually different persons that the individual can achieve perfection in a synthesis of unity and mutual psychophysical completion."[63] In the ontological "givenness" of masculinity and femininity, complementarity is essentialist and classicist.

At the same time, John Paul teaches, man and woman "*become a gift for each other*," forming an "interpersonal relationship" in marriage "that has to be *continually developed*."[64] This *becoming* a gift and *continually developing* an interpersonal relationship through reciprocal complementarity is a historically conscious, progressive, evolving, interpersonal reality, realized in both marriage and conjugal acts.[65] We refer to the historically conscious dimension of complementarity as *existential complementarity*, since it recognizes the specific corporeality of ontological complementarity in a particular, evolving, corporeal, and interpersonal relationship. For John Paul II and magisterial teaching, ontological complementarity is classicist in defining essential human nature, and existential complementarity is historically conscious in defining its evolving nature in an interpersonal relationship.

These two conceptual notions of complementarity are summed up by the Pontifical Council for the Family: "that man and woman are called upon from the beginning to live in a communion of life and love and that this complementarity *will lead to strengthening* the human dignity of the spouses, the good of the children and of society itself."[66] In this statement, there is a tension between two notions of complementarity, the ontological and existential, that have a bearing on defining the sacrament of marriage in light of the historical practice of betrothal in the Christian tradition and the contemporary cultural practice of prenuptial cohabitation, which can be posed as follows. What is the relationship between the ontological complementarity of male and female human "nature" and its existential realization and manifestation in the particular interpersonal relationship between two people in history? What effects the transformation of the universality of complementarity in its essential "nature" to the particularity of complementarity shared between two people in an interpersonal relationship? Investigating the sacrament of marriage from a classicist and historically conscious perspective sheds light on these questions.

MARRIAGE AS SACRAMENT

The Catholic Church has long suffered from what Guindon referred to as a "sacramental automatism," and this is especially apparent in the sacrament of marriage with regard to both consent and to consummation.[67] Marital sacramental automatism is the idea that "the initiation of marriage is a single event," which "tacitly sanctions a vertical, external, and mechanical version of grace . . . which descends on the couple once the formulae of consent and blessing have been heard."[68] According to this view, in Catholic tradition the sacrament of marriage and the grace the couple receives from the sacrament begin *only* at the moment the sacrament is celebrated, that is, at the moment of the exchange of consent. While the exchange of consent at the wedding is certainly an important point in time to remember, sacramentally, theologically, historically, and experientially, an exclusive focus on it overlooks the evolving nature of consent that is "exchanged gradually" from the beginning of the couple's relationship.[69]

Similarly, in canon law, consummation is a single act that ratifies a marriage and makes it indissoluble. This understanding of consummation gives a single act of sexual intercourse the "power to achieve a crucial transformation in the relationship in the sight of God," and consummated relationships cannot be undone.[70] The notion of consent and consummation in the Code of Canon Law and the sacramental theology there represented highlight the difference between canon law and juridical relationship and theology and interpersonal and experiential relationship. There is a tension, if not a disconnect, between canon law, theology, and human experience. It is incomplete and misleading, experientially, interpersonally, and therefore theologically, to claim that a sacramental marriage begins only at this specific point in time. From the canonical perspective, both consent and consummation are single acts given an absolute significance for defining the nature of the relationship between two human beings. This emphasis on the single act and its singularly important meaning is a classicist approach. Marriage and sacrament, however, are not single acts; they are unfolding events in an interpersonal and unfolding relationship. Such interpersonal events are more adequately reflected on from a historically conscious perspective.

CATECHUMENATE FOR MARRIAGE

To combat sacramental, consensual, and consummational automatism, Adrian Thatcher proposes a "Catechumenate for Marriage," which helps to elucidate a historically conscious view of marriage as sacrament.[71] A catechumen is a person receiving religious instruction in the Christian faith with a view to being baptized, and the catechumenate is the body of catechumens awaiting baptism and full initiation into the Church. Historically, catechumens preparing for baptism in the Christian community were considered already inchoate Christians, in the sense that they had already made their commitment in faith to Christ. A catechumen who died before baptism would be given a Christian burial.[72] Though the sacrament of water baptism had not been administered, baptism of desire had been, and the grace of God was already offered to the catechumen in the inchoate but not completed journey of the catechumenate.

According to Thatcher, the term *catechumenate* when used in relation to marriage "is intended to emphasize the parallels between the 'in-between' state of believing Christians seeking baptism, and the 'in-between' state of persons who are no longer single and who wish to bind themselves to one another unreservedly in marriage."[73] Nuptial cohabitation is a modern rite of passage. Nuptial cohabitors, who prior to their cohabitation were in a fixed *single* state, in their cohabitation enter into an "in-between," liminal state, neither single nor fully married. Their wedding ceremony aggregates them into the new fixed state of married.[74] Implementing the catechumenate for marriage "requires a paradigm shift, from treating the ceremony as the beginning of marriage, to treating it as the confirmation, celebration, and blessing of it."[75] In our terms, this is a paradigm shift from the discontinuity between engagement and marriage as discrete events, to the continuity between nuptial betrothal and marriage as events that are part of a marital process. It is the maturation of both their relationship and their faith during their nuptial cohabitation that permits a couple's relationship to attain progressively to the fullness of marriage and, therefore, also sacrament.

The proposed catechumenate for marriage views the transformation from ontological to existential complementarity as a gradual process that begins with betrothal and is confirmed, celebrated, and blessed in the wedding ceremony. This process includes the complementarity between two people in all their human dimensions—biological, psychological, affective, emotional, spiritual—that begins with betrothal and is expressed in sexual acts as well as in an infinite number of other acts that constitute interpersonal relationship. Furthermore, in our model of holistic complementarity, this process is extended to both heterosexual and homosexual couples, depending on whether a person's sexual orientation is heterosexual or homosexual.[76] We defined complementarity as "a multifaceted quality—orientational, physical, affective, personal, and spiritual—possessed by every person, that draws him or her into relationship with another human being, including into the lifelong relationship of marriage, so that both may grow, individually and as a couple, into human well-being and human flourishing." We specify here that existential complementarity is an ever-evolving reality that not only precedes the wedding but also extends far beyond it. In historical consciousness, both existential complementarity and the sacrament of marriage are evolving realities.

CONCLUSION

We can summarize the argument we have been developing in this chapter via the presentation of a schematic proposal. We propose that an option for the process of marrying in the Catholic Church revert to the process accepted in the Church prior to the Council of Trent. That process is as follows.

(A) *Betrothal*, or, in the pre-Tridentine language, *sponsalia*. The betrothal, for which a ritual highlighting free consent to wed in the future could be developed, would be witnessed and blessed on behalf of the church community, preferably, though not necessarily, by a parish priest. The betrothal ritual would differ from the present wedding ceremony only in the fact that the consent would be a consent to marry in the future. Such betrothal, as it did before, would confer on the couple the status of committed spouses with all the rights that the Church grants to spouses, including the right to sexual intercourse. The betrothal ceremony would function also as public enrollment in the catechumenate for marriage. Theologically this marriage catechumenate would be as much a time of grace as the baptismal catechumenate; as baptismal catechumens are already inchoate Christians, so also marriage catechumens are already inchoate spouses.

(B) *Nuptial cohabitation.* In this period, the couple would live together as spouses, would have marital intercourse, including sexual intercourse, with each other in a stable environment, and would continue the lifelong process of establishing their marital relationship as one of love, justice, equality, intimacy, and mutual fulfillment. This inchoate marriage period would be a perfect time for the Church community to assist the couple in honing both their relationship and their faith with an ongoing marriage preparation program aimed precisely at this maturation.[77] This pre-wedding period of marital instruction is the marriage catechumenate, analogous to the established prebaptism period of doctrinal instruction required of catechumens prior to their baptism. It is theologically unthinkable that either catechumenate could happen without the grace of God. Given the expected lifelong character of Christian marriage, the marriage catechumenate is vitally important, for social scientific data indicates that relationship is both the core of long-term spousal and parental success and a reality that can be dangerously flawed by both the self-selecting factors that directed the couple to cohabitation in the first place and the experience of cohabitation itself.

(C) *Fertility.* We are fully conscious that this is the part of our proposal that can cause the most unease among Christians of all denominations. Sexuality and sexual activity have been treated with suspicion in the Christian churches since the days of the early, Stoic-influenced Christians. That suspicion led to the exclusive focus on procreation that once characterized the Church and continues to characterize it even now, when moral approaches among many of its leading thinkers have changed. We have argued, in concert with other Catholic scholars, that this focus on procreation needs to yield to another focus, namely, the focus on the interpersonal relationship at the very root of all spousal and parental success in marriage and family. We stand by what we argued earlier: the moral implications of sexual intercourse, sexual pleasure, and procreation leading to parenthood are best set in the context of stable interpersonal relationship and not in the context of occasional, casual sexual acts. The context of the nuptial cohabitors with whom we are concerned in this chapter is a context of committed, stable, and intentionally lifelong relationship. It is a context that meets the Catholic requirement that sexual intercourse be exclusively within the stable relationship of marriage. It is also a context in which the three dimensions of sexual activity we have mentioned—personal and not just bodily intercourse, mutual pleasure, and procreation leading to not only the biological birth of children but also long-term motherhood and fatherhood—might intersect to the benefit of the relationship. Parenthood, particularly maternal and paternal shared parenthood, expresses and realizes the union of the spouses as much as intercourse and pleasure. In our proposal, it can be the task of nuptial cohabitors as much as of married couples in the received tradition.

(D) *Wedding.* There will come a time when the committed nuptial cohabitors have overcome the socioeconomic restrictions imposed on them by society. There will come a time when their relationship has reached such a level of interpersonal communion that they will wish to ritualize their loving, just, and symmetrical relationship. That is the time for their wedding, when, with their families, friends, and Christian community, they will renew their consent and celebrate their union for what it has become, a symbol or sacrament of the loving union between God and God's people, between Christ and Christ's church. Their wedding can then be considered the consummation of their marriage, the consummation of a relationship they have sought to make as humane and as Christian as possible. The process of marrying would then be complete; consummated marriage would become consummated and ratified marriage.

QUESTIONS FOR REFLECTION

1. What do you understand by the word *cohabitation?* In your judgment, what are the reasons for the great growth of cohabitation in the Western world?

2. This chapter distinguished between *nuptial* and *non-nuptial* cohabitors. Does your experience confirm or reject this as a realistic distinction? Is it true that cohabitation before marriage increases the risk of divorce after marriage?

3. What do you understand by *commitment?* What are the requirements for and implications of commitment for every relationship, including marriage?

4. Has the legal wedding ceremony as we know it today in the Western world always been practiced in the Catholic Church in its present form? If not, why and when did it arise? How did the early practice of betrothal fit into the Catholic notion of marriage?

5. What are the implications of our distinction between classicism and historical consciousness for the sacrament of marriage?

6. What is your judgment about our suggestion that *nuptial cohabitation,* perhaps following engagement or betrothal, is a beginning stage in the process of becoming married and is a sufficiently stable marital stage for sexual intercourse to be moral? Would you personally be interested in enrolling in a pre-marriage catechumenate, with or without the betrothal ceremony we suggest?

7. What other questions arise for you from reading this chapter?

Notes

NOTES

1. Emmanuel Ntakarutimana, "Being a Child in Central Africa Today," in *Little Children Suffer*, ed. Maureen Junker-Kenny and Norbert Mette (London: SCM Press, 1996), 15.
2. Kevin T. Kelly, "Cohabitation: Living in Sin or Occasion of Grace?" *Furrow* 56 (2005): 652.
3. See USCCB Committee on Doctrine, "Inadequacies in the Theological Methodology and Conclusions of *The Sexual Person: Toward a Renewed Catholic Anthropology* by Todd A. Salzman and Michael G. Lawler" (September 15, 2010), http://old.usccb.org/doctrine/Sexual_Person_2010-09-15.pdf (accessed January 2, 2012).
4. Larry L. Bumpass, "What's Happening to the Family? Interactions between Demographic and Institutional Change," *Demography* 27 (1990): 486; Larry L. Bumpass, *The Declining Significance of Marriage: Changing Family Life in the United States* (Madison: University of Wisconsin-Madison: Center for Demography and Ecology, 1995), 8; Larry L. Bumpass and Hsien-Hen Lu, *Trends in Cohabitation and Implications for Children's Family Contexts* (Madison: University of Wisconsin-Madison: Center for Demography and Ecology, 1998), 7; Larry L. Bumpass and James A. Sweet, "National Estimates of Cohabitation," *Demography* 26 (1989): 619; Larry L. Bumpass, James A. Sweet, and Andrew Cherlin, "The Role of Cohabitation in Declining Rates of Marriage," *Journal of Marriage and the Family* 53 (1991): 914; Center for Marriage and Family, *Time, Sex, and Money: The First Five Years of Marriage* (Omaha: Creighton University, Center for Marriage and Family, 2000); David Popenoe and Barbara Dafoe Whitehead, *Should We Live Together? What Young Adults Need to Know about Cohabitation before Marriage* (Rutgers: State University of New Jersey, The National Marriage Project, 1999), 6; Linda J. Waite, ed., *The Ties That Bind* (New York: De Gruyter, 2000).
5. John Haskey, "Patterns of Marriage, Divorce, and Cohabitation in the Different Countries of Europe," *Population Trends* 69 (1992): 27–36; F. Hopflinger, "The Future of Household and Family Structures in Europe," seminar on present demographic trends and lifestyles in Europe, Council of Europe, Strasbourg, 1991; Louis Roussel, *La famille incertaine* (Paris: Editions Odile Jacob, 1989); Hans-Joachim Hoffmann-Nowotny, "The Future of the Family," in *European Population Conference 1987* (Helsinki: IUSSP, Central Statistical Office of Finland, 1987); John Haskey, "Pre-marital Cohabitation and the Probability of Subsequent Divorce: Analyses Using the New Data from the General Household Survey," *Population Trends* 68 (1992): 10–19; Oystein Kravdal, "Does Marriage Require a Stronger Economic Underpinning than Informal Cohabitation?" *Population Studies* 53 (1999): 63–80; Neil G. Bennett, Ann Klimas Blanc, and David E. Bloom, "Commitment and the Modern Union: Assessing the Link between Premarital Cohabitation and Subsequent Marital Stability," *American Sociological Review* 53 (1988): 127–38; Ann-Zofie E. Duvander, "The Transition from Cohabitation to Marriage: A Longitudinal Study of the Propensity to Marry in Sweden in the Early 1990s,"

Journal of Family Issues 20 (1999): 698–717; Aart C. Liefbroer, "The Choice between a Married or Unmarried First Union by Young Adults," *European Journal of Population* 7 (1991): 273–98; Aart C. Liefbroer and Jenny De Jong Gierveld, "The Impact of Rational Considerations and Perceived Opinions on Young Adults' Union Formation Intentions," *Journal of Family Issues* 14 (1993): 213–35; Henri Leridon, "Cohabitation, Marriage, Separation: An Analysis of Life Histories of French Cohorts from 1968 to 1985," *Population Studies* 44 (1990): 127–44; Ron Lesthaeghe, Guy Moors, and Loek Halman, "Living Arrangements and Values among Young Adults in the Netherlands, Belgium, France and Germany, 1990," paper presented at the annual meetings of the Population Association of America, Cincinnati, April 1–3, 1993; Charles Hobart and Frank Grigel, "Cohabitation among Canadian Students at the End of the Eighties," *Journal of Comparative Family Studies* 23 (1992): 311–37; T. R. Balakrishnan, K. V. Rao, Evelyne Lapierre-Adamcyk, and Karol J. Krotki, "A Hazard Model Analysis of the Covariates of Marriage Dissolution in Canada," *Demography* 24 (1987): 395–406; Michael Bracher, Gigi Santow, S. Philip Morgan, and James Trussell, "Marriage Dissolution in Australia: Models and Explanations," *Population Studies* 47 (1993): 403–25.

6. Bumpass and Sweet, "National Estimates of Cohabitation," *Demography* 26 (1989): 615–25; Bumpass and Lu, *Trends in Cohabitation.*

7. Bumpass, *Declining Significance of Marriage*; Larry L. Bumpass, R. Kelly Raley, and James A. Sweet, "The Changing Character of Stepfamilies: Implications of Cohabitation and Nonmarital Childbearing," *Demography* 32 (1995): 425–36; Bumpass and Sweet, "National Estimates of Cohabitation," 615–30; Bumpass, Sweet, and Cherlin, "Role of Cohabitation," 913–27; Arland Thornton, "Cohabitation and Marriage in the 1980s," *Demography* 25 (1988): 497–508; William G. Axinn and Arland Thornton, "The Relationship between Cohabitation and Divorce: Selectivity or Causal Influence," *Demography* 29 (1992): 357–74; Robert Schoen, "First Unions and the Stability of First Marriages," *Journal of Marriage and Family* 54 (1992): 281–84; Elizabeth Thomson and Ugo Colella, "Cohabitation and Marital Stability," *Journal of Marriage and Family* 54 (1992): 259–67; Neil G. Bennett, Ann Klimas Blanc, and David E. Bloom, "Commitment and the Modern Union: Assessing the Link between Premarital Cohabitation and Subsequent Marital Instability," *American Sociological Review* 53 (1988): 127–38; David R. Hall and John Z. Zhao, "Cohabitation and Divorce in Canada: Testing the Selectivity Hypothesis," *Journal of Marriage and Family* 57 (1997): 421–27.

8. See, as an example replicated in diocesan policies across the United States, National Conference of Bishops, Committee on Marriage and Family, *Marriage Preparation and Cohabiting Couples* (Washington, DC: USCC, 1999), 10. See also Pontifical Council for the Family, *Marriage, Family, and De Facto Unions* (Roma: Typis Polyglottis Vaticanis, 2000), 4.

9. Schoen, "First Unions and the Stability of First Marriages," 283.

10. Susan McRae, "Cohabitation: A Trial Run for Marriage?," *Sexual and Marital Therapy* 12 (1997): 259.

11. Lakeesha N. Woods and Robert E. Emery, "The Cohabitation Effect on Divorce: Causation or Selection?," *Journal of Divorce and Remarriage* 37 (2002): 101–21.

12. David de Vaus, Lixia Qu, and Ruth Weston, "Does Pre-marital Cohabitation Affect the Chances of Marriage Lasting?," paper presented at the Eighth Australian Institute of Family Studies Conference, Melbourne, February 2003. May be accessed at www.aifs.org.au.

13. Jay Teachman, "Premarital Sex, Premarital Cohabitation, and the Risk of Subsequent Marital Dissolution among Women," *Journal of Marriage and the Family* 65 (2002): 63.

14. Scott M. Stanley, communication to the Smart Marriages website, April 21, 2003, www.smartmarriages.com.

15. Linda J. Waite, "Cohabitation: A Communitarian Perspective," in *Marriage in America: A Communitarian Perspective*, ed. Martin King Whyte (Lanham, MD: Rowman and Littlefield, 2000), 26.

16. Ibid., 18. See also Steven L. Nock, "A Comparison of Marriages and Cohabiting Relationships," *Journal of Family Issues* 16 (1995): 53; Susan L. Brown and Alan Booth, "Cohabitation versus Marriage: A Comparison of Relationship Quality," *Journal of Marriage and the Family* 58 (1996): 668–78; Susan L. Brown, "Relationship Quality Dynamics," *Journal of Family Issues* 24 (2003): 583–601; David Popenoe and Barbara Defoe Whitehead, "Ten Important Research Findings on Marriage and Choosing a Marriage Partner," http://marriage.rutgers.edu (November 2004), Research Note 6.

17. See National Marriage Project, *The State of Our Unions 2001* (Rutgers: State University of New Jersey, 2001) for the variety of reasons that people cohabit.

18. Paula Y. Goodwin, William D. Moshe, and Anjani Chandra, "Marriage and Cohabitation in the United States: A Statistical Portrait Based on Cycle 6 (2002) of the National Survey of Family Growth," *Vital and Health Statistics* 23 (2010), www.cdc.gov/nchs/data/series/sr 23/sr23 028 (accessed January 4, 2012).

19. See www.smartmarriages.com/app/newsletter (accessed May 24, 2010).

20. *FC*, 13.

21. Kelly, "Cohabitation: Living in Sin or Occasion of Grace?," 652.

22. Scott M. Stanley, *The Power of Commitment: A Guide to Active, Lifelong Love* (San Francisco: Jossey-Bass, 2005), 23; emphasis added.

23. Ibid., 24.

24. See Blaine Fowers, *Beyond the Myth of Marital Happiness* (San Francisco: Jossey-Bass, 2000).

25. Stanley, *Power of Commitment*, 24.

26. Ibid., 62–63.

27. Ibid., 93–95. See also W. Bradford Wilcox, *Soft Patriarchs, New Men: How Christianity Shapes Fathers and Husbands* (Chicago: University of Chicago Press, 2004); Wilcox and Steven L. Nock, "What's Love Got to Do with It? Equality, Equity, Commitment, and Women's Marital Quality," *Social Forces* 84 (2006): 1321–45.

28. Stanley, *Power of Commitment*, 126.
29. Ibid., 176–79.
30. See Second Vatican Council, GS, 44, 58, 59, and especially 62. John Paul II frequently teaches that the cultural situation is a major source for theological reflection. He explains that "since God's plan for marriage and family touches men and women in the concreteness of their daily existence in specific social and cultural situations, the Church ought to apply herself to understanding the situations within which marriage and family are lived today, in order to fulfill her task of serving" (FC, 4). Elsewhere he states that "a faith which does not become culture is a faith not fully accepted, not entirely thought out, not faithfully lived" (*L'Osservatore Romano*, March 8, 1982, 8).
31. See Michael G. Lawler, "Toward a Theology of Christian Family," in Lawler, *Marriage and the Catholic Church: Disputed Questions* (Collegeville, MN: Liturgical Press, 2002), 193–219.
32. It is of note that in 1996, under the pressure of the movement to legalize same-sex marriages, the United States Congress passed the Defense of Marriage Act, which repeated the assertions of these Roman definitions that marriage was a union between a man and a woman.
33. Jean Remy, "The Family: Contemporary Models and Historical Perspective," in *The Family in Crisis or Transition, Concilium* 121, ed. Andrew Greeley (New York: Seabury, 1979), 9.
34. See Ntakarutimana, "Being a Child in Central Africa Today," 15; Michel Legrain, *Mariage chrétien, modèle unique? Questions venues d'Afrique* (Paris: Chalet, 1978).
35. Lawrence Stone, *The Family, Sex, and Marriage in England: 1500–1800* (London: Weidenfeld and Nicolson, 1979), 626.
36. Alan Macfarlane, *Marriage and Love in England: Modes of Reproduction 1300–1840* (Oxford: Blackwell, 1987), 291.
37. G. R. Quaife, *Wanton Wives and Wayward Wenches: Peasants and Illicit Sex in Early Seventeenth Century England* (London: Croom Helm, 1979), 59.
38. Ibid., 61.
39. *DS*, 1813–16.
40. This chapter focuses on heterosexual cohabitation. The conclusions reached here, however, apply *mutatis mutandi*, to homosexual cohabitation.
41. Adrian Thatcher, *Marriage after Modernity: Christian Marriage in Postmodern Times* (Sheffield, UK: Academic Press, 1999), 119; emphasis in original.
42. André Guindon, "Case for a 'Consummated' Sexual Bond before a 'Ratified' Marriage," *Eglise et Théologie* 8 (1977), 137–82; Legrain, *Mariage chrétien*.
43. Legrain, *Mariage chrétien*, 62.
44. Ibid., 77.
45. Jean-Claude Kaufmann coined a perfect phrase to describe this stage theory, "*couple à petits pas*," couple by small steps. See his *Sociologie du couple* (Paris: Presses Universitaires de France, 1993), 44. The phrase was picked up by Pierre-Olivier Bressoud in his *Eglise et couple à petits pas* (Fribourg: Editions Universitaires Fribourg Suisse, 1998).

46. *PH*, 7.
47. See Christine E. Gudorf, *Body, Sex, and Pleasure: Reconstructing Christian Sexual Ethics* (Cleveland: Pilgrim Press, 1994), 29–50.
48. See, for instance, Clement of Alexandria, *Stromatum*, 3, 23, PG 8, 1086 and 1090; Origen, *In Gen Hom*, 3, 6, PG 12, 180; Augustine, *De Gen ad Litt*, 9, 7, 12, PL 34, 397; *De Bono Coniug*, 24, 32, PL 40, 394; *De Bono Coniug*, 9, 9, PL 40, 380.
49. See Joan Roughgarden, *Evolution's Rainbow: Diversity, Nature, and Sexuality in Nature and in People* (Berkeley and Los Angeles: University of California Press, 2004).
50. Karl Barth, *Church Dogmatics* (Edinburgh: T. and T. Clark, 1961), vol. 3, pt. 4, 186.
51. See Judith S. Wallerstein and Sandra Blakeslee, *Second Chances: Men, Women, and Children a Decade after Divorce* (New York: Ticknor and Fields, 1989); Judith S. Wallerstein, "Children of Divorce: Preliminary Report of a Ten-Year Follow-Up of Older Children and Adolescents," *Journal of the American Academy of Child Psychiatry* 24 (1985), 545–53; Judith S. Wallerstein, Julia M. Lewis, and Sandra Blakeslee, *The Unexpected Legacy of Divorce: A 25 Year Landmark Study* (New York: Hyperion, 2000); Sara McLanahan and Gary Sandefur, *Growing Up with a Single Parent* (Cambridge: Harvard University Press, 1994), 65–68.
52. See, for instance, Carl Rogers, *Becoming Partners: Marriage and Its Alternatives* (New York: Delacorte Press, 1972); McLanahan and Sandefur, *Growing Up with a Single Parent*.
53. Bressoud, *Eglise et couples a petits pas*; and "Eglise catholique et couples non mariés: Suggestions en vue d'une réévaluation théologique," *INTAMS Review* 6 (2000): 105–9. The latter piece is a contribution to a debate on cohabitation that includes essays from Lisa Sowle Cahill ("Living Together, Christian Morality, and Pastoral Care") and Hubert Windisch ("Ehe-Wege").
54. See Michael G. Lawler, "A Marital Catechumenate: A Proposal," *INTAMS Review* 13 (2007): 161–77.
55. See Kelly, "Cohabitation: Living in Sin or Occasion of Grace?," 652–58.
56. Christine E. Gudorf, *Body, Sex, and Pleasure*, 14–18; Charles E. Curran, "Sexuality and Sin: A Current Appraisal," in *Moral Theology No. 8: Dialogue about Catholic Sexual Teaching*, eds. Charles E. Curran and Richard A. McCormick (New York; Paulist, 1993), 411–14; Vincent Genovesi, *In Pursuit of Love: Catholic Morality and Human Sexuality* (Wilmington, DE: Glazier, 1987), 154–55; Philip Keane, *Sexual Morality: A Catholic View* (New York: Paulist, 1977), 98; Xavier Lacroix, *Le corps de chair: Les dimensions éthique, esthétique, et spirituelle de l'amour* (Paris: Editions du Cerf, 1992), 346–50.
57. Lisa Sowle Cahill, *Sex, Gender and Christian Ethics* (New York: Cambridge University Press, 1996), 112.
58. Ibid., 11.
59. Philip Keane, *Sexual Morality*, 107.
60. John Paul II, *The Theology of the Body: Human Love in the Divine Plan*, foreword by John S. Grabowski (Boston: Pauline, 1997), 48.

COHABITATION AND THE PROCESS OF MARRYING

61. Ibid.; emphasis in original; *FC*, 19. It is important to note that the distinction between biological sex (male/female) and socially conditioned gender (masculine/feminine) is frequently absent in magisterial discussions of complementarity. See Susan A. Ross, "The Bridegroom and the Bride: The Theological Anthropology of John Paul II and Its Relation to the Bible and Homosexuality," in *Sexual Diversity and Catholicism: Toward the Development of Moral Theology*, ed. Patricia Beattie Jung with Joseph Andrew Coray (Collegeville, MN: Liturgical Press, 2001), 56, n. 5.

62. Kevin Kelly, *New Directions in Sexual Ethics* (London: Cassell, 1999), 51. Kelly goes on to critique ontological complementarity as ultimately "oppressive and deterministic" (52).

63. John Paul II, "Authentic Concept of Conjugal Love," *Origins* 28 (1999): 655–56.

64. John Paul II, *Theology of the Body*, 58; emphasis added; John Paul II, *FC*, 66; Pontifical Council for the Family, *Preparation for the Sacrament of Marriage*, 1996, 46, www.cin.org/vatcong/prepmarr.html.

65. John Paul II, "Authentic Concept of Conjugal Love," 655–56.

66. Pontifical Council for the Family, *Preparation for the Sacrament of Marriage*, 7. Emphasis added.

67. Guindon, "Case for a 'Consummated' Sexual Bond," 157.

68. Adrian Thatcher, *Living Together and Christian Ethics: New Studies in Christian Ethics* (Cambridge: Cambridge University Press, 2002), 217.

69. Ibid., 249.

70. Ibid., 228.

71. Ibid., ch. 8.

72. Ibid., 242.

73. Ibid., 252.

74. See Arnold Van Gennep, *The Rites of Passage* (London: Routledge and Kegan Paul, 1960).

75. Thatcher, *Living Together and Christian Ethics*, 252.

76. We refer here only to same-sex *relationship*, not to the contemporary concept of same-sex *marriage*. In this book, we repeat, we do not enter into the discussion of same-sex marriage. The possible implications of our foundational principle for same-sex marriage remain to be worked out.

77. See Center for Marriage and Family, *Marriage Preparation in the Catholic Church: Getting It Right* (Omaha: Creighton University, 1995); Scott M. Stanley, "Making a Case for Premarital Education," *Family Relations* 50 (2001): 272–80.

CHAPTER 5

Homosexuality

One sexual issue is today tearing the Christian churches apart. It is the issue of homosexuality. In this chapter we consider this issue in the context of scripture and the Catholic moral tradition interpreted in contemporary historical context. Our approach is that mapped out by Pope Benedict XVI when he was Professor Joseph Ratzinger. "Not everything that exists in the Church must for that reason be also a legitimate tradition. . . . There is a distorting, as well as legitimate, tradition . . . [and] . . . [c]onsequently tradition must not be considered only affirmatively but also critically."[1] We critically reflect on traditional teaching on homosexuality and propose a revised norm in light of that reflection.

The theological tools for this critical reflection draw from four sources of moral knowledge, scripture, tradition, reason, and experience.[2] Traditionally, Catholic moral theology has relied upon these four sources of moral knowledge in developing its natural-law approach and to formulate norms guiding human behavior. Both traditionalists and revisionists have recourse to these four sources. What distinguishes these two groups in their approaches to ethics in general, and in the issue of homosexual acts in particular, is their interpretation and prioritization of those sources. Traditionalists use a hierarchical approach to the sources of moral knowledge and tend to interpret tradition in the narrow sense of magisterial teaching, especially as this teaching pertains to moral absolutes. Scripture, reason, and experience, in that order, are all subject to the Magisterium's interpretation. Revisionists, while assigning a very important role to tradition, understand it in a broad sense to include the Magisterium and the other aspects that make up an ecclesiastical tradition, and they use a dialectical approach among the four sources of moral knowledge. There is a presumption of truth in favor of magisterial teaching, but that teaching is to be critically reflected upon in light of theologically sound scriptural exegesis, the reasonable input of science in areas where it has competence, and the cultural, historical, and relational experiences of the faithful. When there is a conflict between these sources, a process of research, dialogue, and discernment must be undertaken to determine where truth resides. This is a complex and involved process, which takes time, patience, and a commitment to dialogue.[3]

The received tradition of the Catholic Church condemns homosexual acts as "intrinsically disordered" and gravely immoral and does so on the basis of three foundations.[4] First, the teaching of scripture in which such acts "are condemned as a serious depravity and even presented as the sad consequence of rejecting God;" second, "the constant teaching of the magisterium;" third, "the moral sense of the Christian people."[5] That theological tradition is not, and cannot be, in question in any contemporary discussion. Following Ratzinger, however, and the scientific and experiential insights available to us, that tradition can be and must be approached critically, to clarify its foundation and continued meaningfulness in the changed circumstances of the contemporary world. The clarification of each foundation is sought in this chapter. While we respect the theological tradition on this issue, on the basis of empirical theology and a dialogue between the sources of moral knowledge, we maintain that the teaching on the intrinsic immorality of homosexual acts represents a distorting tradition. We conclude by defending our principle of holistic complementarity and argue that *some* homosexual acts *may* be morally right.

THE BIBLE AND HOMOSEXUALITY

Since Christianity is a religion of the Book, Christians automatically turn to their Bible, believed to be the word of God, for guidance in ethical matters. The issue of homosexuality is no exception. The CDF turns to the Bible in its discussion of the "problem of homosexuality," and rhetorically asserts that "there is . . . a clear consistency within the sacred scriptures for judging the moral issue of homosexual behavior. The Church's doctrine regarding this issue is thus based, not only on isolated phrases taken out of context, from which could be developed uncertain theological arguments, but rather on the solid foundation of a constant biblical testimony."[6] It lists the texts on which this "solid foundation" is built: Genesis 19:1–11; Leviticus 18:22 and 20:13; Romans 1:26–27; 1 Corinthians 6:9; and 1 Timothy 1:10.[7] Interestingly, when the *Catechism of the Catholic Church* lists the biblical texts that present "homosexual acts as acts of great depravity," it omits the Leviticus texts.[8]

In the light of contemporary biblical scholarship, Catholic included, it is impossible to agree that the texts on which this Catholic tradition of the immorality of homosexual acts is based are "unambiguous" and provide "solid foundation." We believe that, when read as the Magisterium requires they be read, that is, in the "literary forms" of the writer's "time and culture," the texts that are advanced as a clear and unambiguous foundation of the Catholic teaching on homosexual acts are far from clear and unambiguous.[9] They are, rather, complex, historically conditioned literary forms that demand careful analysis that raises questions in the informed and inquiring theological minds of Catholic laypeople.

Three questions are central to this issue. First, does the Bible say anything about homosexuality as we understand it today? Second, if it does say something, what does it say and what does it mean? Third, can the Bible speak to and enlighten the confusion that characterizes contemporary Christian dialogue about homosexuality? Ultimately, the real issue in this section is one we confronted in our opening chapter; not what does the Bible say or not say about homosexuality, but how are we to read the Bible in order to inform our contemporary Christian lives? This issue is central as we confront our three questions in turn.

HOMOSEXUAL ORIENTATION AND THE BIBLE

The first question, does the Bible say anything about homosexuality as we understand it today, is really a question of definition. What do we mean today by the words *homosexuality* and *homosexual?* The answer to that question is embedded in what the sciences and the Magisterium now take for granted, namely, the distinction between homosexual *orientation* and homosexual *behavior*.[10] In contemporary scientific and theological literature, *homosexuality* and *homosexual* are used to refer to a person's *psychosexual condition*, produced by a mix of genetic, psychological, and social "loading," not to refer to a person's sexual behavior.[11] Sexual orientation is defined as "the sustained erotic attraction to members of one's own gender, the opposite gender, or both—homosexual, heterosexual, or bisexual respectively."[12] Homosexual orientation is "a *condition* characterized by an emotional and psycho-sexual propensity towards others of the same sex."[13] A homosexual is "a person who feels a most urgent sexual desire which *in the main* is directed towards gratification with the same sex."[14] In its modern connotation, homosexuality is a way of *being* before it is a way of *behaving*.

Neither the Bible nor the Christian tradition rooted in it prior to the twentieth century ever considered the homosexual condition; they took for granted that everyone was heterosexual. To look for any mention in the biblical texts of what today is called "homosexual orientation" is simply anachronism. One might as well search the Bible for advice on buying a car or a computer. The biblical passages most frequently cited as condemning *homosexuality* actually condemn homosexual *behaviors*, and they condemn these behaviors specifically as a *perversion* of the heterosexual condition they assume to be the natural condition of every human person. In its modern meaning, homosexuality is not and cannot be a perversion of the heterosexual condition, because homosexuals, by natural orientation, do not share that condition. Homosexuality is, rather, an *inversion* of the heterosexual condition, which psychosexual homosexuals, by no choice of their own, do not naturally share, and they cannot be held morally accountable for something they did not choose.[15]

The context in which both Testaments condemn homosexual behavior is a false assumption that all human beings naturally share the heterosexual condition and that, therefore, any homosexual behavior is a perversion of "nature" and immoral. Since that biblical assumption is now scientifically shown to be incorrect, the Bible has little to contribute to the discussion of homosexuality and homosexuals as we understand them today. That conclusion will become clearer when we consider our second question: What does the Bible say about homosexual behavior, and what does it mean when it says that?[16] We might add, with Edward Vacek, what is obvious, namely, that the Bible contains many moral teachings, on sex during menstruation, stoning adulterers, women's roles, slavery, and a host of others, all of which have been rejected by the modern Catholic Church.[17]

INTERPRETING THE BIBLE ON HOMOSEXUALITY

The Old Testament on Homosexuality

The single most influential strand in the Western tradition leading to the condemnation of homosexual acts is probably the *interpretation* given to the biblical story of Sodom. Western churches have taught that the fiery destruction of Sodom was caused by the immoral male homosexual behaviors practiced there, and understandably Christians have passively and uncritically believed what their churches taught. Sodom has even given its name to one form of male homosexual activity, *sodomy*. Two reasonable questions may be raised with respect to this widespread interpretation, the first about its accuracy, the second about its basis in the biblical text. Our contextual interpretation of the Bible will show that the homosexual interpretation of the Sodom story is not accurate and is not supported by a reading of the text in its historical and literary context.

The biblical story is not as straightforward as it appears to the untrained reader. The context of the story and its meaning begins not with Lot and the men of Sodom in chapter 19, but with the story of Abraham's hospitality to "three men," one of whom is identified as "the Lord," in chapter 18.[18] Three "men" pass by Abraham's tent on their way to Sodom, and Abraham offers the strangers the hospitality required by the Levitical law: "When a stranger sojourns with you in your land, you shall not do him wrong . . . you shall love him as yourself."[19] Abraham invites the strangers to his tent. "Let a little water be brought and wash your feet, and rest yourself under the tree while I fetch a morsel of bread that you may refresh yourselves."[20] Abraham has his wife, Sara, bake cakes for them; he kills a calf "tender and good" for them; and he himself serves them. Abraham's goodness is established by his hospitable reception of the three strangers, and so too is his nephew Lot's goodness established in the sequel. After they were fed, two of the men left for Sodom, while the Lord remained behind to have with Abraham the famous discussion about how many righteous men would be required to save Sodom from destruction.

The two "men," now identified as two "angels," "came to Sodom in the evening and Lot was sitting in the gate of Sodom."[21] Lot offered the two angels the required hospitality, bringing them to his house and feeding them, but before they retired for the night, the men of Sodom surrounded the house and called for Lot to bring the two men out "that we may know them (*yadha*)."[22] That word *yadha* is critical for understanding what the men of Sodom were asking. *Yadha* is the ordinary Hebrew word for the English *know*, as it is translated in the Revised Standard Version, but it is also used on occasion to mean specifically sexual intercourse. The question then is which meaning is intended in this text.

The Hebrew-English Lexicon of the Old Testament notes that *yadha* is used 943 times, and in only 10 of those instances is it used with any sexual connotation. Taking his stance on this datum, G. A. Barton argues that in this text it is not clear that *yadha* is to be interpreted in its sexual connotation and that it could just as easily mean that the men of Sodom simply wished to get to know the two strangers.[23] We do not find Barton's interpretation convincing. The sexual meaning of the word seems, at least, to be insinuated by two facts. First, if all the men of Sodom wanted to do was to learn the identity of the strangers, why would Lot beg them "do not act so wickedly."[24] Second, the same word *yadha* is used in a clearly sexual sense when Lot offers his two daughters to the crowd: "Behold I have two daughters who have not known man (*yadha*), let me bring them out to you . . . only do nothing to these men *for they have come under the shelter of my roof.*"[25] We believe there is clear insinuation of homogenital intent against the two strangers at Sodom, which does not mean that the sin of the men of Sodom was the sin of homosexual behavior.

The clearer sin in both the Hebrew text and context is the sin of inhospitality. That Lot is concerned about hospitality is made evident in the phrase we have underscored above, "do nothing to these men for they have come under the shelter of my roof," that is, under the shelter of my hospitality, which embraces protecting them against the wrongful designs of the crowd. The men of Sodom are as bound by the law of hospitality as is Lot, but they demonstrate their wantonness by not living up to the law. If *yadha* is to be understood in its sexual connotation, and we believe it is, then the men of Sodom demonstrate the extent of their inhospitality by seeking violent rape of the strangers. If any action is condemned in the text, it is the crime of wrongful, violent, and inhospitable rape carried out by perverted *heterosexual* men. Moore's principle for argument about the morality or immorality of homosexual behavior is apropos here: "Argue with the best of homosexual practice, not with the worst."[26] Even if male rape perpetrated by heterosexuals is condemned in this text, that is a long way from a clear and unambiguous condemnation of the just and loving homosexual acts of men and women with a homosexual orientation.

The interpretation of the text we propose is supported by the fact that in the rest of the Old Testament, where Sodom is regularly mentioned, not once is its crime said to be homosexual behavior. Ezekiel describes it as "pride, surfeit of food, and prosperous ease, but [that] did not aid the poor and the needy."[27] Isaiah advises the rulers of Sodom, insinuating the standard Old Testament equivalence between God and the poor, to "seek justice, correct oppression, defend the fatherless, plead for the widow."[28] The Book of Wisdom explicitly charges both the men of Sodom and the Egyptians with inhospitality: "Others [the men of Sodom] had refused to receive strangers when they came to them, but these [the Egyptians] made slaves of guests who were their benefactors."[29] Jesus mentions Sodom in the same breath as the inhospitality accorded his disciples.[30] He also makes hospitality or inhospitality a major cause of salvation or damnation in the great judgment scene in Matthew.[31]

If the Sodom story is about inhospitable and not homosexual acts, no such reservation can be made about the prescriptions of the Holiness Code in Leviticus. "You shall not lie with a male as with a woman; it is an abomination," and "If a man lies with a male as with a woman both of them have committed an abomination; they shall be put to death."[32] What the Holiness Code says could not be clearer: *male homosexual behavior* is an abomination. Note that it is *male* acts that are prohibited in these texts; lesbian acts are not part of the prohibition. That restriction yields some insight into both the historical context in which Leviticus says what it says and what it might mean when it says it.

The first thing to be noted about the Hebrew context is bad biology. The ancient Hebrew, Greek, and Roman understanding was that the male gave "seed" that contained the whole of life; the female simply provided the "ground" or the "field" in which the "seed," a true homunculus, was sown to develop into a fully fledged human.[33] To spill that seed or nascent homunculus anywhere it could not develop properly, on the ground or in a male body, for instance, was regarded as tantamount to murder, and murder was always held as an abomination. Those guilty of murder suffered the same penalty as our present text prescribes for male homosexual behavior, namely, death.[34] Since women waste no seed or life—perhaps also because women in a patriarchal society simply do not count—female homosexual acts are not considered worthy of consideration in the Holiness Code or anywhere else in the Old Testament.

That only male homosexual acts are declared an abomination introduces another contextual consideration, that of male honor and the actions appropriate to it.

Extended family was and is "the primary economic, religious, educational, and social network" in Mediterranean society.[35] Within the social network, family was also the locus of honor, carried exclusively by males, particularly the patriarch, who headed the family and, for all intents and purposes, owned the females in it, whether they were daughters or wives. For a male to "lie with" another male, that is, to act passively and allow himself to be penetrated like a female, seriously compromised male honor, not only that of the male being penetrated but also that of every male in the family or clan. The passivity of a male, who was expected to be active in all things, including the sexual, was always abhorred and dishonorable. In such a sociohistorical context, of course, male homosexual acts would be an abomination—not, however, qua homosexual acts but qua passive and therefore dishonorable acts that threatened the patriarchal and hierarchical sexual arrangement that pervaded the Old Testament.[36]

But what of an utterly different social context: a context in which not every human being is assumed to be by "nature" heterosexual, and some are known to be by "nature" homosexual; a context in which honor is not a dominant concern; a context in which male and female are understood to contribute equally to the procreation of new life? In such a context, male homogenital behavior need not be judged as dishonorable and, from this fact, immoral; just and loving homosexual behavior, flowing from an innate homosexual orientation, cannot be regarded as a perversion of a universal heterosexual condition and, therefore, cannot be judged from this fact immoral; and the spilling of male semen, or seed, would no longer be regarded as the spilling of life, murder, and an abomination. In short, when the interpreter considers what the Bible says about male homosexual behavior and the cultural context in which it says it, it is difficult to consider the Bible as saying anything more instructive in contemporary cultural context than what it says about kosher laws.[37] Male homosexual behavior, as understood today, may or may not be immoral, but any contemporary judgment of its morality cannot be based on what the Old Testament says about it in the context of its own time and place.

The New Testament on Homosexuality

Since many Christians consider the Old Testament fulfilled, or even superseded, by the New, they automatically give more credence to what the New Testament says about homosexual acts. We must therefore consider what the New Testament says, and in particular we must consider what many deem its definitive statement about homogenitality, namely, chapter 1 of Paul's letter to the Romans. It is important again to note the context, and that is a Pauline attack not on homosexual acts in particular, but on degenerate, especially idolatrous, Gentile society in general.

After introductory greetings, Paul launches into standard Jewish accusations about Gentile idolatry. "What can be known about God is plain to them [Gentiles] because God has shown it to them."[38] But, however plain the existence of the true God of Israel might be, and however much Gentiles ought to have known that God from the things God made, they did not acknowledge God, they "did not honor God as God or give thanks to God." Rather, "they exchanged the glory of the immortal God for images resembling a mortal human being or birds or four-footed animals or reptiles."[39] What is radically wrong with Gentiles, Paul believes, is that they do not worship the true God of Israel, that they are idolaters, and he immediately moves on to describe the behavior of such idolaters. *Because* they are idolaters, in some divine punishment, "God *gave them up* in the lusts of their heart to impurity, to the dishonoring of their bodies. . . . God *gave them up* to dishonorable passions. . . . God *gave them up* to a base mind and to improper conduct."[40] The dishonorable passions and the male and female homosexual acts performed by perverted heterosexuals are God's punishment on Gentiles for their idolatry. It is Gentile *idolatry* that is directly at stake in the Pauline text, and the perverted homosexual behavior of heterosexuals to which it is presumed to lead, not the homosexual acts of those who by "nature" share the homosexual condition and the just and loving homosexual acts in which it might issue.[41]

The two remaining texts cited by the CDF as solid foundation for the Church's teaching on the immorality of homosexual acts, 1 Cor. 6:9–10 and 1 Tim. 1:10, present a serious difficulty of translation. We need consider only the former text in detail, for the difficulty is the same in both texts. Paul presents to the Corinthians a list of those who will not inherit the kingdom of God. "Do you not know that the unjust will not inherit the kingdom of God? Do not be deceived: neither fornicators, nor idolaters, nor adulterers, nor *malakoi*, nor *arsenokoitai*, nor thieves, the greedy, nor drunkards, nor slanderers, nor robbers will inherit the kingdom of God." The translation difficulty lies with both *malakoi* and *arsenokoitai*, and we shall have to consider each in some detail.

Malakos, the easier word to translate, literally means *soft*, and its cognate *malakia* means softness. It can be applied to people in a metaphorical sense, as it is, for instance, in Matthew 11:8 when Jesus asks about John the Baptizer: "Why then did you go out? To see a man clothed in soft raiment (*en malakois*)?" How does Paul use the word? There is some evidence that both *malakos* and *malakia* were used metaphorically of feminine sexual behavior without, however, being restricted to that meaning.[42] The Vulgate translated it as *molles* (the effeminate); the King James translated it along the same lines as *effeminacy*; the 1973 Revised Standard Version translated it as *adulterers*; the new Revised Standard Version translates it as *male prostitutes*; and the New English Bible translates it as *adultery*. Clearly, there is no solid unanimity of translation.

Malakos is difficult to translate, but bearing in mind the Hebrew context we discussed in connection with Leviticus 18:22, there is a legitimate and clear contextual translation. Honor was a primary value in Hebrew culture, especially male honor that was earned and preserved by a man behaving like a man; masculinity was honored and femininity was correspondingly disparaged. Softness or effeminacy in men, therefore, qua effeminacy without any suggestion of homosexual behavior, was held in horror as an "abomination." Mary Rose D'Angelo articulates this reading when she writes that "the biblical texts that have been read as condemnations of homosexuality originated in part as guardians of the kinds of sexual hierarchy that [are] violated when *a male is 'reduced' to the status of a woman.*"[43]

One feminine way of behaving is, undoubtedly, to act passively like a woman rather than actively like a man in the act of sexual intercourse (we are speaking of Paul's first-century culture, not our twenty-first-century culture with its different understanding of male and female sexuality), but that does not yet mean that the passive act of intercourse is what is condemned. It is more likely that what is condemned is masculine effeminacy in any of its forms. That reading is confirmed by the other difficult word, *arsenokoitai*, a most uncommon word, maybe even a word coined by Paul himself. The common opinion is that it is inspired by the Septuagint version of Leviticus 18:22. If that is true, then Paul uses it in the context of the sexual acts between men prohibited in Leviticus, but again that does not mean that it is precisely those acts qua homosexual that are an abomination. The abomination may be again the more general cultural disvalue of a man behaving like a woman. Paul condemns *malakoi* and *arsenokoitai* (which is also the word at stake in 1 Tim. 1:10), not for perverted homosexual behaviors, as the Revised Standard Version insinuates, but for the feminization of men whom the Creator God calls to be masculine.

The Bible and Contemporary Discourse on Homosexuality

This leads us to our third question and its answer: Can the Bible speak to the confusion that characterizes contemporary Christians with respect to homosexuality? It should first be noted that homosexual behavior is not a prominent biblical concern. There is no mention of it in Israel's earliest moral codes; there is nothing about it in the Decalogue; the Gospels record no saying of Jesus about it; there is not even a word for it in either Hebrew or Greek. Malina's conclusion about the Romans text is difficult to gainsay. "If we return to the twenty-first century after this excursion into the first century we can see that Paul's perspectives, if taken consistently, simply do not make sense."[44] Paul does not live in our context in which homosexuality is scientifically recognized as a *natural* condition; we do not live in Paul's context of bad biology or cultural value; and the ancient context does not translate easily across time to the modern context of homosexuality. The same conclusion applies to the even more distant texts of the Old Testament. They are articulated in the same context as Paul's texts. Everyone is presumed to be heterosexual; therefore, any male homosexual act is a freely chosen perversion. The male is the sole source of life; therefore, any spilling of the homunculus in a place where it cannot develop is murder and therefore an abomination. The male is also the source of honor in the society, and for a male to behave as a female, sexually or otherwise, shames not only him but every other male in the family or corporate clan. "The Old Testament narratives about the men of Sodom in Genesis 19 and the Levite's concubine in Judges 19 are more concerned with egregious failures in hospitality and gang rape than with homosexuality per se."[45]

Because of the difficulty of translating meanings across time, the Christian traditions are moving away from a *biblical rules* approach to moral judgments and are exploring a more profound, and perhaps more morally ambiguous, interrelationship among rules, norms, values, and virtues. There is a movement away from the simplistic judgment that what the Bible says is, without discussion, definitive for all time and is therefore the universal moral norm. Historically, Eugene Rodgers notes that this movement can be found in Aquinas's *Commentary on Romans*, which when read closely demonstrates a keen awareness of the interrelationship among scripture, anthropology, experience, natural law, and virtue, which has implications for interpreting scripture on homosexuality and "*requires* theologians to keep the matter open."[46] Lisa Cahill puts the matter succinctly: "Realizing the impossibility of transposing rules from biblical times to our own, interpreters look for larger themes, values or ideals which can inform moral reflection without determining specific practices in advance."[47] Victor Furnish articulates well the larger theme that we can abstract from both the Old and New Testament texts on homosexual behavior: "Paul, in common with the tradition by which he was influenced and in accord with the wisdom of his day, saw the wickedness of homosexual practice to adhere in its lust and its perversion of the natural order."[48]

The same wickedness, suggested as homosexual rape, and the same judgment of perversion of the presumed natural order are found in the Sodom account. Those judgments against uncontrolled and violent lust and a perversion of the natural order cannot automatically be applied to just and loving homosexual acts in persons whose natural sexual orientation is to persons of the same sex. Those acts may or may not be immoral, but any judgment of immorality will have to be substantiated on bases other than the simple fact that the Bible condemns the homosexual acts of heterosexual males. Richard Sparks's judgment is also ours: "On scriptural evidence alone we are left short of a clear and clean condemnation of what might be called committed or covenantal homosexual acts."[49]

At this point in our discernment of the morality of homosexuality, the theological news for contemporary Christians is twofold: first, the Bible is undeniably subject to historicity, and therefore, second, there are no definitive absolute norms about sexuality or homosexuality uncritically translatable from the cultural contexts of the Bible to those of contemporary times. Christians will therefore have to discern moral judgments about natural homosexuals and homosexual behavior on bases other than what the Bible says. These bases include magisterial teaching and the reflection of the empirical sciences on human experience. To these we now turn.

MAGISTERIAL TEACHING ON HOMOSEXUAL ACTS AND RELATIONSHIPS

Our analysis of the biblical texts, which can be extended to the equally historically and socially constructed theological texts of the Magisterium, points to the direction of moral discernment we propose as a way to arrive at a conscience-judgment about the morality or immorality of homosexual acts and homosexual relationships. Tradition teaches that homosexual acts are intrinsically disordered for the following reasons:

they "are contrary to the natural law," the principles of which are reflected in human nature itself; "they close the sexual act to the gift of life;" and "they do not proceed from a genuine affective and sexual complementarity."[50] We will consider each of these teachings in turn.

Natural Law Argument

First, there is in every human being by "nature" a sexual orientation, but remember that "nature" is always an interpreted category, and therefore there may be different judgments about what is and what is not "nature." The meaning of the phrase "sexual orientation" is complex and not universally agreed upon, but the Magisterium offers a description. It distinguishes between "a homosexual 'tendency,' which proves to be 'transitory,' and 'homosexuals who are definitively such because of some kind of innate instinct.'" It goes on to declare that "it seems appropriate to understand sexual orientation as a *deep-seated* dimension of one's personality and to recognize its *relative stability* in a person."[51] Sexual orientation is predominantly heterosexual, homosexual, or bisexual. This "natural" and scientifically discovered reality may be obscured by the obvious statistical preponderance of persons of heterosexual orientation, but it is in no way negated by that statistical preponderance. We are in complete agreement with the CDF when it teaches that "there can be no true promotion of man's [and woman's] dignity unless the essential order of his nature is respected."[52] We disagree with the CDF, however, on its exclusively heterosexual interpretation of that "essential order of nature."

"Nature" and natural law have always had a prominent place in Catholic moral theology. In official Church teaching, not only homosexuality but also premarital, extramarital, contraceptive, and nonreproductive types of marital sexual activity are condemned as contrary to the natural law. Any sexual activity that deviates from God's "wisely ordered laws of nature" and is not open to the transmission of life, the Magisterium teaches, is morally wrong.[53] The principles that dictate this moral judgment are contained "in the divine law—eternal, objective, and universal—whereby God orders, directs, and governs the entire universe and all the ways of the human community . . . . This divine law is *accessible to our minds.*[54] It is precisely this "accessible to our minds," however, as we explained in our prologue, that raises serious interpretive questions. Already in the thirteenth century, Thomas Aquinas taught that the natural law is "nothing other than the light of understanding [or reason] placed in us by God."[55] He also argues, however, that, although the precepts of the natural law are universal and immutable, their application varies according to the circumstances of people's existence. We argued the same in our prologue.

Because every interpretation of "nature" is a socially constructed reality dependent on human, rational, perspectival interpretations, the reality of "nature" is always to be subjected to scrutiny, even if the interpretation be advanced by the Magisterium of the Catholic Church. Our sexual anthropology recognizes sexual orientation as an intrinsic dimension of human "nature." As such, what is "natural" in sexual activity, which is an expression of the sexual person, will vary depending on whether or not the person's sexual orientation is homosexual or heterosexual. Homosexual acts are "natural" for people with a homosexual orientation just as heterosexual acts are "natural" for people with a heterosexual orientation. They are natural because they coincide with, and reflect, the fundamental human "nature" of a person created in the image and likeness of God. We are not arguing here that homosexual activity is moral because it is natural for those with a homosexual orientation; that would be to treat natural facts as moral justification. To be moral, any sexual act, whether homosexual or heterosexual, must be not only natural but also, as we explained in chapter 2, just, loving, and in accord with holistic complementarity.

Procreation Argument

Second, the magisterial claim that homosexual acts "close the sexual act to the gift of life" has been addressed in chapter 2, and we need not repeat it here. Suffice to say that if one explores "the gift of life" in biological terms, then potentially reproductive and permanently or temporarily nonreproductive heterosexual acts are essentially different types of acts. As Andrew Koppleman points out, a "sterile person's genitals are no more suitable for generation than a gun with a broken firing pin is suitable for shooting." It is a conceptual stretch, he goes on, "to insist that the sexual acts of the incurably infertile are of the same kind as the sexual acts of fertile organs that occasionally fail to deliver the goods."[56] Heterogenital complementarity is the essential difference that distinguishes nonreproductive heterosexual intercourse from homosexual intercourse. If one explores "the gift of life" in metaphorical terms, however, where embodied sexual beings offer themselves to one another in interpersonal union that is a gift of relational life, one to another, then both homosexual and heterosexual couples can realize this gift in sexual acts.

In other words, on the basis of human experience it can be argued that in their witness, homosexual couples manifest "the gift of life" in their sexuality through embodied interpersonal union, just as heterosexual couples, both fertile and infertile, manifest "the gift of life" in their sexuality in their embodied interpersonal union. Heterogenital complementarity is not a determining factor. Rather, two genitally embodied persons, heterosexual or homosexual, in permanent interpersonal union, who reflect God's constant love and steadfast fidelity, are the determining factor. In the case of fertile heterosexual couples, embodied interpersonal union is potentially procreative; in the case of infertile heterosexual couples and in the case of homosexual couples, embodied interpersonal union is not potentially procreative. Embodiment and interpersonal union, however, are essential to all.

Complementarity Argument

Third, while the Magisterium consistently condemns homosexual acts on the grounds that they violate heterogenital and reproductive complementarity, it does not explain why they also violate personal complementarity other than to assert that homosexual acts "do not proceed from a genuine affective and sexual complementarity."[57] This statement, however, raises the question of whether such acts can ever be truly human on the level of personal complementarity. Though the Magisterium refuses to confront this question, monogamous, loving, committed, homosexual couples have confronted it experientially and testify that they do experience affective and communion complementarity in and through their homosexual acts. Margaret Farley notes that the experiential testimonies of these couples witness "to the role of such loves and relationships in sustaining human well-being and opening to human flourishing" and "extends to the contributions that individuals and partners make to families, the church, and society as a whole."[58] This coincides precisely with our foundational principle on the immediate relational impact of truly human sexual acts. "Expressed in a manner which is truly human, these actions signify and promote that mutual self-giving by which spouses enrich each other with a joyful and a thankful will."[59] Farley's claim is amply supported by anecdotal and scientific research on the nature of homosexual relationships.

Some twenty years ago, while acknowledging that the question of same-sex relations is a question of dispute, Farley noted anecdotal experiences of homosexual couples and commented that we "have some clear and profound testimonies to the life-enhancing possibilities of same-sex relations and the integrating possibilities of sexual activity within these relations. We have the witness that homosexuality can be a way of embodying responsible love and sustaining human friendship." She concludes, logically, that "this witness alone is enough to demand of the Christian [and political] community that it reflect anew on the norms [and laws] for homosexual love."[60] Her judgment accords with that of Bernard Ratigan, a gay, English consulting psychotherapist, who notes that "the gap between the caricature of us [gays] in Church documents and our lived reality seems so huge." He asks legitimately "on what evidence does the Vatican base its assertions" about gays and goes on to point out that psychoanalysis "has moved on from being solely concerned with genital sex to thinking much more about human relationships and love."[61] So, too, has revisionist Catholic moral theology.

This call for evidence can also be posed to the United States Conference of Catholic Bishops' most recent statement on homosexuality. Speaking of a homosexual inclination, the bishops note that it "predisposes one toward what is truly not good for the human person." The predisposition is toward homosexual acts that are "not ordered toward the fulfillment of the natural ends of human sexuality," and therefore "acting in accord with such an inclination simply cannot contribute to the true good of the human person."[62] The statement that homosexual acts, by definition, cannot contribute to the good of the human person seems to contradict the relational experiences of committed, monogamous, homosexual couples. While this statement does not cite scientific studies to verify its claim, there are a number of studies that explicitly contradict it.

Lawrence Kurdek has done extensive research on gay and lesbian couples and notes the following characteristics when comparing these relationships with married heterosexual couples. Gay and lesbian couples tend to have a more equitable distribution of household labor, demonstrate greater conflict resolution skills, have less support from members of their own families but greater support from friends, and, most significantly, experience similar levels of relational satisfaction compared to heterosexual couples.[63]

There is also a growing body of social scientific data that shows that partnered gays and lesbians raise children to be every bit as well developed (and heterosexual) as the children of heterosexual parents. Already in 1995 Charlotte Patterson summarized the evidence in a twenty-year retrospective. "There is no evidence to suggest that lesbians and gay men are unfit to be parents or that psychosocial [including sexual] development among children of gay men or lesbians is compromised in any respect relative to that of heterosexual parents."[64] Anne Brewaeys's 1997 study in the Netherlands and Raymond Chan's 1998 study in the United States confirmed that there was no reason to be concerned about the psychological development of children raised by lesbian mothers.[65] Tasker and Golombok and Bailey and Dawood reported from Britain and North America, respectively, that the vast majority of children of homosexual parents grow up to be heterosexual young adults.[66] On the basis of the scientific evidence, the American Academy of Pediatrics judged in 2002 that children of gay parents "fare as well in emotional, cognitive, social, and sexual functioning as do children whose parents are heterosexual."[67] The American Psychological Association rendered the same judgment in 2004.[68]

In 2009, a major study by Paige Averett demonstrated that there is no significant difference in emotional problems experienced by children adopted by heterosexual, gay, and lesbian parents, and that the children of gay and lesbian parents had strength levels equal to or exceeding scale norms. Gay and lesbian parents also fell into the desirable range of the Parent-as-Teacher Inventory.[69] In 2010, Nanette Gartrell and Henry Bos published the results of a longitudinal study on the seventeen-year-old sons and daughters of lesbian mothers who have been raised in lesbian households since birth. They report that these adolescents "are well-adjusted, demonstrating more competencies [social, academic, and total] and fewer behavioral problems than their peers in the normative American population."[70]

There is, therefore, abundant social-scientific data to support the claim that personal, unitive complementarity is experienced in committed, stable, and justly loving homosexual relationships and that, in the case of homosexual parents, these complementarities facilitate the positive nurture of children.[71] Yet the Magisterium of the Catholic Church continues to deliver ideological judgments contrary to the scientific evidence. The CDF asserts that "as experience has shown [!], the absence of sexual complementarity in [same-sex] unions creates obstacles in the normal development of children who would be placed in the care of such persons. . . . Allowing children to be adopted by persons living in such unions would actually mean doing violence to these children."[72] The *Catechism of the Catholic Church* asserts that homosexual acts "do not proceed from a genuine affective and sexual complementarity."[73] Speaking to the Pontifical Council for the Family in February 2010, Pope Benedict XVI continues to propagate the myth that "children needed to be raised in a traditional family consisting of a stable union between a man and a woman if they were going to have a healthy development."[74] These magisterial positions are so contrary to the overwhelming scientific evidence that they must be judged under John Courtney Murray's famous principle: practical, as distinct from theoretical, intelligence is preserved from ideology by having a close relation to concrete experience.[75] Catholic magisterial positions on both the unions and the children of gays and lesbians are very much ideology divorced from the well-documented experience of those gays and lesbians and their children. This divorce between ideology and experience warrants, at least, a theological reconsideration of gay and lesbian unions.

The Second Vatican Council praises the advances of the social sciences that bring the human community "improved self-knowledge" and "influence on the life of social groups."[76] Pope John Paul II teaches that "the Church values sociological and statistical research when it proves helpful in understanding the historical context in which pastoral action has to be developed and when it leads to a better understanding of the truth."[77] The present question, namely, the effect of homosexual parents on their children, is a classic case in which the social sciences have clearly led to a better understanding of the truth. There is abundant social scientific data to support the claim that communion and affective complementarity are evident in homosexual relationships and that, in the case of homosexual parents, these complementarities facilitate both parental complementarity and the positive nurture of children.

THE MORAL SENSE OF THE CHRISTIAN PEOPLE AND HOMOSEXUAL ACTS

Data from the social sciences also suggests that the third foundation on which the CDF grounds its judgment on the immorality of homosexual acts, "the moral sense of the Christian people," is now as open to critique as the reading of biblical texts and the natural-law argument. In a 1997 study, James Davidson and his colleagues describe "how American Catholics approach faith and morals."[78] They found, with respect to homosexual activity, that 41 percent of parishioners agree with the Magisterium that homosexual acts are always wrong, and that 49 percent believe that, at least in certain circumstances, the decision to engage in such acts is up to the individual.[79] A 2001 study replicated that figure of 49 percent, believing the decision to engage in homosexual acts belongs to the individual; only 20 percent believed it had anything to do with the Magisterium.[80] The authors comment that their data "depicts a trend away from conformity and toward personal autonomy" (that is, personal conscience) with respect to sexual issues.[81] That trend was most marked in "Post-Vatican II Catholics," those aged thirty-eight and younger.[82] Dean Hoge and his colleagues also document this trend away from authority to personal conscience in matters of morality. In his study, he found that 73 percent of Latino Catholics and 71percent of non-Latino Catholics judged that, in matters of morality, the final authority is the individual's informed conscience.[83] The same trend is well documented in other Western countries.[84] A reasonable theological question then arises: Does sociological data of this sort tell us anything about magisterial teaching and the faith of the Church?

An immediate and crucial answer is that sociological data is not an expression of the belief and teaching of the Catholic Church. Nor does it tell us what the Church ought to believe and teach, for 50 percent, and even 100 percent, of Catholics could be wrong. The empirical data reported above, however, does two important things. It tells us what the beliefs of Catholics actually are with respect to the morality of homosexual acts, and it demonstrates that these beliefs are at variance with the teachings of the Magisterium. It ought neither be accepted uncritically nor dismissed out of hand as if it had no relevance to the life of the Church. Pope John Paul II teaches that "the Church values sociological and statistical research" but immediately adds the proviso that "such research is not to be considered in itself an expression of the *sensus fidei*."[85] The pope is correct. Empirical research neither expresses nor creates the faith of the Church, but it does manifest what Catholics actually believe and do not believe, and that experiential reality is a basis for critical reflection on any claim about what "the Church believes." It is that critical reflection, always required of the Church's theologians, we undertake in this chapter and throughout this book.[86]

Theologian and sociologist Robin Gill complains that Christian ethicists have been "reluctant to admit that sociology has any constructive role to play in their discipline. It is rare to find a Christian ethicist prepared to examine data about the moral effects of churchgoing. Christian communities have become *far too idealized*."[87] "Christian communities" may be a euphemism for Catholic Magisterium, which tends to talk theoretically of the belief of the Church, perhaps as it has been rather than as it is. If, as the Second Vatican Council clearly taught, "the body of the faithful as a whole cannot err in matters of belief," then they must be infallible in the beliefs they *actually* believe.[88] It is that actual belief that is uncovered by sociological research. Avery Cardinal Dulles argues that to determine *sensus fidei*, which has important relevance in this discussion, "we must look not so much at the statistics, as at the quality of the witnesses and the motivation for their assent."[89] We agree. *Sensus fidei*, the connatural capacity to discern the truth into which the Spirit of God is leading the Church, must be carefully discerned by all who are competent. John Paul II is correct: a simple head count does not necessarily express the faith of the Church. A head count, however, that would include virtually all of the faithful, especially virtually all the competent theological faithful, would most certainly manifest the actual faith of the whole Church. All we claim here about the sociological data with respect to the belief of the Church about the morality of homosexual acts is that it may manifest a development that Church theologians and Magisterium ought to examine carefully.

What is clear from the above investigation of biblical and magisterial teaching on homosexual acts and homosexual relationships is the importance of experience as a source of moral knowledge. In the dialogue between the four sources of moral knowledge for morally assessing homosexual acts and relationships—scripture, tradition, reason, and experience—Farley notes and we agree that experience "is an important part of the content of each of the other sources, and it is always a factor in interpreting the others."[90] It provides a sociohistorical context for interpreting the other sources of moral knowledge and illuminates whether, and to what extent, the sources and the normative conclusions that they reach "make sense" and "ring true" in terms of "our deepest capacity for truth and goodness."[91] Furthermore, "given the arguable inconclusiveness of Scripture, tradition, and secular disciplines" on the immorality of homosexual relationships, "concrete experience becomes a determining source on this issue."[92]

THE MORALITY OF HOMOSEXUAL ACTS RECONSIDERED

We propose a revision of magisterial teaching on the intrinsic immorality of all homosexual acts based on what we believe to be a more adequate foundational principle, grounded in sound biblical exegesis, the best of magisterial teaching on human sexuality, and the data on human experience elucidated by the empirical sciences. Bearing in mind our revised foundational principle and everything we said about complementary, just, and loving sexual intercourse in chapter 2, we conclude this section by, again, approving of Farley's judgment. "Sex between two persons of the same sex (just as between two persons of the opposite sex) should not be used in a way that exploits, objectifies, or dominates; homosexual (like heterosexual) rape, violence, or any harmful use of power against unwilling victims (or those incapacitated by reason of age, etc.) is never justified; freedom, integrity, privacy are values to be affirmed in every homosexual (as heterosexual) relationship; all in all, individuals are not to be harmed, and the common good is to be promoted."[93]

Heterosexual orientation is an innate, deep-seated, and stable orientation to, predominantly, persons of the opposite sex; homosexual orientation is a similarly innate, deep-seated, and stable orientation to, predominantly, persons of the same sex. "Ethics can have for its object only acts that are free, acts that can be imputed to personal responsibility. Whatever is determined, *insofar as it is determined*, is neither moral nor immoral; it simply *is*."[94] Sexual orientation is neither chosen nor readily changeable; it simply is. It is, therefore, in itself neither moral nor immoral. The sexual behaviors that flow from it, however, may be moral or immoral. We apply the principle we have already enunciated to arrive at the judgment of the morality or immorality of all heterosexual or homosexual acts.

Sexual acts are moral when they are natural, reasonable, and expressed in a truly human, just, and loving manner. All terms of this articulation are important and must be carefully understood. Sexual acts are moral when they are *natural*, and they are natural when they coincide with the "*nature*" of the human person according to right reason and what facilitates human flourishing.[95] For men and women who are by "nature" heterosexual, heterosexual acts are natural, reasonable, and therefore moral when all other requirements for moral acts are safeguarded, and homosexual acts are unnatural, unreasonable, and therefore immoral, even if all other requirements for moral acts are safeguarded. For those who are by "nature" homosexual, it is the reverse. Homosexual acts are natural, reasonable, and moral, and heterosexual acts are unnatural, unreasonable, and immoral. Sexual acts are moral when they are *reasonable*, and they are reasonable when, as a result of careful attention to and understanding of all the relevant human circumstances, a person makes an informed conscience-judgment that a given sexual action is according to right reason and facilitates human flourishing. The circumstances to be attended to will include sexual orientation and holistic, that is, orientation, personal, and biological, complementarity. Sexual acts are moral when they are *truly human*, that is, when they fulfill all the requirements of holistic complementarity.[96]

Heterosexual acts are truly human, and therefore reasonable and moral, when they are in line with holistic complementarity, which embraces orientation, personal, and genital (though not necessarily reproductive) complementarity. Personal complementarity embraces everything we considered in chapter 2 under the headings of the physical, emotional, psychological, spiritual, and relational dimensions of truly human sexuality. Any sexual act that violates any of these dimensions will be deemed immoral; any sexual act which is true to all these dimensions will be deemed moral. Heterosexual rape, therefore, or any heterosexual intercourse which is not just and loving, will be deemed immoral, and so too will homosexual rape. Heterosexual intercourse without relational connection—casual sex, for instance, or sex with a prostitute—will be similarly deemed immoral, because it violates personal complementarity, and so too will homosexual intercourse without relational connection. Heterosexual intercourse that is predetermined to be free of responsibility for its outcome—the birth of a child, for instance, or the communication of a sexually transmitted disease—will be deemed immoral because it violates personal complementarity as justice; and so too will homosexual intercourse. Heterosexual intercourse, however, that is mutually freely chosen, just, and loving will be deemed moral, whether it is actually reproductive or not, and so too will homosexual intercourse.

CONCLUSION

We argued earlier in this book that, given the essential historicity of every human teaching, what Augustine and Aquinas, Trent and Vatican II, Paul and John Paul taught in the past about human sexuality cannot be the *exclusive* basis for conscientious moral judgment about sexuality today. All must be subjected to critical scrutiny. We have attempted that scrutiny throughout this book, and again in this chapter with respect to homosexuality, enlightened by Cardinal Ratzinger's judgment that remains true today. "Not everything that exists in the Church must for that reason be also a legitimate tradition. . . . Consequently tradition must not be considered only affirmatively but also critically."[97] With respect to historicity, the CDF teaches that "the meaning of the pronouncements of faith depends partly upon the expressive power of the language used at a given time and in given circumstances"; that being so, a truth that is first expressed incompletely may, "at a later date, when considered in a broader context of faith or human knowledge, [be] expressed more fully and perfectly."[98] In the light of contemporary scientific and human knowledge about homosexual orientation, we have examined in this chapter the threefold bases on which the Catholic Church rests its judgment that homosexual acts are intrinsically disordered and gravely immoral, namely, the teaching of scripture, the teaching of the Magisterium, and the moral sense of the Christian people. On all three bases, we argued, the Church's teaching needs serious reevaluation.

We believe we have comprehensively shown that the biblical texts cited in support of the serious depravity of the homosexual activity of persons of genuine homosexual orientation, which was simply unknown when the scriptures in question were written, do not support such a judgment. The same approach that was used to demonstrate the meanings of the biblical texts in their historical contexts applies equally to the historically conditioned texts of the Magisterium. We believe we have shown that the Magisterium's argument for the immorality of all homosexual acts on the basis of a biological interpretation of "nature" is also unsound and open to critique, as is the absolute assertion that homosexual acts can never "proceed from a genuine affective and sexual complementarity." So too is its argument on the basis of the constant belief of the Christian people, when faced with the data of contemporary research into what Catholics actually believe.

Lack of understanding, indeed misunderstanding, of the full scope of sexuality in a human life until very recent history; lack of understanding, indeed misunderstanding, of the essential contribution of both male and female in human reproduction until the latter half of the nineteenth century; lack of understanding, indeed misunderstanding, of the natural reality of heterosexual and homosexual orientation until the twentieth century—these are not good bases for making any normative judgment about sexuality in general or about heterosexuality and homosexuality in particular. Nothing we have argued in this chapter proves that *all* homosexual acts are morally right. We have argued only that the arguments advanced by the Church's Magisterium to sustain the judgment that *all* homosexual acts are morally wrong are unsound and need to be revisited.

Our present judgment endorses Farley's judgment. "At this point . . . it is difficult to see how on the basis of sheer rationality alone, and all of its disciplines [including theology], an absolute prohibition of same-sex relationships or activities can be maintained." She goes on to point out,

"We are still pressed to the task of discerning what must characterize same-sex relationships if they are to conduce to human flourishing."[99] Again we agree, though we also believe we have developed criteria in previous chapters for the judgment that *some* homosexual acts may be morally right. We content ourselves here by repeating the criteria with which we concluded a previous chapter. *Some* homosexual and *some* heterosexual acts, those that meet the requirements of holistically complementary, just, and loving sexual relations, are truly human and moral; and *some* homosexual and *some* heterosexual acts, those that do not meet the requirements of holistically complementary, just, and loving sexual relations, are immoral. This judgment, we believe, stands in spite of the rhetorical assertions of the Catholic Magisterium, and stands for the good of the whole Church. We embrace Moore's judgment. "This is not a matter of dissent . . . ; it is simply that the Church at the moment produces no good arguments to assent to. Regrettably, in this area, the Church teaches badly."[100]

QUESTIONS FOR REFLECTION

1. What do you understand by the term *sexual orientation*? In your best judgment, is sexual orientation truly a natural fact of human sexuality? If you judge that it is, how can homosexual acts for persons of homosexual orientation be, as the Catholic Church teaches them to be, "intrinsically disordered"?

2. Did the writers of both Old and New Testament have any idea of what today we call sexual orientation? If they did not, can they make any judgment on people with a homosexual orientation who engage in homosexual acts as we understand them today? What is to be said about the Catholic Church's teaching that biblical texts provide a "solid foundation" for its condemnation of homosexual acts as "acts of great depravity"?

3. One reason the Catholic Church condemns homosexual acts as immoral is that they "close the sexual act to the gift of life." Should,

then, the sexual acts of permanently or temporarily infertile heterosexuals, which clearly are equally closed to the gift of life, be also condemned as immoral? On what basis are they not so condemned?

4. It is clear that homosexuals cannot ever achieve the procreative
   end of marriage, except perhaps by adoption or the use of artificial
   reproductive technologies (see chapter 6). But can they, do you think,
   achieve that partnership of life and love that is the unitive end of
   marriage? Is there any social-scientific evidence to support the claim
   that they can? Does the abundant social-scientific evidence that
   shows that stable, committed, and loving gay and lesbian couples
   raise children to be as normal as those raised by heterosexuals have
   anything to contribute to this question?

5. Joseph Ratzinger, now Pope Benedict XVI, wrote: "Not everything
   that exists in the Church must be for that reason also a legitimate
   tradition. . . . There is a distorting as well as legitimate tradition. . . .
   Consequently tradition must not be considered only affirmatively
   but also critically." In your judgment, does Ratzinger's judgment
   apply also to the moral teaching of the Catholic Church, including
   its teaching on homosexuality? If it does, what are the implications
   of this judgment for the Church's teaching on homosexuality?

6. What other questions arise for you from reading this chapter?

NOTES

1. Joseph Ratzinger, "The Transmission of Divine Revelation," in *Commentary on the Documents of Vatican II*, ed. Herbert Vorgrimler (New York: Herder and Herder, 1969), 3:185.
2. In Catholic theological discourse, *tradition* refers not simply to the process of handing down teachings, but also to those teachings themselves. See Yves Congar, *Tradition and Traditions* (New York: Macmillan, 1967). Even within this discourse, however, there is fluidity in interpreting the word. For instance, the International Theological Commission, in its article "The Interpretation of Dogmas," uses the term *tradition* throughout the text but provides no explanation of it. See "De Interpretatione Dogmatum," *Gregorianum* 72 (1991): 5–37.
3. See Todd A. Salzman, "The Basic Goods Theory and Revisionism: A Methodological Comparison on the Use of Tradition as a Source of Moral Knowledge," *Studia*

Moralia 40 (2002): 171–204, and *What Are They Saying about Roman Catholic Ethical Method?* (Mahwah, NJ: Paulist Press, 2003).

4. *PH*, 8; CCC, 2357.

5. *PH*, 8.

6. *Letter to the Bishops of the Catholic Church on the Pastoral Care of Homosexual Persons*, 5, *AAS* 79 (1987), 545.

7. Ibid., 546.

8. CCC, 2357.

9. *DV*, 12. See also Pius XII, *Divino Afflante Spiritu, AAS* 35 (1943), 297–325.

10. See William J. Paul, James Weinreich, John Gonsiorek, and Mary E. Motvedt, eds., *Homosexuality: Social, Psychological, and Biological Issues* (Beverly Hills, CA: Sage, 1982); Pim Pronk, *Against Nature? Types of Moral Argumentation regarding Homosexuality* (Grand Rapids, MI: Eerdmans, 1993); Richard C. Pillard and J. Michael Bailey, "A Biological Perspective on Sexual Orientation," *Clinical Sexuality* 18 (1995): 1–14; Lee Ellis and Linda Ebertz, *Sexual Orientation: Toward Biological Understanding* (Westport, CT: Praeger, 1997); Richard C. Friedman and Jennifer I. Downey, *Sexual Orientation and Psychoanalysis: Sexual Science and Clinical Practice* (New York: Columbia, 2002); CDF, *Letter to the Bishops of the Catholic Church on the Pastoral Care of Homosexual Persons, AAS* 79 (1987), 543–54; USCCB, *Always Our Children* (Washington, DC: USCCB, 1997).

11. This terminology articulates our position that homosexual orientation is neither exclusively genetic nor exclusively social in origin. See John E. Perito, *Contemporary Catholic Sexuality: What Is Taught and What Is Practiced* (New York: Crossroad, 2003), 96.

12. Pillard and Bailey, "Biological Perspective on Sexual Orientation," 1.

13. D. Sherwin Bailey, *Homosexuality and the Western Christian Tradition* (New York: Longman's, 1955), x; emphasis added.

14. Donald W. Cory, *The Homosexual in America* (New York: Julian Press, 1951), 8; emphasis in original.

15. See *HP*, 10; and United States Catholic Conference, *Always Our Children*.

16. Our argument in what follows is in full agreement with Gareth Moore, that "there are no good arguments, from either scripture or natural law, against what have come to be known as homosexual relationships. The arguments put forward to show that such relationships are immoral are bad. Either their premises are false or the argument by means of which the conclusion is drawn from them itself contains errors." See his *A Question of Truth: Christianity and Homosexuality* (London: Continuum, 2003), x. See also Robin Scroggs, *The New Testament and Homosexuality* (Philadelphia: Fortress, 1983).

17. See Edward Vacek, "A Christian Homosexuality," *Commonweal*, December 5, 1980, 681–84.

18. Gen. 18:2, 3, 10, 13, 14, 17, 22.

19. Lev. 20:33–34.

20. Gen. 18:4–5.
21. Gen. 19:1.
22. Gen. 19:5.
23. G. A. Barton, "Sodomy," in *Encyclopedia of Religion and Ethics*, ed. James Hastings, (Whitefish, MT: Kessinger, 2003) 11, 672. Derrick Sherwin Bailey (*Homosexuality in the Western Christian Tradition* [London: Darton, Longman, Green, 1955], 1–6) advances the same argument; the men of Sodom simply wanted to know the identity of the strangers.
24. Gen. 19:7.
25. Gen. 19:8; emphasis added.
26. Moore, *Question of Truth*, 5.
27. Ezek. 16:49.
28. See Michael G. Lawler, "Being Christ-ian and the Service of Love and Justice," in *Liturgical Ministry* 13 (2004): 10–22; Is. 1:17.
29. Wisdom 19:14.
30. Luke 10:10–12; cp. Matt 10:14–15.
31. Matt. 25:34–46.
32. Lev. 18:22; 20:13.
33. For Greek society, see Paige duBois, *Sowing the Body: Psychoanalysis and Ancient Representations of Women* (Chicago: University of Chicago Press, 1988), 39–85. For Jewish society, see Sirach 26:19; *Mishna*, Ketuboth, 1, 6. For Muslim society, see Carol Delaney, *The Seed and the Soil: Gender and Cosmology in Turkish Village Society* (Berkeley and Los Angeles: University of California Press, 1991).
34. Lev. 24:17, 21; Num. 35:30; Exod. 20:13.
35. Bruce J. Malina and Richard L. Rohrbaugh, *Social Science Commentary on the Synoptic Gospels* (Minneapolis: Fortress Press, 1992), 202. See also Carolyn Osiek and David L. Balch, *Families in the New Testament World: Households and House Churches* (Louisville: Westminster/John Knox Press, 1997); and Halvor Moxnes, *Constructing Early Christian Families* (London: Routledge, 1997).
36. The same system of honor and shame existed among the Greeks. Though it was acceptable for a boy to behave passively sexually, it was not acceptable for an adult male. Taking the passive, female role in sexual activity brought him dishonor and negatively impacted his status and role in society. See Foucault, *The Use of Pleasure: The History of Sexuality*, vol. 2, trans. Robert Hurley (New York: Pantheon, 1985), 187–225.
37. Lev. 11.
38. Rom. 1:19.
39. Rom. 1:21–23.
40. Rom. 1:24–28; emphasis added.
41. See Dale B. Martin, "Heterosexism and the Interpretation of Romans 1:18–31," *Biblical Interpretation* 3 (1995): 332–55. For a contrary reading, see Richard Hays, "Relations Natural and Unnatural: A Response to John Boswell's 'Exegesis of

Romans 1,' *Journal of Religious Ethics* 14 (1986): 184–215;" and *The Moral Vision of the New Testament: Community, Cross, New Creation: A Contemporary Introduction to the New Testament* (San Francisco: Harper, 1996), especially chapter 16.

42. See Scroggs, *New Testament and Homosexuality*, 62–65.

43. Mary Rose D'Angelo, "Perfect Fear Casteth Out Love: Reading, Citing, and Rape," in *Sexual Diversity and Catholicism: Toward the Development of Moral Theology*, ed. Patricia Beattie Jung with Joseph A. Corey (Collegeville, MN: Liturgical Press, 2001), 181; emphasis added.

44. Bruce J. Malina, "The New Testament and Homosexuality," in *Sexual Diversity and Catholicism*, 168.

45. Daniel Harrington and James Keenan, *Jesus and Virtue Ethics: Building Bridges between New Testament Studies and Moral Theology* (Lanham, MD: Sheed and Ward, 2002), 166.

46. Eugene F. Rogers Jr., "Aquinas on Natural Law and the Virtues in Biblical Context," *Journal of Religious Ethics* 27 (1999): 52.

47. Lisa Sowle Cahill, "Is Catholic Ethics Biblical?" Warren Lecture Series in Catholic Studies, no. 20 (Tulsa, OK: University of Tulsa), 5–6.

48. Victor Paul Furnish, *The Moral Teaching of Paul: Selected Issues* (Louisville: Abingdon, 1985), 78.

49. Richard Sparks, *Contemporary Christian Morality* (New York: Crossroad, 1996), 81.

50. CCC, 2357; CRP, 4.

51. USCCB, *Always Our Children*, 4–5; emphasis added. See also PH, 8.

52. PH, 3.

53. HV, 11.

54. Ibid., 3; emphasis added.

55. CCC, 426.

56. Andrew Koppleman, "Natural Law (New)," in *Sex from Plato to Paglia: A Philosophical Encyclopedia*, ed. Alan Soble (Westport, CT: Greenwood Press, 2006), 2:708.

57. CCC, 2357.

58. Margaret A. Farley, *Just Love: A Framework for Christian Sexual Ethics* (New York: Continuum, 2006), 287. Frans Vosman affirms this claim as well, noting that homosexuals contribute to the "social good" in terms of "mutual support, care, and justice," for example ("Can the Church Recognize Homosexual Couples in the Public Sphere?" *INTAMS Review* 12 [2006]: 37).

59. GS, 49.

60. Margaret A. Farley, "An Ethic for Same-Sex Relations," in *A Challenge to Love: Gay and Lesbian Catholics in the Church*, ed. Robert Nugent (New York: Crossroad, 1983), 99–100. In her most recent book, Farley returns to the question of gay and lesbian experience and judges that "we do have strong witnesses to the role of such [gay and lesbian] relationships in sustaining human well-being and opening to human flourishing. This same witness extends to the contributions that individuals

and partners make to families, the church, and society as a whole" (Margaret A. Farley, *Just Love: A Framework for Christian Ethics* [New York: Continuum, 2006], 287). The recent Vatican "Document on Homosexuality and the Priesthood" is also guilty of ignoring the experience of many gay men. After having stated that gay men "must be accepted with respect and sensitivity; every sign of unjust discrimination in their regard should be avoided," the document proceeds to assert unjustly that such men "find themselves in a situation that seriously obstructs them from properly relating to men and women" (CCE, *Instruction concerning the Criteria for the Discernment of Vocations with Regard to Persons with Homosexual Tendencies*, 2, www.vatican.va/roman_curia/congregations/ [accessed July 5, 2006.]. No evidence is advanced for such a sweeping statement; contrary evidence, known to anyone who accepts gays and lesbians with "respect and sensitivity," is ignored.

61. Bernard Ratigan, "When Faith and Feelings Conflict," *Tablet* (December 10, 2005), 13.

62. USCCB, "Ministry to Persons with a Homosexual Inclination: Guidelines for Pastoral Care," *Origins* 24 (2006):381.

63. Lawrence A. Kurdek, "What Do We Know about Gay and Lesbian Couples?" *Current Directions in Psychological Science* 14 (2005): 251; "Differences between Partners from Heterosexual, Gay, and Lesbian Cohabiting Couples," *Journal of Marriage and Family* 68 (2006): 509–28; "Lesbian and Gay Couples," in Anthony R. D'Augelli and Charlotte J. Patterson, *Lesbian, Gay and Bisexual Identities over the Lifespan* (New York: Oxford University, 1995), 243–61; "Are Gay and Lesbian Cohabiting Couples *Really* Different from Heterosexual Married Couples?," *Journal of Marriage and Family* 66 (2004): 880–900. See also Ritch C. Savin-Williams and Kristin G. Esterberg, "Lesbian, Gay, and Bisexual Families," in *Handbook of Family Diversity*, ed. David H. Demo, Katherine R. Allen, and Mark A. Fine (New York: Oxford University, 2000), 207–12; and Philip Blumstein and Pepper Schwartz, *American Couples: Money, Work, Sex* (New York: Morrow, 1983).

64. Charlotte J. Patterson, "Lesbian and Gay Parenting" (APA, 1995), www.apa.org/pi/parent.html, para. D (accessed April 14, 2010); emphasis added. See also Charlotte J. Patterson, Megan Fulcher, and Jennifer Wainright, "Children of Lesbian and Gay Parents: Research, Law, and Policy," in Bette L. Bottoms, Margaret B. Kovera, and Bradley D. McAuliff, *Children, Social Science, and the Law* (Cambridge: Cambridge University Press, 2002), 176–202; Marybeth J. Mattingly and Robert N. Bozick, "Children Raised By Same-Sex Couples: Much Ado about Nothing," paper presented at the Conference of the Southern Sociological Society, 2001.

65. Anne Brewaeys, I. Ponjaert, E. V. Van Hall, and Susan Golombok, "Donor Insemination: Child Development and Family Functioning in Lesbian Mother Families," *Human Reproduction* 12 (1997): 1349–59; Raymond W. Chan, Barbara Raboy, and Charlotte Patterson, "Psychological Adjustment among Children Conceived via Donor Insemination by Lesbian and Heterosexual Mothers," *Child Development* 69 (1998): 443–57.

66. Fiona Tasker and Susan Golombok, *Growing Up in a Lesbian Family* (New York: Guilford Press, 1997); J. M. Bailey and K. Dawood, "Behavior Genetics, Sexual Orientation, and the Family," in *Lesbian, Gay, and Bisexual Identities in Families*, ed. Charlotte J. Patterson and Anthony R. D'Augelli (New York: Oxford University Press, 1998), 3–18.

67. American Academy of Pediatrics, "Technical Report: Coparent or Second-Parent Adoption by Same-Sex Parents," *Pediatrics* 109 (February 2002): 341–44.

68. APA, "Resolution on Sexual Orientation and Marriage" (2004), www.apa.org/about/governance/council/Policy?gay-marriage.pdf (accessed January 3, 2012).

69. Paige Averett, B. Nalavany, and S. Ryan, "Does Sexual Orientation Matter? A Matched Comparison of Adoption Samples," *Adoption Quarterly* 12 (2009): 129–51.

70. Nanette Gartrell and Henry Bos, "US National Longitudinal Lesbian Family Study: Psychological Adjustment of 17-Year-Old Adolescents," *Pediatrics* 26 (2010):1–9, www.nllfs.org/images/uploads/pdf/NLLFS-psychological-adjustment-17-year-olds-2010.pdf.

71. For a review of this data, see Osnat Erel and Bonnie Burman, "Interrelatedness of Marital Relations and Parent–Child Relations: A Meta-Analytic Review," *Psychological Bulletin* 118 (1995): 108–32; Paul R. Amato and Alan Booth, *A Generation at Risk: Growing Up in an Era of Family Upheaval* (Cambridge: Harvard University Press, 1997), 67–83; Stacy J. Rogers and Lynn K. White, "Satisfaction with Parenting: The Role of Marital Happiness, Family Structure, and Parents' Gender," *Journal of Marriage and Family* 60 (1998): 293–316; David H. Demo and Martha J. Cox, "Families with Young Children: A Review of the Research in the 1990s," *Journal of Marriage and Family* 62 (2000): 876–900.

72. CDF, CRP, n. 7.

73. CCC, 2357.

74. Reported in *Tablet*, February 13, 2010, 31.

75. John Courtney Murray, *We Hold These Truths: Catholic Reflections on the American Experience* (New York: Sheed and Ward, 1960), 106.

76. GS, 5.

77. FC, 5.

78. James D. Davidson, Patricia Wittberg, William J. Whalen, Kathleen Mass Weigert, Andrea S. Williams, Richard A. Lamanna, and Jan Stenftenagel, *The Search for Common Ground: What Unites and Divides Catholic Americans* (Huntington, IN: Our Sunday Visitor, 1997), 11.

79. Ibid., 47.

80. William V. D'Antonio, Dean R. Hoge, James D. Davidson, and Katherine Meyer, *American Catholics: Gender, Generation, and Commitment* (Lanham, MD: Altamira Press, 2001), 76.

81. Ibid., 85.

82. Ibid., 84.

83. Dean R. Hoge, Mary Johnson, and William Dinges, *Young Adult Catholics: Religion in the Culture of Choice* (Notre Dame, IN: University of Notre Dame Press, 2001), 59–60.

84. See Michael Hornsby-Smith, *Roman Catholicism in England: Customary Catholicism and Transformation of Religious Authority* (Cambridge: Cambridge University Press, 1991); Timothy J. Buckley, *What Binds Marriage? Roman Catholic Theology in Practice* (London: Chapman, 1997); John Fulton, ed., *Young Catholics at the New Millennium: The Religion and Morality of Young Adults in Western Countries* (Dublin: University College Press, 2000).

85. *FC*, 5.

86. See International Theological Commission, *Theses on the Relationship between the Ecclesiastical Magisterium and Theology* (Washington, DC: USCCB, 1977), thesis 8, 6.

87. Robin Gill, *Churchgoing and Christian Ethics* (Cambridge: Cambridge University Press, 1999), 1; emphasis added.

88. *LG*, 12.

89. Avery Dulles, "*Sensus Fidelium*," *America* (November 1, 1986), 242.

90. Farley, *Just Love*, 190. See also Michael G. Lawler and Todd A. Salzman, "Human Experience and Catholic Moral Theology," *Irish Theological Quarterly* 76 (2011): 35–56.

91. Ibid., 195–96.

92. Ibid., 287.

93. Farley, "An Ethic for Same-Sex Relations," in *A Challenge to Love: Gay and Lesbian Catholics in the Church*, ed. Robert Nugent (New York: Crossroad, 1983), 105.

94. Xavier Lacroix, "Une parole éthique recevable par tous ?," in *L'amour du semblable: Questions sur l'homosexualité* (Paris : Cerf, 2001), 148 ; emphasis in original.

95. See Stephen J. Pope, "Scientific and Natural Law Analyses of Homosexuality: A Methodological Study," *Journal of Religious Ethics* 25 (1997): 110–11.

96. See Todd A. Salzman and Michael G. Lawler, "New Natural Law Theory and Foundational Sexual Ethical Principles: A Critique and a Proposal," *Heythrop Journal* 47 (2006): 182–205; "Catholic Sexual Ethics: Complementarity and the Truly Human," *TS* 67 (2006): 625–52; and James F. Keenan, "Can We Talk? Theological Ethics and Sexuality," *TS* 68 (2007): 113–31.

97. Ratzinger, "Transmission of Divine Revelation," 185.

98. CDF, *Mysterium Ecclesiae*, AAS 65 (1973), 402–3.

99. Farley, *Just Love*, 286.

100. Moore, *A Question of Truth*, 282.

CHAPTER 6

❦

Artificial Reproductive Technologies

In the 1950s, the marketing of effective oral contraceptives made it possible to have sexual intercourse without reproduction; in the 1980s, the marketing of artificial reproductive technologies (ARTs) made it possible to reproduce without having sexual intercourse. The Catholic Magisterium argues against the morality of both artificial contraceptives and ARTs on the basis of its principle of the inseparability of the unitive and procreative meanings of sexual intercourse. We have already dealt at length with the teaching on contraception. In this chapter, we deal with the teaching on ARTs. The CDF's *Instruction, Donum Vitae*, enunciates the principle: "The Church's teaching on marriage and human procreation affirms the 'inseparable connection, willed by God and unable to be broken by man on his own initiative, between the two meanings of the conjugal act: the unitive meaning and the procreative meaning.'"[1] This inseparability principle prohibits "artificial procreation" or "artificial fertilization," understood as "the different technical procedures directed towards obtaining a human conception in a manner other than the sexual union of man and woman."[2]

From the beginning of this book, we have insisted that traditional Catholic sexual morality is essentially marital morality; sexuality is confined within marriage and is moral when open to procreation. There is a trinity that is intrinsically and inseparably interconnected: marriage, sexuality, and procreation. For the Magisterium, artificial reproductive technologies, defined as "non-coital methods of conception that involve manipulation of both eggs and sperm," interfere with this intrinsic connection by separating the unitive and procreative meanings of sexual intercourse.[3] Revisionist theologians tend to think that, although ARTs often do not rely on sexual intercourse for reproduction, they may still fulfill on occasion both the unitive and procreative ends of *marriage* considered as an intimate interpersonal whole. When the marital relationship is seen, as it has been seen since Vatican II in contemporary Catholic theology, as an interpersonal, procreative whole, and not just as a genital act, it seems reasonable to argue that at least some ARTs utilize modern science and technology to facilitate both the unitive and procreative meanings of the relationship. *Gaudium et spes* notes that "children really are the supreme gift of marriage," and if they are, and ARTs can help infertile couples realize this supreme gift, we may legitimately ask about the credibility of the Magisterium's inseparability principle in condemning *all* ARTs that separate the two meanings of the conjugal act.[4] This, then, concretely, is the debate in this chapter. First, we define various types of ARTs; second, we explain and critique magisterial teaching on ARTs, focusing primarily on the CDF's *Instruction*; third, we analyze and evaluate ARTs in light of our foundational principle for the morality of any sexual activity.

DEFINING ARTIFICIAL
REPRODUCTIVE TECHNOLOGIES

ARTs are used when at least one spouse in a marriage is believed to be infertile. The American Society for Reproductive Medicine puts the level of infertility, "generally defined as the inability of a couple to conceive after 12 months of intercourse without contraception," at around 10 percent.[5] The causes of infertility are varied. They include hormonal imbalance, endometriosis, venereal infection (20%), contraceptive practices, abortions, incompatibility of gametes, cancer, and other causes, but scientific developments in the last forty years have offered couples the ability to overcome infertility.[6] These developments include fertility drugs, which cause the woman to produce a number of ripe ova that can result in multiple pregnancies, and surgical operations, which can remove blockages in, for example, the fallopian tubes. The most popular of these modern developments is, however, the ARTs.[7]

One of the earliest ARTs to be used was artificial insemination. In this procedure male sperm is collected, from either masturbation or a condom used in sexual intercourse, and is inserted into the woman's cervical canal at or near the time of ovulation in order to fertilize the released ovum. The collected sperm may be used within a few hours of collection or frozen for later use. When fertilization takes place within the woman's body, the procedure is known as *in vivo* (in the body) artificial insemination. When the sperm is collected from the woman's husband, the entire procedure is known as *homologous insemination*; when it is collected from a donor not the woman's husband, it is *heterologous insemination*.

Another ART, one that differs from in vivo in terms of where fertilization takes place, is *in vitro fertilization with embryo transfer* (IVF-ET). In this procedure, used in over 70 percent of all ART procedures, both sperm and ova are collected, and fertilization takes place outside the woman's body in a laboratory. There are various ways to collect the ova. Hormonal treatments with human menopausal gonadotropin (HMG) cause ova to mature in the woman's body, and these ripe eggs, or oocytes, are harvested via laparoscopic surgery or transportation by ultrasound guidance to the vagina. Once sperm and ova are collected, the sperm is washed or *capacitated* to enhance penetration and fertilization of several oocytes, creating several zygotes in a lab container. Since fertilization in this case takes place outside the woman's body in a laboratory container, the procedure is known as in vitro (in glass) fertilization. After fertilization and about forty hours of development, during which time the zygote is scientifically in the *pre-embryo* stage, one to six healthy embryos are selected and transferred through the woman's cervix to her uterus anticipating implantation and development.[8] Excess healthy embryos can be frozen, a process known as *cryopreservation*, and used later if the embryo transfer is unsuccessful or if the couple desires another pregnancy. They may also be used for research. Unhealthy embryos are typically destroyed. The processes of destruction, use in research, and the cryopreservation of fertilized embryos raise their own moral issues with regard to respect for human life. The Catholic principle on these issues is firm: "The human being must be respected—as a person—from the very first instant of his existence."[9]

Moral theologians who argue against the morality of ARTs in general do so on the basis that "fertilization is not directly the result of the marital act, since the semen used is not deposited by that act in the vagina, but by a technician's manipulation which substitutes for the marital act."[10] We argue that it is the intention of the couple, in conjunction with their sexual intercourse, *to maintain the unitive and procreative meanings of their overall marital, interpersonal relationship* that defines, in whole or in part, the moral meaning of any artificial technique. Since the integrity of marital intercourse and its direct relationship with reproduction is at the heart of the Magisterium's moral analysis of ARTs, we next explore this analysis as it is articulated in the CDF's *Instruction*.

THE CDF'S *INSTRUCTION* AND ARTS

The *Instruction* was issued by the CDF in 1987 in response to questions posed by bishops, theologians, doctors, and scientists about the scientific and biomedical ability to intervene in the process of procreation.[11] It draws some clear lines on the morality of fertility-related interventions. These technologies "must be given a moral evaluation in reference to the dignity of the human person, who is called to realize his vocation from God to the gift of love and the gift of life."[12]

As its full title indicates, the *Instruction* addresses two main issues. The first is the fundamental respect due to human life and the long-standing Catholic principle that "human life must be absolutely respected and protected from the moment of conception."[13] This principle rules out by definition any destruction of, experimentation with, and cryo-preservation of embryos. The second issue, "Interventions upon Human

Procreation," specifically addresses artificial insemination and IVF-ET.[14] Interventions are to be assessed morally on the basis of "the respect, defense and promotion of man, his dignity as a person who is endowed with a spiritual soul and with moral responsibility," but no definition is offered for the dignity of the human person in relation to either natural law or the meaning and nature of marriage, human sexuality, procreation, and parenthood.[15] All these dimensions of the question will be considered next.

Natural Law: Biological and Personalist Interpretations

In general, the CDF's *Instruction* "argues its case in terms of the traditional natural-law teaching of the Catholic Church, amplified by revelation and mediated though papal and magisterial teaching."[16] Much of the same critique we have leveled against traditionalist interpretations of natural law throughout this book, therefore, applies to the foundational principles the *Instruction* derives from natural law to condemn certain ARTs. The American Fertility Society, which met in 1987 to reconsider its statement about the morality of ARTs in light of the CDF's *Instruction*, questioned the procedure used by the CDF to derive its conclusions from the stated premises. "While stating that 'the individual integrally and adequately considered' is to be the basis of the moral judgment, the fact is that most conclusions are based on and referred to past Catholic statements."[17] We question the teaching of the *Instruction* largely because of its biological and physicalist approach to natural law.

Like *Gaudium et spes* and *Humanae vitae*, however, the *Instruction* evinces a tension between biological, that is, the physical process of reproduction, and personalist, that is, the relational meaning of reproduction, approaches to natural law. Thomas Shannon articulates this tension in relation to *Gaudium et spes* and Vatican II. The Second Vatican Council "vacillated between a less biological and more personalistic understanding of natural law, suggesting that, while physical reality is important, one also needs to look at the good of humanity and one's vocation in that context."[18] It is never a question of either/or, either the biological or the personal in natural law, but a question of both/and, both biological and personal. The personalist account of natural law in *Gaudium et spes*, however, has yet to be fully integrated into magisterial teachings on both human sexuality and reproduction.

Though it does offer intimately personalist reflections on the unitive meaning of marital sexual intercourse, *Humanae vitae's* absolute prohibition of artificial means of regulating conception demonstrates a clear prioritization of the biological over the personalist approach to natural law. This prioritization allows for "therapeutic means necessary to cure bodily diseases, even if a foreseeable impediment to procreation should result therefrom," but does not allow such means to facilitate the unitive meaning of the marital relationship.[19] For example, if for "serious reasons" a couple chooses not to reproduce, or for the sake of responsible parenthood chooses not to have more children, and practicing natural family planning (NFP) proves to be detrimental to the unitive meaning of the marital relationship, artificial contraceptives are not permitted. In this situation, treating a biological pathology justifies using artificial contraceptives, but addressing relational complications that may arise from practicing NFP does not.

The *Instruction* also demonstrates a clear prioritization of the biological over the personalist emphasis in natural law, but it vacillates between these two interpretations in assessing different types of reproductive technologies. This vacillation is clearly evident in its different analysis of heterologous artificial fertilization (AFD), in which the semen and/or ova come from a third-party male or female, and homologous artificial fertilization (AFH), in which the semen and ova come from the male and female in the coupled relationship.[20] While the *Instruction* draws on personalist interpretations in its reflections on marriage, marital union, and parenthood, it is unwilling to follow through with the logical and normative implications of that interpretation in the case of certain ARTs. We explore how it vacillates in its use of natural law when addressing AFD and AFH.

HETEROLOGOUS ARTIFICIAL INSEMINATION
AND THE PERSONALIST PRINCIPLE

While the *Instruction* utilizes personalist language to explain marriage and human sexuality, the tension between the personalist and biological interpretations of natural law is evident in its treatment of heterologous (AFD) and homologous (AFH) artificial insemination. The *Instruction* begins its treatment of AFD by answering the question: "Why must human procreation take place in marriage?" Procreation "must be the fruit and the sign of the mutual self-giving of the spouses, of their love and of their fidelity."[21] Notice that the emphasis is not on the biological act of intercourse, but on the interpersonal marital *relationship*, its mutual self-giving, love, and fidelity. Fidelity pertains to the marital relationship, where there is "reciprocal respect of their right to become a father and a mother only through each other."[22] The *Instruction* grounds its moral assessment of AFD in the personalist dimension of natural law. Procreation must take place in marriage because of the personal and relational implications for the spouses with one another, "mutual self-giving," and with the child, "the child is the living image of their love," the "permanent sign of their conjugal union."[23] The clear focus of the *Instruction's* treatment of AFD is on the personal and relational dimensions of the spouses, their union, and their relationship with the child.

In light of these relational criteria, the *Instruction* then asks whether AFD conforms to the "dignity of the couple and to the truth of marriage" and illustrates its negative answer by highlighting several ways in which AFD violates marital and familial relationships. First, AFD violates the marital relationship. "Heterologous artificial fertilization is contrary to the unity of marriage, to the dignity of the spouses, to the vocation proper to parents, and to the child's right to be conceived and brought into the world in marriage and from marriage."[24] Second, the introduction of a third party into reproduction through the use of donor gametes "constitutes a violation of the reciprocal commitment of the spouses and a grave lack in regard to that essential property of marriage which is its unity."

Third, AFD "violates the rights of the child; it deprives him of his filial relationship with his parental origins and can hinder the maturing of his personal identity." Fourth, AFD threatens the vocation to parenthood since "it offends the common vocation of the spouses who are called to fatherhood and motherhood . . . it brings about and manifests a rupture between genetic parenthood, gestational parenthood and responsibility for upbringing." Finally, AFD negatively impacts broader social relationships. "Such damage to the personal relationships within the family has repercussions on civil society: what threatens the unity and stability of the family is a source of dissension, disorder and injustice in the whole of social life." The fundamental violation of all of these relationships leads "to a negative moral judgment concerning heterologous artificial fertilization."[25]

This entire section of the *Instruction* focuses on the various relationships the spouses have to each other, to their child, and to their society, and argues to the immorality of AFD on the basis that it fundamentally violates those relationships. If the *Instruction* were consistent in its ethical reasoning, it would continue with this personalist, relational principle in morally evaluating homologous artificial insemination. It does not. When it addresses AFH, it shifts emphasis to a different foundational principle.

HOMOLOGOUS ARTIFICIAL INSEMINATION AND THE BIOLOGICAL PRINCIPLE

The CDF's treatment of AFH opens with the question "What connection is required from the moral point of view between procreation and the conjugal act?"[26] The shift in the question from "dignity of the couple and the truth of marriage" to "procreation and the conjugal act" reflects a methodological shift from the primacy of a relational, personalist emphasis to the primacy of an act-centered, biological emphasis. Three questions emerge regarding the *Instruction*'s shift. First, why does the *Instruction* make this methodological shift from a focus on *relationship* when morally evaluating AFD to focus on the *act* of intercourse when morally evaluating AFH? Second, what are the weaknesses of this inseparability principle with regard to AFH? Third, what would be the moral implications for AFH if the *Instruction* were methodologically consistent?

First, while the arguments against AFD seem reasonable to us given the relational complications of donor gametes and their potential impact on the marital relationship, the relationship of the parents with the child, the donor's relationship with both the parents and the child, and the social implications with regard to the nature of the family, the same relational complications do not apply in AFH. Where the gametes belong to the spouses, and a surrogate is not used to carry the embryo, the relational complications do not exist. All that can be claimed with certainty in the case of AFH is that the act of sexual intercourse is not *immediately* responsible for procreation. This point, however, while it gives us insight into the *procedure* facilitating reproduction, gives us no insight into the *moral meaning* of that procedure. As was indicated earlier, moral meaning is discerned not through the *givenness* of reality, in this case the givenness of the use of technology and science to assist reproduction, but in the *meaning* of those facts for human relationships. If the same personalist principle applied to AFD were applied to AFH, one could come to a different conclusion about the morality of AFH.

Second, by focusing on the act of intercourse and the inseparability principle in its discussion of AFH, the *Instruction* clearly recognizes that there is a shift in the foundational moral principle in analyzing and morally evaluating AFH and AFD. The *Instruction*'s condemnation of AFH is strictly dependent on the inseparability principle, that is, the inseparability of the unitive and procreative meanings of sexual intercourse. It follows from the *Instruction*'s strict dependence on this principle to justify its moral argument against AFH that the argument is only as strong as the principle; if the principle is weak, so too is any moral conclusion drawn from the principle.

We believe the "inseparability principle" used to prohibit AFH (and contraception) is a weak principle on several counts. First, there is no essentially procreative meaning to each and every sexual act. As we have noted several times, sexual acts in an infertile or postmenopausal relationship, or sexual acts during the lengthy periods when the woman is known to be infertile, do not have an essentially procreative meaning.

Second, the basis for the inseparability principle is a product of the biologism and physicalism that has controlled the Catholic natural-law tradition, grounded in both a flawed biology and a flawed theology of marriage. In the Catholic tradition up until the Second Vatican Council, the *primary end* of marriage was always said to be procreation. This teaching reflected a long history that recognized procreation as the only legitimate meaning and purpose for sexual intercourse.[27] Our modern understanding of biology and human sexuality, however, teaches us that procreation is not even possible in the vast majority of sexual acts. A couple can morally justify having sexual intercourse without the procreative meaning, but they can never justify having sexual intercourse without the unitive meaning. It is logical, therefore, to argue that not only are the unitive and material procreative meanings of the sexual act separable, and on occasion in fact legitimately separated, but also that the unitive meaning is now primary, and the procreative meaning secondary.

Third, while the *Instruction* correctly notes that "the one conceived must be the fruit of the parent's love," it has not adequately explained how the one conceived in AFH is not the fruit of the parents' love. It is not enough simply to state that AFH separates the unitive and procreative meanings of the sexual act and to conclude, therefore, that the child conceived in AFH is not the fruit of the parents' love, for that conclusion is a non sequitur; it does not follow from the premise. The forty-year experience with artificial insemination appears to show that the desperation of infertile couples, and the emotional, physical, and economic inconvenience they are willing to undergo, is frequently a very powerful sign of their mutual love and their desire to offer to one another "the supreme gift of marriage," namely, a child.[28] The meaning of ARTs and the intentions for choosing them are determined concretely, case by case, within the context of particular human relationships; meaning and intention are determined by the motives, desires, hopes, dreams, and reasons of the particular couple choosing ARTs.

Fourth, the tension between the personalist principle used to morally evaluate AFD and the inseparability principle used to morally evaluate AFH is highlighted all the more when the *Instruction* claims that "homologous IVF and ET fertilization is not marked by all that ethical negativity found in extra-conjugal procreation; the family and marriage continue to constitute the setting for the birth and upbringing of the children."[29] The relational considerations of AFD make it more morally objectionable than the violation of the inseparability principle in AFH. By its own admission, then, the inseparability principle on the basis of which the *Instruction* condemns AFH does not carry the same moral weight as the relational principle condemning AFD. The *Instruction* focuses on the marital act to argue against AFH; it focuses on relational dimensions to argue to the "ethical negativity" of AFD. It is relational considerations that make AFH less morally reprehensible than AFD. Since there may be no conjugal act in AFH, however, why would the *Instruction* base its moral condemnation of AFH on the conjugal act and the inseparability principle? It must do so because the relational considerations do not warrant an absolute prohibition of AFH, though the inseparability principle may so warrant if one accepts the principle as morally compelling. We do not find it morally compelling.

THE MORALITY OF AFH

Based on the foregoing analysis, we draw what we believe is a logical conclusion about the morality of homologous artificial insemination. As we noted at the beginning of our discussion of AFH, if the premise, in this case the inseparability principle, is weak, then any conclusion drawn from that premise will also be weak. We believe the inseparability principle cannot bear the weight of the *Instruction*'s conclusions absolutely prohibiting AFH. Given the desperation of an infertile couple to have a child, and their intention, grounded in justice, mutual love, respect, responsibility, and human dignity, to have their marital relationship "crowned" by their child, we believe the use of AFH can be moral and facilitate both the unitive and procreative meanings of marriage.[30]

ARTIFICIAL REPRODUCTIVE TECHNOLOGIES

We are in agreement here with Lisa Cahill. Many Catholics, she notes, "perceive a difference larger than the Vatican allows between therapies used in marriage, even if they do temporarily circumvent sexual intercourse, and methods which bring donors into the marital procreative venture. . . . Donor methods are more morally objectionable because they do not appreciate the unity as *relationships* of sexual expression, committed partnership, and parenthood."[31] While procreation in AFH would not be the result of one act of marital coitus, it would be the fruit of an overall *marital relational act* that expresses and facilitates the just love, commitment, care, concern, and dignity of the couple shared with a new human being, their child. Our argument defending the moral acceptability of AFH is grounded not in the inseparability of the unitive and procreative meanings of a sexual act, but in the meaning and nature of marital relationship, marital sexuality, and parenthood that is its crown. It is in the overall marital relationship, not in each and every sexual act, that the unitive and procreative meanings may be legitimately inseparable.[32] With the *Instruction*, we affirm the intrinsic connection of marriage, sexual love, and parenthood. We judge, however, that its claim that genuine marital love is absolutely incompatible with the occasional use of artificial means to bring about conception without an immediate sexual act, or to avoid conception with a sexual act, is unsupported and meaningless apart from consideration of the context of particular marital relationships.

The Meaning and Nature of Parenthood

While the *Instruction* uses the inseparability principle to condemn AFH, it indicates a parallel consideration between this principle and the relational emphasis it uses to condemn AFD. This parallel consideration revolves, first, around the relationship between the conjugal act and parenthood and, second, around the meaning and nature of parenthood itself. After positing the inseparability principle as the foundational principle prohibiting AFH, the *Instruction* quotes *Humanae vitae*: "By safeguarding both these essential aspects, the unitive and the procreative, the conjugal act preserves in its fullness the sense of true mutual love and its ordination towards man's exalted vocation to parenthood."[33] In addressing AFD, the *Instruction* notes that "it offends the common vocation of the spouses who are called to fatherhood and motherhood: it objectively deprives conjugal fruitfulness of its unity and integrity; it brings about and manifests a rupture between genetic parenthood, gestational parenthood, and responsibility for upbringing."[34] Two points need to be addressed when parenthood is offered as a parallel consideration in the condemnation of AFD and AFH. First, we must investigate the *Instruction's* assertion that the conjugal act is ordained toward parenthood. Second, we must investigate parenthood in its genetic, gestational, and social dimensions.[35]

Gaudium et spes teaches that "children are really the supreme gift of marriage."[36] In the abstract and in general, one can say there is an essential relationship between the conjugal act and parenthood in its three dimensions, genetic, gestational, and social. Approximately one out of ten couples in the United States, however, is infertile, and for these infertile couples it is impossible that any conjugal act will lead to genetic, gestational, or social parenthood.[37] The CDF's teaching on ARTs that replace the marital act prescribes that the only morally acceptable path to parenthood for these infertile couples is through adoption or fostering.

The Magisterium applauds the moral validity and nobility of postnatal adoption, which incarnates the fundamental Christian imperative to care "for the least of these."[38] In the case of an adopted child, however, the nature of the relationship between the conjugal act and parenthood is fundamentally transformed. The sexual acts of infertile couples can never result in genetic or gestational parenthood, but they do express and promote the union of the spouses, thereby strengthening their ordination to social parenthood, that is, the nurturing of a child into functional adulthood. In and through just and loving sexual intercourse, a couple promotes shared life in their relationship, and that shared life permeates all their relationships, including a possible relationship with an adopted child in social parenthood. It also, of course, makes possible a sacramental relationship with God, a fact deeply important for Catholics. While adoption may not preserve "in its fullness" the relationship between sexual intercourse and genetic and gestational parenthood, it certainly preserves the unitive, relational dimension of the marriage and, therefore, the social dimension of parenthood.

Technology has complicated the definition of parenthood. Couples who utilize IVF-ET or its technological equivalents generally produce excess embryos that are frozen.[39] If a couple decides not to have more children, these embryos remain frozen, to be eventually destroyed, used for stem cell research, or adopted. The *Instruction*, as we have seen, clearly condemns destroying embryos or any experimentation that will damage or destroy them. The first successful birth of an adopted frozen embryo occurred in Australia in 1984. Even though the publication of the *Instruction* followed that first case of frozen embryo adoption by three years, it did not address embryo adoption. The question of adopting frozen embryos has been discussed by theologians, but the Magisterium's silence on the question continues.[40] The reality of the possible adoption of frozen embryos, however, challenges us to rethink the meaning and nature of parenthood.

The *Instruction* notes that AFD "brings about and manifests a rupture between genetic parenthood, gestational parenthood and responsibility for upbringing," but it does not explain the moral meaning of that rupture.[41] Nor does it explain the interrelationship among the three dimensions of parenthood or suggest any hierarchy among them. We offer two comments. First, as is indicated in both pre- and postnatal adoption, there is no intrinsic relationship between the various dimensions of parenthood. A couple can experience one, two, or all three dimensions. Second, in the case of AFD, the *Instruction* makes no moral distinction between the three dimensions of parenthood. It would seem that these dimensions are of equal value and constitute various dimensions of the vocation of parenthood. In both pre- and postnatal adoption, no genetic parenthood is involved; in prenatal adoption there is both gestational and social parenthood; in postnatal adoption, there is neither genetic nor gestational but only social parenthood. Social parenthood is common to all three scenarios and, in fact, is the most important dimension of parenthood. On this we agree with Paul Lauritzen, who writes that the core of parenthood is "the commitment to, and the activities of, caring for a child in a way that promotes human flourishing," and with Germain Grisez, who writes that "parenthood is far more a moral than a biological relationship: its essence is not so much in begetting and giving birth as in readiness to accept the gift of life, commitment to nurture it, and faithful fulfillment of that commitment through many years."[42]

The primacy of social parenthood has moral implications for the definition of the rupture between the three types of parenthood the *Instruction* notes and for the relationship between parenthood and the conjugal act. The rupture *may* have moral implications for AFD, but its deliberate rupture in the case of embryo adoption leads to an untenable position in the case of AFH. John Berkman highlights this position. "Catholic teaching seems to allow [adoptive embryo transfer] which separates genetic parenthood from gestational and 'raising' parenthood, but prohibits [AFH embryo transfer] that would maintain the bond between genetic, gestational, and 'raising' parenthood."[43] While AFH does not rely on the act of sexual intercourse for its realization, it does realize parenthood "in its fullness." The rupture between the three types of parenthood may be *descriptively* relevant, but it is not necessarily *morally* relevant in evaluating ARTs.

The Magisterium's apparent approval of embryo adoption, and undoubted approval of postnatal adoption, also recognizes the moral legitimacy of separating the conjugal act from genetic parenthood. In the case of AFH, as with pre- and postnatal adoption, there is not a conjugal act of the parents immediately responsible for procreation. The conjugal act between the spouses, however, is unitive in that it sustains and nurtures both the marital relationship between the spouses and the parental relationship between the parents and the child.

Parental Complementarity, Relational
Considerations, and Social Ethics

Since the Magisterium's principle of the inseparability of the procreative and unitive meanings of the marital act, used to prohibit AFH, is subject to fundamental critiques, a credible moral analysis of ARTs needs to focus more on the relational dimensions and implications of these procedures. We agree with the *Instruction's* prioritization of the relational considerations of ARTs over the inseparability principle in its moral assessment of AFD, and, for the sake of internal consistency and credibility, we use the relational principle to analyze and evaluate all ARTs. Since there is not an act of spousal sexual intercourse immediately responsible for reproduction in most ARTs, since the genetic link is severed from the act of intercourse and parenthood in prenatal adoption, and since the genetic and gestational link is severed from the conjugal act in postnatal adoption, our option for this principle, we believe, is compelling. Focus on personal relationships is at the heart of the foundational, sexual, moral principle we have articulated in this book. Since reproduction is fundamentally about parenthood, we focus on the meaning of parenthood in morally assessing ARTs. Parenthood includes the relationship between the spouses, the relationship between the parents and their child, and the broader social relationships in which the family exists, functions, finds support, and contributes to society.

Since the relationship between husband and wife, the "coupled-we" in marriage, is the foundational relationship in which children are procreated, nurtured, and educated, this relationship requires special focus and attention in the case of ARTs. We share with many theologians and the CDF concerns about the potential relational complications associated with AFD. While it is not necessarily the case that the use of donor gametes is destructive of the marital, parental, or child–parent relationship, there are legitimate relational concerns that warrant a *presumption against* the use of donor gametes. At the root of these concerns is the notion that "conjugal exclusivity should include the genetic, gestational and rearing dimensions of parenthood. Separating these dimensions (except through rescue, as in adoption) too easily contains a subtle diminishment of some aspect of the human person" and the spousal relationship.[44] The diminishment of the human person could take many different forms: feelings of reproductive inadequacy, loss of the self-esteem so necessary for a healthy sexual life, and resentment toward the other spouse. These personal issues may affect the marital relationship and create disharmony between the spouses. Where donor gametes are the only means for a couple to reproduce, the couple must discern the impact of gamete donation on their relationship and their mutual relationship with any child that might be born. This discernment process requires open and honest reflection, dialogue, and prayer. A realistic assessment of the issues and their potential impact on human relationships must be made, and, in light of this assessment, a responsible decision can be reached.

The great challenge in speculating about the relational implications and consequences of reproductive choices is, of course, that we are finite human beings, and our vision, knowledge, and understanding are limited. This is especially true of any reality that lies in the future. We cannot fully understand or accurately assess all the complications or blessings that may arise from our decisions on reproductive, or any other, issues. Though certitude is not an absolute requirement for moral judgment, prudence always is. We believe an infertile couple could make, in good conscience, a prudential moral judgment to use AFD. The couple would, however, bear the burden of proof that the concerns voiced by the *Instruction* about the use of donor gametes would not endanger their various relationships.

If, after reflection, an infertile couple comes to the conclusion that AFD would entail a disproportionate risk to their human relationships, there are alternatives for reproduction. Rather than using AFD and creating new embryos or practicing artificial insemination, a couple could adopt existing, cryopreserved embryos. While, technically, the woman is carrying the embryo of another couple, there is a fundamental difference between embryo adoption and surrogacy. In the former, the gestational mother will give birth to and nurture a wanted child; in the latter, the gestational mother will "surrender the child once it is born to the party who commissioned or made the agreement for the pregnancy."[45] Surrogacy is a means to an end, in which the gestational mother's obligations to the child end shortly after the child's birth, and the responsibility of nurturing the child is taken over by another person or persons. Embryo adoption, on the other hand, includes both the gestational and social dimensions of parenthood.

The distinction between surrogacy and embryo adoption is helpful for addressing the issue of ARTs and same-sex parenthood. Some argue that if AFD is permitted as a moral option, then there is nothing to prevent lesbian or gay couples (through surrogacy) from reproducing children. The same relational concerns we highlighted in the case of heterosexual couples and their marital relationship, with the exception of reproductive inadequacy, apply to homosexual couples and their union. While these concerns do not rule out, ipso facto, AFD for homosexual couples, there is a presumption against such procedures. Embryo adoption, however, is another matter and would provide, for lesbian couples, an opportunity to participate in both the gestational and nurturing dimensions of parenthood. As we indicated in an earlier chapter, there is no credible social-scientific evidence to support the claim that homosexual parenting has a negative impact on the children.[46]

There is no doubt that genes are biological material, but there is a more profound relational consideration that defines the moral meaning of the genetic, biological consideration. If biological, genetic material were the only morally determinative reason that AFD is morally acceptable or unacceptable, then spousal rape that results in pregnancy could be morally justified, since parenthood is respected genetically, gestationally, and socially. No one, however, would ever condone spousal rape, even if it does fulfill all three dimensions of parenthood. Spousal rape is absolutely wrong because of the unjust violence and relational implications of the act. Similarly, in the case of AFD, where the biological genes are not from one or both of the partners, the moral assessment of the procedure rests not in the presence or absence of the requisite genes, but in the relational implications of the genetic connection for the partners individually, for the couple, and for their relation to a possible child. The genetic dimension of parenthood is morally relevant only in light of these relational considerations. If it could be demonstrated that the genetic dimension does not have a negative influence on these relationships, then, in theory, AFD could be morally acceptable. We hold, however, a presumption against AFD. The burden of proof, as we have already argued, rests with the couple to demonstrate that there would not be negative relational complications due to AFD and that there would be positive implications for the couple in relation to each other, the child, and the common good. While these concerns would apply to AFD, they would not apply to embryo adoption.

ARTS AND HEALTH COMPLICATIONS AMONG CHILDREN

While the relational implications of AFH and adoptive surrogacy for the spouses as individuals, as a couple, and as parents do not establish an *absolute* moral prohibition against either AFH or AFD, other considerations seem to indicate caution in their use. The first important consideration is the multiple pregnancies that result from the use of an ART, and the medical complications for the mother and child that accompany those pregnancies. In the United States in 2008, 33 percent of all fresh embryo, non-donor cycles utilizing ARTs were multiple births, and about 4 percent involved triplets or more.[47] This statistic contrasts with 3 percent of multiple birth rates in natural reproduction. For the mother, the medical complications include anemia, increased risks of hypertensive disorders, premature labor and delivery, the possibility of cesarean section with the accompanying risks, and death. For infants the major risks include low birth weight, prematurity, congenital anomalies, and death.[48]

The second important consideration, which expands on medical risks to the child, is scientific studies that seem to indicate a direct correlation between ARTs and the heightened risk of birth defects among children. A systematic metareview of the literature investigating the prevalence of birth defects in infants conceived through the use of IVF suggests "that infants born following ART treatment are at increased risk [30–40%] of birth defects, compared to spontaneously conceived infants."[49] While the increase in the likelihood of birth defects would not influence the moral assessment of embryo adoption for either heterosexual or homosexual couples, it would certainly have moral implications for those who choose to use ARTs for reproductive purposes. Using ARTs knowing that such procedures have a higher incidence of birth defects may demonstrate a lack of care and concern for a child's human dignity. Studies that demonstrate this correlation recommend that couples seeking ARTs should be informed of this possibility.[50] We would expand this recommendation to require reproductive clinics to inform potential parents about the increased likelihood of birth defects from using ARTs. Informed parental ethical choice demands knowledge that is accurate, complete, and readily understood. This provides a strong argument for more legislation and moral guidelines in an industry that remains largely unlegislated.[51]

In addition to consideration of a couple's emotional, psychological, and relational capabilities to care for a child with a birth defect, whether that child is the result of ART or of natural procreation, there is also an economic consideration. The ethical challenge of factoring the financial consideration into the discernment process is that those who can afford to use ARTs can have access to the technology and those who cannot afford to do so are usually denied access. In addition, those who can afford to use ARTs may or may not be able to afford to pay for the short- and long-term health complications that may result from those technologies. The social-justice issues become more prevalent the more we explore the issues surrounding ARTs.

FAMILY AND SOCIETY: ARTS AND THE COMMON GOOD

Another consideration related to the moral acceptability of ARTs is the relationship between the procedures and the Catholic tradition of the common good. A recent estimate puts the cost of in vitro fertilization with a woman's own eggs at $12,500 to $25,000, and the cost with donor eggs up to $35,000, and "less than 25% of cycles involving fresh, non-donor eggs result in a live birth."[52] Some insurance companies cover part of the initial costs. By far the greatest costs of ARTs, however, are associated with multiple births and postnatal care for those infants. In 2000, multiple births from ARTs accounted for more than $640 million dollars in additional hospital costs, an amount that does not include the cost of caring for a child with a lifelong disability that may result from the use of an ART.[53]

This is where an important Catholic ethical question arises. The biblical prophets consistently proclaim that to know and love God requires action against the injustice perpetrated against God's people.[54] The reciprocation between God and the poor "underside" reaches its high point in Jesus of Nazareth, who, in Guttierez's pregnant words, is "precisely God become poor."[55] In the Catholic ethical tradition, this reciprocation is framed in the language of the common good and includes distributive justice, a preferential option for the poor, and solidarity.[56] Given the equal dignity of every human being before God, distributive justice demands that each and every person be accorded equal right to have their minimum human needs satisfied. Ambrose of Milan articulates the root principle: "The earth belongs to all, not to the rich."[57] His disciple Augustine of Hippo agreed: "God commands sharing, not as being from the property of those he commands but as being from his own property, so that those who offer something to the poor should not think they are doing so from what is their own."[58] Strange language in the contemporary highly individualistic Western world, but thoroughly consonant with the biblical action and teaching of Jesus.

Two items of statistical information frame the present question. First, besides the financial costs of ARTs and postnatal care to families, insurance companies, and hospitals, there are also major costs in medical resources, professional talent, and research and development. According to the Centers for Disease Control, there were 428 fertility clinics in the United States in 2002, an exponential increase from the 30 or so in 1995. Second, there are approximately fifty million people in the United States without health insurance, many of them among the poorest in the nation. A serious question is whether fertility treatment for well-off individuals, almost exclusively in the first world, is the wisest and most efficient use of limited medical resources and personnel. Are ARTs a luxury that should be offered only after we have provided necessary minimum health care for everyone, in the third as well as in the first world?

If we grant that ARTs are a luxury, second to basic health care for all on a medical hierarchy, does this national hierarchy have international implications as well? What about basic health care resources in third world countries? Should financial and medical aid to third world countries come before infertility treatments in our medical hierarchy? While these considerations may seem to be blowing the moral question surrounding ART out of proportion, we believe that just as the sexual relationship between a couple has both personal and social implications, so too the reproductive choices a couple makes have both personal and social implications. A holistic moral evaluation of ARTs requires that we take the common-good implications of their use into consideration when rendering a moral judgment on a couple's reproductive decisions. "[T]he procreative interests of infertile persons have to be evaluated in light of the obligation of society to provide universal access to a decent minimum level of care. From our reading of Catholic social teaching . . . guaranteeing basic primary and emergency care takes precedence over curative therapies that benefit a small number of individuals."[59]

The approach we recommend to this hierarchical question and to the questions surrounding the Catholic debate about ARTs is to shift the focus from sexual ethics and a biological understanding of natural law to social ethics, and a personalist, relational understanding of natural law. When the focus shifts, so also the questions and the answers found acceptable shift. We submit that discussions about the moral acceptability of ARTs should not revolve exclusively around individual sexual acts. Reproduction is never simply a private, individual matter; the birth of a child, whether by natural intercourse or ART, is always a social reality. It establishes inescapable social relations—between the parent and the child, between the child and society, and between individuals and the social or common good. Maura Ryan frames the question: "How should we understand the relationship between individual wants, needs, and desires, and the social or 'common' good? How do we weigh the importance of 'saving' lives versus 'creating' lives?"[60] We agree with Cahill. "Low success rates, disproportionate expense, the priority of other medical needs, and the availability of other solutions should be part of public deliberation about the ethics and practice of assisted reproduction."[61] We suggest that the approach to questions about ARTs from a perspective in which distributive justice, preferential option for the poor, and agapaic love of neighbor hold priority is a more fruitful approach than the approach from the meaning of individual sexual acts and would help to restore much-needed credibility in the public forum to the Catholic voice on reproductive issues.

CONCLUSION

In this chapter we explained artificial reproductive technologies (ARTs), considered and critiqued the CDF's judgment on their morality, and examined their morality in light of our foundational principle guiding human sexual morality. We considered also the relational considerations between parents and between parents and their children that might impact judgments about the morality of ARTs. Although we judge that the use of the Magisterium's inseparability principle to condemn homologous artificial fertilization (AFH) lacks credibility, we also judge that the personalist and relational considerations of the CDF's *Instruction* are in line with our foundational principle guiding human sexuality.

According to this principle, we argued that AFH is morally acceptable *in se*, though we warn that the issues of multiple embryos and their human right to life, the higher probability of birth defects, and social justice must be factored into a couple's discernment process. These latter considerations, however, do not ipso facto prohibit the moral use of AFH. We further argued that, though there is a presumption against heterologous artificial fertilization (AFD) because of the potential relational complications between the spouses, the spouses and child, and the family and society, these considerations do not lead to an *absolute* norm prohibiting the use of AFD. A couple is required to discern the relational implications of their reproductive choices on these various relationships and to make a conscientious, socially just, prudent, and responsible moral decision. These considerations apply to both heterosexual and homosexual couples, though we warn that there are further complications with gay couples and surrogacy. Embryonic adoption may be morally acceptable for all couples, though again, the surrogacy issue would arise for gay couples. We believe that, again, the strength of our argument rests in the consistency of a holistic, interpersonal approach to human anthropology, sexuality, and reproductive decisions, rather than in an act-centered, biological understanding of human sexuality grounded in exclusive heterogenital or organic complementarity.

QUESTIONS FOR REFLECTION

1. What do you understand by the term *artificial reproductive technologies* (ARTs)? One ART, in vitro fertilization with embryo transfer (IVF-ET), is used more than any other. What is the process of IVF-ET?

2. Artificial insemination may be either heterologous (AFD) or homologous (AFH). In AFD, the male semen or female ova come from a third party extraneous to the couple's relationship, and the Catholic Church condemns AFD on the basis of this third-party intrusion into the couple's relationship. What possible relationship problems do you foresee for the couple and for any child that may be conceived from AFD? Are such problems sufficient, in your judgment, to condemn AFD as immoral? Why or why not?

3. The Church also condemns AFH, not on the personal basis of possible relationship problems but on the biological basis that it destroys the supposed inseparable connection between the procreative and unitive meanings of marriage. Do you know any couples that have conceived via AFH? Do you believe it is true that, as traditionalists

sometimes argue, their child is a "product of technology" rather than of their love? Do you think their relationship is any more or less loving and their child any less loved if conceived by AFH? Do your answers to the previous questions have any moral implications for evaluating AFH?

4. There are three kinds of parenthood: genetic, gestational, and social. AFD ruptures the connection between genetic and gestational parenthood, but AFH does not. It is generally agreed that the most important parenthood is social parenthood, "the commitment to, and the activities of, caring for a child in a way that promotes human flourishing." Does this judgment have any moral implications for evaluating AFH, and for pre- and postnatal adoption?

5. Scientific studies appear to indicate a direct correlation between the use of ARTs and heightened risks of birth defects among children. These risks, the high costs of dealing with birth defects for a lifetime, and the cost of ARTs cause us to raise moral questions about the common good related to the use of ARTs. Do you believe these related costs raise any moral questions about justice and the common good in the United States and even internationally? Or do you believe, rather, that the risks and the costs are questions only for the couple seeking IVF? If you believe the latter to be the case, how then do you deal with the biblical calls for action on behalf of the poor?

6. What other questions arise for you from reading this chapter?

NOTES

1. CDF, *Instruction on Respect for Human Life in Its Origin and on the Dignity of Procreation: Replies to Certain Questions of the Day* (Washington, DC: Office of Publishing and Promotion Services, United States Catholic Conference, 1987), II, B, 4, a. Cited henceforth as *Instruction*.

2. Ibid., II.

3. Linda J. Beckman and S. Marie Harvey, "Current Reproductive Technologies: Increased Access and Choice?," *Journal of Social Issues* 61 (2005): 2.

4. GS, 50.

5. Office of Technology Assessment, *Infertility, Medical and Social Choices* (Washington, DC: OTA, 1988), 3; Mary B. Mahowald, "Ethical Considerations in Infertility," in *Infertility: A Comprehensive Text*, 2nd ed., ed. Machelle M. Seibel (Stamford, CT: Appleton and Lange, 1997), 823; American Society for Reproductive Medicine, "Frequently Asked Questions about Infertility," www.asrm.org/awards/index.aspx?id=3012 (accessed January 3, 2012). See also Seibel, *Infertility*, 4.

6. Benedict Ashley and Kevin O'Rourke, *Health Care Ethics: A Theological Analysis*, 4th ed. (Washington, DC: Georgetown University Press, 1997), 241. For a historical overview of ARTs, see Don P. Wolf and Martin M. Quigley, "Historical Background and Essentials for a Program in *In Vitro* Fertilization and Embryo Transfer," in *Human in Vitro Fertilization and Embryo Transfer*, ed. Don P. Wolf and Martin M. Quigley (New York: Plenum Press, 1984), 1–11; and Annette Burfoot, ed., *Encyclopedia of Reproductive Technologies* (Boulder, CO: Westview Press, 1999).

7. For more detailed descriptions of ARTs, see Burfoot, ed., *Encyclopedia of Reproductive Technologies*; Ashley and O'Rourke, *Health Care Ethics*, 240–48; and Peter J. Cataldo, "Reproductive Technologies," *Ethics & Medics* 21 (1996), 1–3.

8. The pre-embryo stage lasts from the completion of fertilization to the development of the primitive streak, which occurs "on about the fourteenth day of development" (Howard W. Jones and Susan L. Crockin, "On Assisted Reproduction, Religion and Civil Law," *Fertility and Sterility* 73 [2000]: 450).

9. *Instruction*, I, 1.

10. Ashley and O'Rourke, *Health Care Ethics*, 247. See also Germain Grisez, *Difficult Moral Questions: The Way of the Lord Jesus*, vol. 3 (Quincy, IL: Franciscan Press, 1997), 244–49; Donald T. DeMarco, "Catholic Moral Teaching and TOT/GIFT," in *Reproductive Technologies, Marriage and the Church*, ed. Donald G. McCarthy (Braintree, MA: Pope John Center, 1988), 122–39; and John M. Haas, "GIFT? No!" *Ethics & Medics* 18 (1993): 1–2.

11. *Instruction*, foreword.

12. Ibid., Introduction, 3.

13. Ibid., I, 1.

14. Ibid., II.

15. Ibid., 1.

16. Thomas A. Shannon and Lisa Sowle Cahill, *Religion and Artificial Reproduction: An Inquiry into the Vatican "Instruction on Respect for Human Life in Its Origin and on the Dignity of Human Reproduction"* (New York: Crossroad, 1988), 55.

17. Cited in Jones and Crockin, "On Assisted Reproduction," 449.

18. Thomas A. Shannon, "Reproductive Technologies: Ethical and Religious Issues," in *Reproductive Technologies: A Reader*, ed. Thomas A. Shannon (New York: Sheed and Ward, 2004), 47.

19. *HV*, 15.

20. The *Instruction* distinguishes between heterologous artificial fertilization or procreation and homologous artificial fertilization or procreation. Within each classification, it addresses two types of reproductive technology: artificial insemination

(AI) and in vitro fertilization and embryo transfer (IVF-ET). In this chapter, we will use AFD to designate both types of heterologous artificial fertilization, and AFH to designate both types of homologous artificial fertilization. We will specifically distinguish between AI or IVF-ET when it is necessary for a point of clarification.

21. Ibid., II, A, 1.
22. Ibid.
23. Ibid.
24. Ibid., II, A, 2.
25. Ibid.
26. Ibid., II, B, 4.
27. See Michael G. Lawler, *Marriage and the Catholic Church: Disputed Questions* (Collegeville, MN: Liturgical Press, 2002), 27–42.
28. GS, 50.
29. *Instruction*, II, B, 5.
30. See GS, 48.
31. Lisa Sowle Cahill, *Women and Sexuality* (New York: Paulist, 1992), 75; emphasis in original. See also Shannon and Cahill, *Religion and Artificial Reproduction*, 103–32.
32. The Ethics Committee of the American Fertility Society accuses the CDF of "barnyard physiology." "This means that the concept that intercourse is intended entirely for reproduction derives from observation of those animals who exhibit 'heat' and give an external sign of ovulation during which period the female will accept the male and at no other time." Cited in Jones and Crockin, "On Assisted Reproduction," 449.
33. *Instruction*, II, B, 4, a.
34. Ibid., II, A, 2.
35. The classic legal case that demonstrates the *Instruction's* legitimate concern for the relational complications of surrogacy is the case of "Baby M" and the contractual and custodial dispute between Elizabeth and William Stern, who contracted with Mrs. Whitehead to both donate her egg and her womb to bear a child for the Sterns. The bond that Mrs. Whitehead developed over the nine-month gestational period as well as through the genetic link with "Baby M" led her to deny her contractual obligations to the Sterns. In turn, this denial led to a complex legal custody battle that illustrates well the relational complications of AFD and surrogacy in which the *Instruction* is legitimately concerned. In the end, the New Jersey Supreme Court nullified the surrogacy contract, arguing that commercial surrogacy was tantamount to selling babies and unethical. The basis for deciding the case was on the parental considerations of genetic, gestational, and social parenthood. While Mrs. Whitehead fulfilled the first two criteria of parenthood, social parenthood seems to be morally decisive. We agree with Glannon: "the social mother (or father) is arguably more important than genetic or gestational mothers, because the social mother is responsible for the welfare of the child from birth onward" (*Biomedical*

Ethics [New York: Oxford University Press, 2005], 84). In the end, the Supreme Court granted full custody to Mr. Stern, and Mrs. Whitehead was granted visitation rights. For our purposes, the important points in this case are twofold: first, the importance of the distinction the New Jersey Supreme Court made between different types of parenthood, genetic, gestational, and social, a distinction that the *Instruction* highlights as well; second, the primacy of social parenthood over genetic and gestational parenthood.

36. GS, 50.

37. Cataldo, "Reproductive Technologies," 1.

38. FC, 14; Matt. 25:40.

39. For a full listing of these equivalents, see Todd A. Salzman and Michael G. Lawler, *The Sexual Person: Toward a Renewed Catholic Anthropology* (Washington, DC: Georgetown University Press, 2008), 237–40.

40. See John Berkman, "The Morality of Adopting Frozen Embryos," *Studia Moralia* 40 (2002): 11–41; Grisez, *Difficult Moral Questions*, 239–44; Mary Geach, "Are There Any Circumstances in Which It Would Be Morally Admirable for a Woman to Seek to Have an Orphan Embryo Implanted in Her Womb? – 1," in *Issues for a Catholic Bioethic*, ed. Luke Gormally (London: Linacre Centre, 1999), 341–46; William B. Smith, "Rescue the Frozen?," *Homiletic and Pastoral Review* 96 (1995): 72–74; Smith, "Response," *Homiletic and Pastoral Review* 96 (1995): 16–17; Geoffrey Surtees, "Adoption of a Frozen Embryo," *Homiletic and Pastoral Review* 96 (1995): 7–16, and Sarah-Vaughan Brakman and Darlene Fozard Weaver, eds., *The Ethics of Embryo Adoption and the Catholic Tradition: Moral Arguments, Economic Reality, and Social Analysis* (New York: Springer, 2007).

41. *Instruction*, II, A, 2.

42. Paul Lauritzen, *Pursuing Parenthood: Ethical Issues in Assisted Reproduction* (Bloomington: Indiana University Press, 1993), 76–84; Germain Grisez, *The Way of the Lord Jesus*, vol. 2: *Living a Christian Life* (Quincy, IL: Franciscan Herald Press, 1993), 689.

43. Berkman, "Morality of Adopting," 132.

44. Richard A. McCormick, *Critical Calling: Reflections on Moral Dilemmas since Vatican II* (Washington, DC: Georgetown University Press, 1987), 341.

45. *Instruction*, II, A, 3.

46. See Charlotte J. Patterson, "Lesbian and Gay Parenting," *American Psychological Association* (1995), 9; Joan Laird, "Lesbian and Gay Families," in *Normal Family Processes*, ed. Froma Walsh (New York: Guilford Press, 1993), 316–17; APA, "Resolution on Sexual Orientation and Marriage" (2004), 7, apa.org/about/governance/council/Policy/gay-marriage.pdf; Ann Sullivan, ed., *Issues in Gay and Lesbian Adoption: Proceedings of the Fourth Annual Peirce-Warwick Adoption Symposium* (Washington, DC: Child Welfare League of America, 1995), 24–28. See also Elizabeth D. Gibbs, "Psychosocial Development of Children Raised by Lesbian Mothers: A Review of Research," *Women and Therapy* 8 (1988): 65–68; Patricia J. Falk, "Lesbian Mothers: Psychosocial Assumptions in Family Law,"

American Psychologist 44 (1989): 941–47; Fiona Tasker and Susan Golombok, "Children Raised by Lesbian Mothers: The Empirical Evidence," *Family Law* (1991): 184–87; Fiona Tasker and Susan Golombok, *Growing Up in a Lesbian Family: Effects on Child Development* (New York: Guilford, 1997); Susan Golombok and Fiona Tasker, "Children in Lesbian and Gay Families: Theories and Evidence," *Annual Review of Sex Research* 5 (1994): 73–100; Jeffrey Weeks, Brian Heaphy, and Catherine Donovan, *Same-Sex Intimacies: Families of Choice and Other Life Experiments* (London: Routledge, 2001); Stephen Hicks, "The Christian Right and Homophobic Discourse: A Response to 'Evidence' That Lesbian and Gay Parenting Damages Children," *Sociological Research Online* 8, no. 4 (2003), www.socresonline. org.uk/8/4/hicks.html (accessed January 3, 2012); Lawrence A. Kurdek, "Are Gay and Lesbian Cohabiting Couples Really Different from Heterosexual Married Couples?," *Journal of Marriage and Family* 66 (2004): 880–900.

47. CDC, American Society for Reproductive Medicine, Society for Reproductive Technology, "2008 Assisted Reproductive Technology Success Rates: National Summary and Fertility Clinic Reports," www.cdc.gov/art/ART2008/PDF/01/ ArtSuccessRates08-FM.pdf (accessed January 3, 2010), 25.

48. Robert W. Rebar and Alan H. DeCherney, "Assisted Reproductive Technology in the United States," *New England Journal of Medicine* 350 (2004): 1603.

49. Michèle Hansen, Carol Bower, Elizabeth Milne, Nicholas de Klerk, and Jennifer J. Korinczuk, "Assisted Reproductive Technologies and the Risk of Birth Defects—A Systematic Review," in *Human Reproduction* 20 (2005): 335; Z. Kozinsky, "Obstetric and Neonatal Risk of Pregnancies after Assisted Reproductive Technology: A Matched Control Study," in *Acta Obstetrica Gynecologica Scandinavica* 82 (2003): 850–56. These studies contradict earlier studies that indicate there is minimal, if any, risk to IVF-ET embryos. See Thomas A. Shannon and Lisa Sowle Cahill, *Religion and Artificial Reproduction* (New York: Crossroad, 1988), 7–9, and their references, including John D. Biggers, "Risks of In Vitro Fertilization and Embryo Transfer in Humans," in *In Vitro Fertilization and Embryo Transfer*, ed. R. F. Harrison et al. (London: Academic Press, 1983), 393–409; and Ian L. Pike, "Biological Risks of In Vitro Fertilization and Embryo Transfer," in *Clinical In Vitro Fertilization*, ed. Carl Wood and Alan Trounson (Berlin: Springer-Verlag, 1984), 137–46.

50. Hansen et al., "Assisted Reproductive Technologies."

51. Rebar and DeCherney ("Assisted Reproductive Technology in the United States," 1603–4) note that while assisted reproduction in the United States "is not legislated . . . it is highly regulated" (1604). One source of this regulation passed by Congress in 1992 to curb misleading advertising on success rates by fertility clinics as well as ethical, financial, and scientific scandals, is the Fertility Clinic Success Rate and Certification Act (also known as the "Wyden Law," which is a misnomer since reporting is voluntary). This act "promotes uniformity in data reporting and requires the listing of clinics that do not report their data" (1604), but it does not require clinics to participate. See also Wendy Y. Chang and Alan H. DeCherney, "History of Regulation of Assisted Reproductive Technology (ART) in the USA: A Work

in Progress," *Human Fertility* 6 (2003): 64–70; Andrea D. Gurmankin, Arthur L. Caplan, and Andrea M. Braverman, "Screening Practices and Beliefs of Assisted Reproductive Technology Programs," *Fertility and Sterility* 83 (2005): 61–67.

52. Gina Kolata, "The Heart's Desire," *New York Times*, May 11, 2004, D1; see also Maura A. Ryan, *Ethics and Economics of Assisted Reproduction: The Cost of Longing* (Washington, DC: Georgetown University Press, 2001), 2; Linda J. Beckman and S. Marie Harvey, "Current Reproductive Technologies: Increased Access and Choice?," *Journal of Social Issues* 61 (2005): 2.

53. Carol J. Rowland Hogue, "Successful Assisted Reproductive Technology: The Beauty of One," *Obstetrics and Gynecology* 100 (2002): 1017. See also John A. Collins, "Reproductive Technology: The Price of Progress," *New England Journal of Medicine* 331 (1994): 270–71.

54. See Deut. 24:18–22; Jer. 7:2–7; Is. 61:1–8; Matt. 25: 31–46.

55. We borrow this metaphor from Jorg Rieder, *Remember the Poor: The Challenge to Theology in the Twenty-First Century* (Harrisburg, PA: Trinity Press International, 1998), 1–5. Gustavo Guttierez, *The Power of the Poor in History* (New York: Orbis, 1983), 13.

56. See *SRS*, 39–42; Christina Traina, *Feminist Ethics and Natural Law* (Washington, DC: Georgetown University Press, 1999); David Hollenbach, *The Common Good and Christian Ethics* (Cambridge: Cambridge University Press, 2002).

57. Ambrose, *De Nabuthe Jezraelita*, 1, PL, 14, 747.

58. Augustine, *Sermo L*, 1, PL 38, 326.

59. Ryan, *Ethics and Economics of Assisted Reproduction*, 134.

60. Ibid., 8

61. Lisa Sowle Cahill, *Theological Bioethics: Participation, Justice, Change* (Washington, DC: Georgetown University Press, 2005), 210.

Epilogue

Throughout this book, we argue that Catholic sexual morality is institutionalized within the confines of marriage and procreation, and we examine the foundations of two principles that articulate the essence of that Catholic morality. The first principle states that "each and every marriage act must remain open to the transmission of life."[1] The second states that "any human genital act whatsoever may be placed only within the confines of marriage."[2] In contemporary Catholic moral theology, two approaches to understanding these principles demarcate two schools of Catholic moral theology. There is, first, the classicist approach, which holds the principles as universal, permanent, and unchangeable; this classicist approach defines what we called the traditionalist school. There is, second, the empirical or historically conscious approach, which holds that the principles *may* be unchangeable and unchanged or *may* be in the process of development or resolution in the contemporary historical context. This historically conscious approach defines what we called the revisionist school. Throughout the book, we have intentionally opted for a historically conscious and revisionist approach.

It is misleading, as we point out, to speak about reason *and* nature, as if they were two completely separate categories. They are not. Thinkers in the past, including sainted theologians, did not know the full reality of the human person as it has unfolded over the centuries, nor did they know the full reality of human biology and sexuality physiologically and psychologically. This restricted knowledge relates directly to the subject matter of this book, namely, in general, human anthropology and, in specific, human sexuality, and makes it difficult to gainsay Fuchs's claim that "one cannot take what Augustine or the philosophers of the Middle

Ages knew about sexuality as the exclusive basis of a moral reflection."[3] Nor can one take the presumed facts of nature as the exclusive basis for moral reflection, for "we never simply 'have' nature or that which is given in nature." We know nature, rather, "always as something that has already been interpreted in some way."[4] Put more directly, "nature" is a socially constructed category. To indicate and underscore that socially constructed reality, we have throughout presented "nature" always within quotation marks.

INTRACHURCH DIALOGUE

Because theologians are essentially persons inculturated into a variety of human perspectives, only one of which is theology, this book inevitably engages in a twofold dialogue. The first dialogue is internal to theology and to Church. It asks what a two-thousand-year ecclesial tradition has said theologically about human anthropology and sexuality, and how that ancient tradition is to be mediated to, appropriated by, and transmitted onward in and by the contemporary Church. The young Ratzinger underscores why that internal dialogue must be pursued.

> Not everything that exists in the Church must for that reason be also a legitimate tradition; in other words, not every tradition that arises in the Church is a true celebration of the mystery of Christ. There is a distorting, as well as a legitimate tradition . . . [and] . . . consequently tradition must not be considered only affirmatively but also critically.[5]

Three matters are crucial to both the critical consideration Ratzinger demands and the internal dialogue: the "nature" of Christian theology, the origin of sacred scripture, and the "nature" of the Church that claims its origin in the scriptures and seeks to mediate its meanings to each new Christian generation. For what has transpired in this book, the "nature" of the Church is, perhaps, the most pressing of these three, because how one conceives Church will determine how one conceives the functioning of another theological reality that is central to the internal dialogue, and to this book, namely, *sensus fidei,* "the instinctive capacity of the whole Church to recognize the infallibility of the Spirit's truth."[6]

Before we consider *sensus fidei,* however, we add another word about theology and theologians. Traditional Catholic theology prior to the Second Vatican Council was enclosed within a classicist-traditionalist framework; it was universal, permanent, objective, and only to be learned. It was above all ahistorical, which led to its categorization as "non-historical orthodoxy."[7] That explains its evident lack of creativity. One of the achievements of Bernard Lonergan was to point the way beyond this classicist-traditionalist theology to an empirical, historically conscious, critical, and revisionist theology. Some continue to lament that "some recent Roman Catholic theology seems determined to live in a world that no longer exists," but we have eschewed that lamentation and have chosen the way forward that Lonergan has mapped in detail.[8]

Horizon is an important category in Lonergan's philosophy and theology. In its everyday use, it denotes the line at which the earth and the sky appear to meet, the outer limit of physical vision. Horizon is not immovably fixed. My horizon moves as I move, either receding in front of me or encroaching behind me. It is determined by my perspective and, in turn, determines what I can and cannot see. "Beyond the horizon lie the objects that, at least for the moment, cannot be seen. Within the horizon lie the objects that can now be seen."[9] Physical horizon provides an easy analogy for the personal horizon of knowledge. The perspective that lies within my personal horizon is, to a greater or lesser degree, an object of interest and of knowledge: I can be attentive to it, understand it, make a judgment about its truth, and make a decision about it. What lies outside my perspective and horizon lies outside the range of my interest and knowledge. There is a difference, however, between the physical horizon and my personal horizon. The latter is the product of both past socialization and individual achievement, and it constitutes both the condition and the limitation of any further development. In sociological language, my personal horizon is a socially constructed human product, and different products, different horizons, different perspectives may be opposed dialectically. An understanding, a judgment, and a decision that is intelligible and true in one horizon may be unintelligible and false in another horizon. As I have the freedom to move and adjust within a horizon, so also I have the freedom to move from one horizon to another. The move from one horizon to another is what Lonergan means by conversion.

Conversion, the movement from one horizon to another, may be either intellectual or moral. Intellectual conversion is "the elimination of an exceedingly stubborn and misleading myth concerning reality, objectivity, and knowledge. The myth is that knowing is like looking, that objectivity is seeing what is out there to be seen and not seeing what is not there, and that the real is what is out there to be looked at."[10] This myth confuses the physical world of sensation, the sum of what is experientially seen, heard, touched, tasted, smelled, with the world mediated by meaning, which is a world known, not by the act of sensation alone, but by the cognitive process of sensation, understanding, and judgment. Knowing is not simply seeing, hearing, touching, tasting, smelling; it is sensing, understanding, and judging. Until knowers reach the judgment that their understanding is true or false, there is no true knowledge. The myth that is to be clarified and eliminated has many possible consequences. It can lead to naive realism, thinking that the world of meaning can be known simply by looking at it, thinking that I achieve true knowledge simply by looking at and learning what Paul or John, Augustine or Aquinas, Pius IX or John Paul II said and wrote. Once intellectually converted from this prevalent myth, I come to understand that what Augustine or John Paul or Karl Marx said is only a first step in the process of my coming to know, to be followed by my own understanding and judgment, not only of what was said but also, and especially, of what is true. This converted horizon is what Lonergan means by critical realism.

Besides intellectual conversion, there is also moral conversion. Following judgment and the attainment of truth comes the decision about what to do about the truth. Moral conversion "changes the criterion of one's decisions and choices from satisfactions to values."[11] Moral conversion involves progressively understanding the present situation, exposing and eradicating both individual and societal bias, constantly evaluating my scale of preferred values, paying attention to criticism and protest, and listening to others. Neither one instance of moral conversion nor one moral decision leads to moral perfection, for after one conversion there remains the possibility of either another conversion or relapse, and after moral decision there is still required moral action. Conversion is not to be conceived as a one-off moment but as an ongoing process.

Horizon and conversion have much to do with *sensus fidei* and its cognates, *sensus fidelium, sensus ecclesiae, sensus catholicus. Sensus fidei* is a spiritual charism of discernment, possessed by the whole Church, which recognizes and receives a teaching as apostolic truth and, therefore, to be believed.[12] It has biblical root in Paul's exhortation to the Philippians to "have this [common] mind (*phroneite*) among yourselves, which is yours in Christ Jesus" (2:5). It has modern validation in the Second Vatican Council, which taught that the doctrine of the Catholic Church is preserved in *all* the faithful, laity and hierarchy together.

> The body of the faithful *as a whole*, anointed as they are by the Holy One (1 John 2:20, 27), cannot err in matters of belief [that is, they are infallible]. Thanks to a supernatural sense of the faith [*sensus fidei*] which characterizes the people *as a whole*, it manifests this unerring quality when, 'from the bishops to the last of the faithful,' it manifests its universal agreement in matters of faith and morals.[13]

Catholic doctrine enshrines this belief in the teaching that the Spirit is gifted to the whole Church. That teaching makes sense only in a Church that is believed to be and is lived as a communion instituted by Christ, constituted by the Spirit of Christ, and "composed of all those who receive him in faith and in love," a historical communion "of life, love, and truth."[14] It is from and for such a Church that this book is written to invite conversion.

EXTRACHURCH DIALOGUE

The second dialogue is external to theology and to Church. It takes place between theology and the historical contexts in which theological doctrines develop and take root. Theology is not sociology or any other social science, but that does not mean that the two disciplines are completely unrelated. Sociology is eminently equipped, for instance, to elucidate empirically and scientifically what theologically *is*, forcing theologians to reflect on and evaluate what is and the sociohistorical context in which it is. It forces, for instance, the question we raised in the section on contraception: How can anyone claim that the Church believes that artificial contraception is morally wrong when some 89 percent of the communion-Church does not believe that claim?[15] Yves Congar highlights two approaches to an answer to that question. Obedience to authentic ecclesial authority is called for "if the Church is conceived as a society subject to monarchical authority," and dialogue and consensus are called for "when the universal Church is seen as a communion."[16] The theological fact that, after the Second Vatican Council, the Church is seen predominantly as a communion demands critical dialogue and consensus about the *sensus fidei* of the Church, rather than uncritical obedience. The ecclesiology in which this book is rooted is a communion ecclesiology.[17]

The simple social fact that 89 percent of Catholics in the communion-Church believe that they can practice methods of contraception prohibited by the Church and still be good Catholics proves nothing theologically. It does, however, raise questions that theologians cannot ignore without fulfilling contemporary bias that theologians and their theologies have nothing to do with the real questions of the real world in which real women and men live, among other things, as members of the communion-Church. Another moral question we considered in this book presses the Church in our day, perhaps more than contraception, namely, cohabitation prior to marriage. If the first union for some 75–80 percent of Western women and men is cohabitation and not marriage, again a social fact raises questions for theologians about what the communion-Church believes. The historical and theological fact of the nonreception and nuanced re-reception of long-held Catholic doctrines about usury, slavery, religious freedom, and membership in the Body of Christ points to, and ecclesially legitimates, the direction in which the doctrines prohibiting contraception and premarital cohabitation (and also divorce and remarriage without annulment) *might* develop.[18]

A word here about responsible behavior in the Church. The *Catechism* states that "the Church's social teaching proposes *principles for reflection*; it provides *criteria for judgment*; it gives *guidelines for action*.[19] This trinity, principles for reflection, criteria for judgment, and guidelines for action, came into Catholic social teaching via Pope Paul VI's *Octogesima adveniens* in 1971.[20] It was repeated in the CDF's *Instruction on Freedom and Liberation* in 1986.[21] A year later it was underscored again in John Paul II's *Sollicitudo rei socialis*.[22] This approach to social morality, an authentically established part of the Catholic moral tradition in modern times, introduces a model of converted personal responsibility that underscores the responsibility of each person in the communion-Church. John Paul II accentuates this Catholic perspective by teaching that, in its social teachings, the Church seeks "to *guide* people to *respond*, with the support of rational reflection and of the human sciences, to their vocation as *responsible* builders of earthly society."[23] The relationship between Church teaching and individual-believer learning that this approach advances merits close attention in a Church that is communion. Church teaching *guides*; responsible believers learning—drawing on Church guidance, their own attentiveness, intelligence, rationality, decisiveness, experience, and the findings of the human sciences—*respond*.

The notion of responsibility introduces an important dimension of individual and communal freedom to the unnuanced notion of uncritical obedience. In social reality, the Magisterium does not pretend to pronounce on every last detail or to impose final decisions; it understands itself as informing and guiding believers while leaving judgment, decision, and application to their faithful and responsible conscience.[24] Socio-moral principles are humanly constructed guidelines for attention, intelligence, judgment, and decision, not moral imperatives drawn from

EPILOGUE

divine, natural, or ecclesiastical law, and demanding uncritical obedience to God, nature, or Church. John Paul adds what the Catholic tradition has always taken for granted. On the one hand, the Church's social teaching is "constant." On the other hand, "it is ever new, because it is subject to the necessary and opportune adaptations suggested by the changes in historical conditions and by the unceasing flow of the events which are the setting of the life of people and society."[25] Principles remain constant. Judgments, decisions, and actions, as history amply demonstrates, can change after responsible reflection on changed historical contexts and the ongoing flow of human events illuminated by the social sciences. Since this approach is authoritatively advanced in social morality, and since social and sexual morality pertain to the same human person, it would seem that the same approach would apply to sexual morality. Indeed, since the whole person is more intimately involved in the sexual domain than in the social, should the sexual domain not "be *more than any other* the place where all is referred to the informed conscience?"[26] Part of the proposal of this book has been, under the guidance of ecclesial principles and the illumination of the contemporary sciences, to refer questions about sexual morality to the morally converted and informed conscience.

Christians in general and Christian theologians in specific do not live in a comfortable theological cocoon; they live in the world along with other human beings who appear to have decided that Christians have nothing to tell them about that world, about themselves in the world, or about the forces at work for good and evil in the world. Many of these others have perspectives on the world and answers for the world's questions that are different from Christian theological perspectives and answers. That raises the inevitable question of which perspective is right and true, a question that, in its turn, raises another question about a necessary external dialogue between theology and other socially constructed human perspectives. Individuals and the human world they inhabit are not two independent realities; they are realities that work in an ongoing dialectical and symbiotic interdependence. Human society, culture, and perspective are human products and nothing but human products, and yet these products act back upon their producers to conform and control them. The temptation of intellectually unconverted individuals, be they theologians or not, is always to assume that *our* way is the *right* way and *our* truth is the *real* truth. The sociology of knowledge scotches that unconverted approach.

Human truth, we have argued elsewhere, is relative to a given perspective and is supported by a plausibility structure that derives from that perspective.[27] Each perspective has its own accent of reality, its own cognitive style, its own consistency and compatibility, and outside of a given perspective there is no possibility of grasping the truth held within that perspective. That raises the specter of relativism, so disconcerting to many. Relativism acknowledges that all human truth is inseparably bound to the sociohistorical perspective of the thinker and concludes that, therefore, all human truth is *relative* and unreliable. We do not accept that judgment. All human truth is, indeed, inseparably bound to the sociohistorical perspective of the thinker and is therefore *relational*, but that does not suggest that it is unreliable. It suggests only that truth-within-perspective is partial truth in need of dialectical complementation by truths held in other perspectives. That suggestion is even truer, the Christian traditions universally teach, when it comes to human truth about God, whom "no one has ever seen" (John 1:18; cp. Exod. 33:20–24).

Augustine expresses the basic Christian perspective when he argues *"si comprehendis, non est Deus"*; if you have understood, then what you have understood is not God.[28] Aquinas expresses it in his mature doctrine of analogy: "Now we cannot know what God is but only what God is not; we must, therefore, consider the ways in which God does not exist rather than the ways in which God does exist."[29] Rahner expresses the same perspective in modern theological language when he writes that "revelation does not mean that the mystery is overcome by gnosis bestowed by God. . . . on the contrary, it is the history of the deepening perception of God *as* the mystery."[30] The God whom the communion-Church believes in is always wholly other, *deus absconditus*, a hidden God, a transcendent Mystery, "blessedly present but conceptually inapprehensible, and so God."³¹ Recognizing this Christian theme, the Magisterium of the Church teaches that "the fullness of truth received in Jesus Christ does not give individual Christians the guarantee that they have grasped that truth fully. . . . Christians must be prepared to learn and to receive from and through others the positive values of their traditions. Through dialogue they may be moved to give up ingrained prejudices [psychic conversion], to revise preconceived ideas [intellectual conversion], and even sometimes to allow the understanding of their faith to be purified."³² Pope John Paul II approves. Dialogue, he teaches, as we pointed out in our prologue, "is rooted in the nature and dignity of the human person. . . . [It] is an indispensable step along the path towards *human self-realization*, the self-realization of *each individual* and of *every human community*. . . . It involves the human subject in his or her entirety."³³ We agree. We are wide open to dialogue in this book, and we look forward to the ongoing dialogue for the building up of the holy communion that is the Church.

QUESTIONS FOR REFLECTION

1. In your own life, where is there a need for intellectual conversion to better understand human sexuality? What are the normative implications of this conversion for sexual ethics?
2. What are the top ten ideas you have learned from reading this book? Please discuss them.

NOTES

1. *HV*, 11.
2. *PH*, 7.
3. Joseph Fuchs, *Moral Demands and Personal Obligations* (Washington, DC: Georgetown University Press, 1993), 36.
4. Ibid.
5. Joseph Ratzinger, "The Transmission of Divine Revelation," in *Commentary on the Documents of Vatican II*, ed. Herbert Vorgrimler (New York: Herder and Herder, 1969), 185.
6. John E. Thiel, *Senses of Tradition: Continuity and Development in the Catholic Faith* (New York: Oxford University Press, 2000), 47.
7. See Michael Novak, "The 'Open Church' 40 Years Later: A Reckoning," in *Unfinished Journey: The Church 40 Years after Vatican II*, ed. Austin Ivereigh (New York: Continuum, 2003), 48. Novak comments that the practitioners of this nonhistorical orthodoxy "did not worry overmuch about that system's historical justification, or about making it relevant to the historical present" (ibid.).
8. Robert M. Doran, *Theology and the Dialectics of History* (Toronto: University of Toronto Press), 4.
9. Ibid., 236.
10. Ibid., 238.
11. Ibid., 240.
12. For a fuller analysis of *sensus fidei* and reception, see Michael G. Lawler, *What Is and What Ought to Be: The Dialectic of Experience, Theology, and Church* (New York: Continuum, 2005), 119–34; and Michael G. Lawler and Todd A. Salzman, "Human Experience and Catholic Moral Theology," *Irish Theological Quarterly* 76 (Winter 2010): 35–56.
13. Augustine, *De Praed Sanct.*, 14, 27, *PL* 44, 980; *LG*, 12; emphasis added.
14. *GS*, 32; *LG*, 9; cp. *AG*, 19.
15. See George H. Gallup Jr., *Religion in America 1996* (Princeton: Princeton Religion Research Center, 1996), 44. See also James D. Davidson, Patricia Wittberg, William J. Whalen, Kathleen Mass Weigert, Andrea S. Williams, Richard A. Lamanna, and Jan Stenftenagel, *The Search for Common Ground: What Unites and Divides Catholic Americans* (Huntington, IN: Our Sunday Visitor, 1997); William V. D'Antonio, Dean R. Hoge, James D. Davidson, and Katherine Meyer, *American Catholics: Gender, Generation, and Commitment* (Lanham, MD: Rowman and Littlefield, 2001); Dean R. Hoge, Mary Johnson, and William Dinges, *Young Adult Catholics: Religion in the Culture of Choice* (Notre Dame, IN: University of Notre Dame Press, 2001).
16. Yves M. J. Congar, "Reception as an Ecclesiological Reality," *Concilium* 77 (1965): 62. See also Nicholas Lash, "Teaching or Commanding? When Bishops Instruct the Faithful," *America* December 13, 2010, 17–20.

17. See Yves Congar, *Divided Christendom: A Catholic Study of the Problem of Reunion*, trans. M. Bousfield (London: Bles, 1939); Henri de Lubac, *Catholicism: A Study of Dogma in Relation to the Corporate Destiny of Mankind*, trans. Lancelot Sheppard (New York: Longmans, Green, 1950); Marie Joseph Gouillou, *Mission et unité. Les exigencies de la communion* (Paris: Desclée, 1960); Jerome Hamer, *The Church Is a Communion* (New York: Sheed and Ward, 1965); Gustave Martelet, *Les idées maîtresses de Vatican II* (Paris: Desclée, 1966); Michael G. Lawler and Thomas J. Shanahan, *Church: A Spirited Communion* (Collegeville, MN: Liturgical Press, 1995).

18. See John T. Noonan, *A Church That Can and Cannot Change* (Notre Dame, IN: University of Notre Dame Press, 2005); Lawler, *What Is and What Ought to Be*, 127–29.

19. CCC, 2423; emphasis added.

20. Paul VI, *Octogesima adveniens* 4, *AAS* 63 (197), 403 ff.

21. CDF, *Instruction on Christian Freedom and Liberation* 72, *AAS* 79 (1987), 586.

22. *SRS*, 3.

23. Ibid., 1; emphasis added.

24. This notion of individual responsibility is brilliantly analyzed by Jean-Yves Calvez in his essay "Morale sociale et morale sexuelle," *Etudes* 378 (1993): 642–44.

25. *SRS*, 3.

26. Calvez, "Morale sociale et morale sexuelle," 648; emphasis added.

27. See Lawler, *What Is and What Ought to Be*, 44–67.

28. *Sermo* 52, *PL* 38, 360.

29. *ST*, 1, 3, preface.

30. Karl Rahner, "The Hiddenness of God," *Theological Investigations*, vol. 16 (London: Darton, Longman, and Todd, 1979), 238; emphasis in original.

31. Elizabeth A. Johnson, *She Who Is: The Mystery of God in Feminist Theological Discourse* (New York: Crossroad, 1992), 105.

32. Pontifical Council for Interreligious Dialogue, *Dialogue and Proclamation* (Roma: Typis Polyglottis Vaticanis, 1991), 49.

33. *SRS*, 28.

Index

artificial reproductive technologies (*cont.*) and, 206; natural law and, 200; parental complementarity and, 206; parenthood and, 203

Ashley, Benedict, 216n6

Augustine, 2–3, 8, 22–24, 27, 37, 39, 180, 211, 221, 224, 229; on concupiscence, 24; on the incomprehensibility of God, xxii; on Manichees, 22; on marriage, 22–23; on original sin, 22; on Pelagians, 23; procreation as primary end of marriage, 37, 98; three goods of marriage and, 27

authentic human sexuality, 60

autonomy, 3, 4, 176

Averett, Paige, 174

Baby M, 217n35

Bailey, Sherwin D., 184n13

baptism, 144, 146

Barth, Karl, 14–15, 18, 137

Barton, 160–61

Basil, 21, 26, 98

Benedict XVI, 155, 174, 183; on conscience, xxvi. *See also* Ratzinger, Joseph

Berkman, John, 205, 218n40

betrothal, 127, 129, 130–36, 139, 142, 144–46, 148

Bible, 7–8, 10, 19, 38–39, 157–59, 163, 165–68; on homosexuality 157–68; interpretation of, xvi–xvii, 7; patriarchy in, 10; on women, 10–11. *See also* New Testament; scriptures; *specific books of the Bible*

biblical exegesis, 8, 178

biblical rules, 167

biological complementarity, 64, 74, 81, 84–86, 141

biological materialism, 30

biologism, 200

biology, 39, 77–78, 162, 167, 200, 221; ancient understandings of, 162; Church Fathers and, 39; inseparability principle and, 200; male seed and, 167; reproduction and, 77–78; Thomas Aquinas and, 77

birth control. *See* contraception

birth defects, 209–10, 213, 215

Blakeslee, Sandra, 153n51

Blankenhorn, David, 120n29

body, the, 20, 28–29, 56–57, 141, 193

Bonaventure, 28

Book of Wisdom, 162

Booth, Alan, 91n61

Boswell, John, 41n18

Brakman, Sarah-Vaughan, 218n40

Bumpass, Larry L., 149n4

Cahill, Lisa, 15, 110–11, 139–40, 167, 202, 213, 217n31

Cantor, Peter, xix

cardinal virtues, 86

Casti connubii (Pius XI), 29, 37, 96, 102, 104

Cataldo, Peter J., 216n7

Catcher in the Rye, xiii

Catechism of the Catholic Church (CCC), 3, 60, 67, 157, 174; on conscience, xxv–xxvi; on Sodom and Gomorrah, xvi

Catechism of the Council of Trent, 29, 102

catechumenate, 144, 148

Catholic Press Association, xiii

Catholic tradition, 7; anthropology and, xv, xvii; biblical interpretation and, xvi; cohabitation and, 124; common good and, 210; on conscience, xxv–xxvi; on

organic complementarity, 214

orgasm, 48, 51–52

original sin, 109

O'Rourke, Kevin, 216n6

Papal Birth Control Commission, 35–37

parental complementarity, 64, 71, 175, 206; artificial reproductive technologies and, 206

parenthood, 147; genetic, 198, 203–5; gestational, 198, 203–4, 215; marriage and, 114; social, 203–5, 215; vocation and, 198. *See also* responsible parenthood

parents: homosexuality and, 174

partial truth, xxii, 229

passion, 16, 21, 53, 164

passivity, 6, 163

pastors, xxiv

patriarchy, 10, 12

Patterson, Charlotte J., 173, 187n64

Paul (Saint), 16–18, 50; bad biology and, 167; on covenant, 17; on homosexuality, 164–66; letter to the Romans, 164; on marriage, 16; Philippians, 225; Tertullian on, 21

Paul VI, xiv; on authority of the magisterium, 102; on contraception, 36, 96, 105, 111; on the hierarchy of the ends of marriage, 33; on the inseparability principle, 112–13; on the marriage act, 7, 37, 114; on the meaning of marriage acts, xiv; *Octogesima adveniens*, 3, 227; on Papal Birth Control Commission, 35–37, 100. *See also Humanae vitae*

Payer, Pierre J., 24

Pelagianism, 22

penetrative sexual intercourse, 130

Penitentials, 25–26

periodic continence, 104–5

Perito, John E., 91n66, 184n11

person. *See* human person

Persona humana (CDF), 72

personal complementarity, 74–76, 80, 84–85, 171, 179–80; affective complementarity and, 67; communion complementarity and, 66; heterogenital complementarity and, 68, 71; truly human sexual acts and, 74

personalism, 102, 104; vs. biological, 195; genital complementarity and, 76; heterologous artificial insemination and, 197; homologous artificial insemination and, 198; *Humanae vitae* and, 196; *Instruction on Respect for Human Life* and, 195–96; natural law and, 195; social ethics and, 212

personal relationships. *See* interpersonal

perspectivism, xxi–xxii; Lonergan and, xxii

philosophy, xxii; Gnosticism and, 19; Lonergan and, 223; Stoicism and, 7, 37

physical acts, xxiv, 48, 139

physicalism, 200

pilgrim Church, xx

Pius XI: *Casti connubii*, 29–30; personal procreative-union model, 103

Pius XII: *Address to Italian Midwives*, xiv, 104; on nature and human reason, xiv; on procreation, 114–15, 118

Plato, 6, 15, 27

pleasure, 140. *See also* sexual pleasure

Pontifical Biblical Commission, 7, 38

Pontifical Council for the Family, 142

Pope, Stephen, 81, 92n78

Popenoe, David, 120n29, 149n4